By Marian Salzman

Next: A Vision of Our Lives in the Future
(with Ira Matathia)

Next Now: Trends for the Future
(with Ira Matathia)

The Future of Men: The Rise of the Ubersexual and What He Means for Marketing Today
(with Ira Matathia and Ann O'Reilly)

Buzz: Harness the Power of Influence and Create Demand
(with Ira Matathia and Ann O'Reilly)

Agile PR: Expert Messaging in a Hyper-Connected, Always-On World
(with the team at Havas PR)

The New Megatrends: Seeing Clearly in the Age of Disruption

The New Megatrends

The New Megatrends

Seeing Clearly in the Age of Disruption

Marian Salzman

Currency
New York

Published in the United States by Currency,
an imprint of Random House,
a division of Penguin Random House LLC, New York.

CURRENCY and its colophon are trademarks of
Penguin Random House LLC.

Hardback ISBN 978-0-593-23970-4
Ebook ISBN 978-0-593-23971-1

Printed in the United States of America on acid-free paper

crownpublishing.com

2 4 6 8 9 7 5 3 1

First Edition

Book design by Virginia Norey

For the people over five decades
who convinced me the world could be my oyster—
it has been just that, and so much more.

Preface

You can think of this book as a time traveler's guide.

It will take you back twenty years to the turn of the millennium, unpacking the pivotal events in the period of disruption that followed before transporting you forward to two decades after the "Great Reset" of the present day. With this time span supplying our observational bookends, I will explore how world affairs, technological innovation, social movements, and a pandemic have combined to create trends that are shifting our identities, shaping our collective future, and recasting our past.

Are you keen to understand how the recent past will influence the trends that shape tomorrow? Are you an entrepreneur or a leader looking for an edge by anticipating and responding early to cultural shifts that offer promise or peril? Are you prepared to tackle cold, hard truths today rather than pretending looming catastrophes will magically disappear? If so, this book is for you.

My aim is to help you understand the forces that have led to a world facing widespread dissatisfaction and even the threat of systemic collapse and, crucially, to offer insights into how we might turn things around before it is too late. For reasons I will explain in the introduction, the end point of my forecasts is 2038—a timeframe that allows me to make evidence-based predictions without venturing into the murky territory of science fiction.

I refer throughout to cultural trends, business trends, and consumer trends, using them as illustrations and markers to guide you into a global future that will be characterized by unprecedented change and even chaos. These sightings draw on my experiences as a longtime trendspotter, a professional communicator and observer of people, and someone who lives simultaneously on two continents, in three hometowns, and nowhere at all.

Often the word *trend* carries a superficial connotation, as when it is applied to shifting appetites in entertainment, fashion, and vocabulary. This book will dip into those realms, but they are not its focus. Any serious effort to forecast the future today must necessarily grapple with the weightier issues of climate change, technology use, and polarization—aspects of life that trickle down into every facet of our culture. "Forewarned, forearmed; to be prepared is half the victory." Cervantes had it right.

People often ask what it is like to have worked in and around trends for almost four decades. I am reminded that it has been a journey marked by a series of robust immersions and unexpected (sometimes unwelcome) detours. I learned about globalism and deregulation during the "Big Bang"—a moment of sudden financial deregulation in the 1980s. I hitchhiked the scantly populated information superhighway in the early 1990s and launched the first market-research company in cyberspace. I lived and worked in the Netherlands when European unification was the next big thing and the "polder model," championing consensus decision-making, was coming to the fore. I moved back to New York full-time in 1998 (but kept a base and a team in the Netherlands for a few more years, never completely breaking ties with Holland) and watched the Twin Towers collapse two miles from my loft in September 2001. (When the planes hit, the first person I called after my parents was my executive assistant in Amsterdam; she still recalls my fear and anxiety.) My consumer research into metrosexuality hit a nerve and unleashed a global media explosion. Many years later, I helped promote the launch of Venture for America, whose founder, Andrew Yang, through his unlikely presidential campaign, introduced much of the United States and even some non-Americans to the concept of a universal basic income.

A friend once described me as "Forrest Gump lite." In truth, many people have found themselves similarly caught in multiple threads of history in the making. The difference for me is that these threads are not left unexamined. My job as a trends analyst is to untangle and rearrange these strands into a road map that will help us move forward in a reasoned way.

One caveat before you dig in: It is my style to make nonlinear leaps as I lay out possible and probable scenarios and contemplate what has led up to them and how they might develop. Zigs and zags through peaks and valleys reflect the increasingly complex nature of these times. While I always keep a close eye on the United States, a country that has given rise to countless cultural movements in the past fifty years, the predictions contained herein are global in nature. Much of the beauty of trendspotting lies in soaking in the views along the way. But even with some colorful diversions, I promise that I ultimately will deliver you to a destination worth pondering—and a potential future worth fighting for.

Contents

Preface ix

Introduction: Spotting Trends xv

PART ONE:

The Big Picture 1

Chapter 1. The Bug and the Virus 9

Chapter 2. 2000–2019: A Slow Slide 20

Chapter 3. Climate Truths 33

Chapter 4. The Chaos of Now 45

Chapter 5. America Divided 56

Chapter 6. China Makes Its Move 67

PART TWO:

How We Live 85

Chapter 7. Who's in Your Lifeboat? 89

Chapter 8. Crossing Lines, Resetting Boundaries 101

Chapter 9. Small Is the New Big 111

Chapter 10. The Luxury of Freedom and Time 128

Chapter 11. The Inequity of Wealth 139

PART THREE:

Who We Are 155

Chapter 12. Is the Future Really Female? 159

Chapter 13. Guy Problems 179

Chapter 14. Unmooring from Gender and Cis-Sameness 188

Chapter 15. Me, Myself, and I 197

PART FOUR:
WHAT'S NEXT? 209

CHAPTER 16. OUR WORLD IN 2038 217

CONCLUSION: WHAT'S IN IT FOR ME? 241

ACKNOWLEDGMENTS 247

NOTES 251

INDEX 305

Introduction

Spotting Trends

Before we journey two decades into the past, I want to spend a few minutes illuminating the methods, history, and implications of my somewhat unusual vocation.

Trendspotting is not about setting trends or influencing cultural movements. As the name would suggest, it is about recognizing and understanding emerging shifts, predicting what will happen next, and then using that foresight to inform actions and gain an advantage, whether personal or professional. For those expecting a sexier explanation, I am sorry to say the practice has nothing to do with divination or mysticism. I don't use tarot cards. I don't drink botanical potions to induce visions. I don't have a special connection to a higher power. As for magic, the sleight of my hand is slight indeed.

And yet I do know a few things about the future.

I look ahead by observing and processing incidents and patterns that may reveal trends, much as sailors study charts and look for signs from the sea and sky. I start by peering into the past to perceive how it has flowed into the present, blending the roles of cultural historian and futurist. The goal is to learn from what has passed to guide us into the best possible version of the future.

You may be thinking, What's so unique about this? Isn't everyone's thinking about the present and the future informed by the past? Unfortunately, no. Too many people measure the present against an idealized vision of the past. Some look to a time when straight white males carried unquestioned authority, when immigrants and minorities "knew their place" and a woman's work was in her husband's home. Others envision a past marked by a closeness to the land and the rhythms of nature, a time of personal responsibility and moral rectitude—a past that never truly was, at least not in the way they imagine it. Just because lives were once less technologically turbocharged and slower does not necessarily mean they were simpler, more fulfilling, more equitable, or happier. It is easy to view the "good old days" through rose-colored glasses, overlooking the frustrations of those times. To get a clear view, the trendspotter must shed these biases before interrogating the past or looking ahead to the future. Only by mining the past with precision can we draw insights untainted by rose, or any other color.

People who are serious about understanding trends know we live in a complicated, interconnected world. Trends analysts are uncertain and often uneasy about what is to come. We are not expecting to catch glimpses of robots that will cook us gourmet meals or cash that will drop into our laps from the money trees on Venus, but we would welcome an edge in our financial and career decision-making. We want tools and clues and insights, a peek into possible and probable scenarios that might influence our lives—and that we, in turn, may begin to influence now. If we can correctly discern the forces shaping the future, we can begin to alter their trajectory.

Bottom line, most people want the answer to one question: What's in it for me? That's not as blatantly selfish a query as it may first appear. Sure, it can speak to a personal or business advantage, such as creating precisely the right startup to surf the wave of an emerging trend, making a savvy business decision that anticipates a significant consumer shift ahead of one's competitors—as Emily Weiss did when she leveraged the appeal of beauty blogs into global beauty brand Glossier, or as Beyond Meat founder Ethan Brown did when he anticipated a growing market for plant-based foods. Beyond that, though, having an advance glimpse of the future has societal implications. In a world marked by chaos and challenges that threaten to overwhelm, being prepared for change—emotionally and practically—is a critical advantage.

When looking deeply into the past, it is vital to peer through two lenses. One is quantitative, anchored in statistics and events. The other is qualitative, exploring the emotional overlays—the perspectives—that color what came before. Both quantitative and qualitative inputs inform our experience of the present and contribute to what we collectively regard as our shared past—even if two individuals' perceptions of the past are never wholly aligned. Our thinking and assessments are invariably influenced by race, wealth, gender, culture, life experience, and other factors. Only after seeing how we got here does a trendspotter look forward—and that's how this book will work, too.

The insights I share are necessarily shaped by my personality, my experiences, and the paths I have taken. A relentless curiosity about what is around the corner has defined my character since I was a child in River Edge, New Jersey, population eleven thousand, give or take. Despite being just on the other side of the Hudson River from Manhattan, we did not feel the city's culture there, at least not significantly, when I was growing up in the 1960s and '70s. Even now, River Edge is a snapshot of suburban America—or at least a snapshot of primarily white, educated, upwardly mobile, suburban America.

As a teenager, I was obsessed with escaping suburbia, never to return to what I considered the humdrum of carpools and after-school sports, carefully mowed lawns and annual summer block parties. After I graduated from college, I proceeded directly to Manhattan and found myself working in the advertising industry. Over three decades, I built a career. I wrote or coauthored more than a dozen books and spent most of a decade running a global public relations agency. Along the way, in a move that would have shocked my teenage self, I left New York City behind for several variations on the suburbs. In 2010, I became the life partner of a lawyer and law professor who lives in Arizona and Connecticut, and I picked up an address in each of those states. And then, in early 2018, I added a third address, in Canton Vaud, Switzerland, when I took a job as head of global communications for a multinational corporation.

The truth about my whereabouts, though, is that I live in multiple places and nowhere. Prior to the pandemic, I did so much work in hotels or on airplanes that I sometimes forgot where I was or where I was headed. For many years, like so many frequent flyers (and now like so many remote workers during the pandemic), I connected to my worlds, to people and businesses on various continents, through screens. When someone asks me where I live, I fight the impulse to reply, "The cloud." That's part fact, part joke, and part lament.

My travels inform my trendspotting—I have long found airports and local supermarkets an excellent source of inspiration and insights—and so do all my other life experiences. Perhaps chief among them: the three surgeries (and counting) I have undergone to remove atypical and typical meningiomas, known as the "good kind of brain tumor," as if there were such a thing. Those operations have given me a bit more patience (it is never going to be my thing), a greater ability to cede control to others (only slightly more my thing), and, vital to trendspotting, a perspective about how best to manage the vagaries of life.

This synthesis of the subjective and objective is one of the things I find endlessly fascinating about trendspotting and trends analysis. It is not just a science involving data and clinical observations; it is an art that draws on unique and highly personal experiences—from significant life events to intimate conversations. The man who popularized the art of trendspotting is a prime example of that. John Naisbitt was born in Salt Lake City nine months before the 1929 stock market crash.[1] His father drove a delivery truck; his mother was a seamstress. It would be a stretch to call his childhood comfortable. After high school, he joined the Marines, went to college on the GI Bill, married, ran out of money while his wife was pregnant, and found a job penning speeches for executives at Eastman Kodak. More public relations positions followed. One, for the government, had him studying the impact of Great Society programs. As research, he purchased copies of fifty out-of-town newspapers. "I was absolutely stunned what I learned in three hours about what was going on in America," he recalled.[2] Those revelations inspired Naisbitt to start a consulting business. It failed. He was soon divorced and bankrupt. He continued to give presentations about significant changes that would affect American society—and he collected those ideas in a book called *Megatrends: Ten New Directions Transforming Our Lives.*

Naisbitt's message was pure blue-sky optimism. America's working-class days, he wrote, were over. A postindustrial economy and the values of the sixties counterculture (individualism, feminism, and spiritualism among them) would launch a golden era of economic prosperity and cultural freedom. In 1982, when *Megatrends* was published, those ideas echoed the "morning in America" pronouncements of President Ronald Reagan. *Megatrends* was a *New York Times* bestseller for two years and sold fourteen million copies in fifty-seven countries. Naisbitt became a regular guest at the White House and a friend to British prime minister Margaret Thatcher. And trendspotting became a staple of the media.

Another researcher might have read fifty newspapers and not seen what Naisbitt did. I would argue that what Naisbitt found in those pages struck a nerve because of his hardscrabble childhood, his early failures, and his great desire to succeed. He saw blue skies ahead because signs of them existed, but also because he needed to see them.

I grew up under clear blue skies, but I do not think I realized it until I was shaken—along with many in my generation—by an unexpected event: the 1999 plane crash that killed John F. Kennedy, Jr., his wife, and her sister. (Little did we anticipate that, just two years later, the events of 9/11 would eclipse that tragedy.) Kennedy had been two years behind me at Brown University, and we had friends in common. My schoolmates and I had basked in his halo. To many in our peer group, regardless of political leanings, he represented limitless possibility—the promise of a brighter future. Losing John, his wife, Carolyn, and her sister Lauren Bessette marked the loss of a sense of immortality shared by many who had come of age in the late 1970s and early 1980s—the very years Naisbitt celebrated.

Those of us born in the late 1950s and the first half of the 1960s have existed uneasily on the cusp between the baby boomers and Generation X. We understand the angst of the latter without feeling the entitlement and confidence of the former. What we do share with older boomers is a general optimism and faith in our ability to persevere. We "cuspers" (sometimes called "Generation Jones") graduated from high school or college in a time of high inflation and jobs moving overseas. And now—as is the case for every generation—portents of doom are the mainstay of our media diets, from the pandemic and climate change to the all-too-real prospect of civil war in the no-longer-quite-so-United States; from the rise of populist leaders to cyberterrorism.

And yet, for all the bad news these days, not all seems bleak. "No one can look long at the sun or death," French moralist François de La Rochefoucauld wrote. Optimism and hope are hard to kill. So I am at least an occasional optimist. I am not looking for blindingly happy tomorrows, but neither do I crave doomsday scenarios. What I seek is foresight and some small measure of assurance—a way to navigate uncertainty. A sense of the "why" that helps me to endure—or, better yet, reshape—the "what."

The first step to navigating uncertainty is to keep your ears and eyes wide open. Trend sightings can come from anywhere at any time, so it pays to be attentive (and nosy).

In 2002, I ran into a straight male friend walking his dog in New York's SoHo neighborhood. Nothing unusual in that—but I noticed that the dog's leash was bright pink. Around that time, I also registered more baritone voices during my visits to the hair salon. Soon it was 2003, and I was using sightings of this nature to decode a broader movement of young men embracing fashion, high-end grooming, and home décor. To announce the emerging movement, I borrowed a catchy term (*metrosexual*) first deployed by journalist Mark Simpson to describe a subset of gay men, but I changed its meaning entirely, using it to describe this trend I was seeing among young, straight males. The term and the trend took off, and soon the media requests were endless. You could not avoid metrosexual-mania in 2003—the American Dialect Society even named *metrosexual* its word of the year.

Metrosexualism was not an ephemeral, surface-level craze. It represented a fundamental shift in the way many men define masculinity, a shift that has developed in complex and conflicting ways. From metrosexuals and staunch feminists at one end of the male spectrum to Proud Boys, incels (involuntarily celibate men), and the Taliban at the other, the battle to prescribe what is "manly" continues to rage today.

My work in advertising and communications has encompassed not just cultural shifts such as metrosexuality and "globesity" (the global rise of obesity) but also business and consumer trends, including the always-on media environment, hyperspecialized retail, and narrowcasting. For more than three decades, I have released an annual report that offers a glimpse into the trends of the coming year. I predicted the rise of internet influencers, the loss of privacy, and nature's "revenge" in the climate change era. On the other hand, I was dead wrong when I bought into the buzzword *Chindia*. In many ways, India has faltered while China has become a superpower. And I goofed on "ages without stages"; rather than melding, the generations seem to be at war with one another.

I did not predict the upheaval of COVID-19 in my 2020 forecast, released in late 2019, although I did forecast that more people would start wearing face masks—albeit for reasons of poor air quality rather than a novel coronavirus. I also foresaw more stockpiling of essential goods, but I thought that would be an extension of the "doomsday prepper" movement that has loomed since the 1990s. What I did know for certain when I wrote my 2020 report was that we were living in a world that felt increasingly out of control. "Chaos as the new normal," I called it. Spot-on, but soon intensified beyond what I could have imagined.

If you have ever seen a murmuration of starlings, you likely came away with a fresh appreciation of beauty. These are huge gatherings of as many as a million or more small birds.[3] They swoop and dive and form dazzling patterns while flying so close together they look like a single organism. They do this at high speed. And somehow, they never collide with one another.

The starlings communicate so precisely and instantaneously, it is as if they share a collective brain. This tells us their organization is not top-down; they have no leader. It also tells us they are not aware they are part of the larger group; they are conscious only of the six or seven birds surrounding them.

Why do starlings form a murmuration? Predictably, for protection against predators. The noise they make en masse can be deafening. Their sudden movements are baffling—in a flash, the birds can turn their backs so they look like an impenetrable shield.

In certain respects, these starlings form a perfect society. Intuition is instant, simultaneous for all, and so accurate as to defy belief.

Now for the bad news . . . at least for North Americans.

Starlings are not native to our continent. In the 1890s, Eugene Schieffelin imported a hundred starlings from Europe and uncaged them in New York City's Central Park. For a while, they stayed in New York, but then, because they are migratory, they moved on.

There are now so many starlings in the United States that hordes of hundreds of thousands or more are not uncommon. They can devour entire harvests. Twenty tons of potatoes in a single day. Their droppings contribute to or cause histoplasmosis, a fungal lung ailment, and toxoplasmosis, an infection that afflicts pregnant women and their fetuses.

And they kill. In 1960, a Lockheed Electra was taking off from Logan Airport in Boston when some ten thousand starlings flew straight into the plane, clogging its engines. Sixty-two people died.

Many efforts have been mounted to control the two hundred million starlings in the United States. None has succeeded. The viewers who marvel at YouTube videos of a murmuration may overlook the harsh truth: Beauty comes at a price. And you almost never know in advance what that price will be.

I often think about starlings when I contemplate what the internet has done to culture and society. I recall a vivid prediction written at the turn of the century by internet pundit and Grateful Dead songwriter John Perry Barlow. In "A Declaration of the Independence of Cyberspace," he wrote about a new, egalitarian world in which nonconformity and all beliefs would be welcomed and where traditional legal concepts of property, expression, and identity would no longer apply.[4]

The idealized world Barlow imagined has not come to pass, unfortunately. The songwriter ignored an immutable human statute: the law of unintended consequences.

The story of the past two decades is the story of a murmuration: big dreams, beautiful visions, and unforeseen repercussions.

So, what will the next two decades hold? It is a no-brainer to say that the catastrophic events of 2020–21 kicked off a reset of almost everything. It is more challenging to figure out which changes are short-term and which will have staying power. To separate the two, I will first look back to events from 2000 to 2020 and the cultural shifts we can glean from this recent history. Then I will look forward to a specific date: January 19, 2038. Why that day? For one, it has two code names, *Y2038* and *Epochalypse*. It is a sort of cousin to Y2K, the much-feared computer glitch that put a damper on New Year's Eve celebrations as we moved into the current millennium on January 1, 2000 (a year prior to the official start date, but present-day humans don't have patience for such hair-splitting). The technical explanation of the "year 2038 problem" defies pithy description, but the basic idea is this: Some computer scientists believe that on January 19, 2038, at 03:14:07 UTC, we will run out of room to encode time on whatever digital devices the world is using.

When I first learned about Y2038, it struck me as a natural end point for this book. With Y2K and Y2038 as our bookends, we are left with a span of roughly four decades to unpack, a span that speaks to the heavy handprint of digital technology on virtually every trend you will encounter in these pages—and on all of human life in the twenty-first century.

Fair warning: Some of the predictions in this book may make you want to retreat to a distant cave. I can relate. Gaming out worst-case scenarios has sent me to bed with a bag of chips or a box of cookies more than once. But I always return to the first truth of our contemporary predicament: We may have stone-age minds, but we live in a space-age technology world. And that brings not just challenges but potential solutions.

Let's start with four baseline global observations about where we find ourselves today:

- **"Together apart" is now normal.** Thanks to technology, we can create highly personalized environments in which we listen (alone) to our customized playlists and watch (alone) our streamed entertainment on our devices. If we so choose, we can remain hermetically sealed within our biased media bubbles and echo chambers, existing in worlds of our own making.
- **Economic inequity has increased exponentially** since the mid-1970s in many countries,[5] creating wholly different experiences and expectations for the many at the bottom versus the few at the top. Social safety nets are in tatters, especially in the United States (compared with its industrialized peers), as the disenfranchised and even the diminishing middle class prove impotent against the lobbying might of those who would keep riches and rights for themselves.
- **Self-centeredness has become our worldview,** with everyone, including children, being encouraged to build and nurture their "personal brands."
- At the same time, **we place more value on shared experiences.** Selfies are giving way to friends-and-family video chats—and that runs deeper than pandemic-era needs. In business, too, we see a new emphasis on togetherness. Collaborative-everything reigns.

All around us, we can see that our reality is on the one hand this, on the other hand that. Yin and yang. Hermetically sealed worlds and community. Self-centeredness and increased awareness of the inequities affecting others. Such is the nature of trends: They are balanced to varying degrees by countertrends. Even as we see the rise of nationalism and tribalism among some, there is a new recognition among others of the interconnectedness of the planet's peoples and an understanding that no country will be safe from a virus—or any other massive threat—until all countries are safe. Organized religion is declining even as spirituality and new belief systems are rising.

What else lies in wait for us in 2038? Here is a taste of the trends that I will explore in the chapters ahead.

Government: Society's faith in current systems of government will fracture further. Democracy as the optimal system of governance will be questioned more intensely, most often by politicians who crave absolute power and by citizens who want to return to idealized versions of the past that are dependent on racial, economic, and social inequality.

A new world order: In his 2006 book, *Mind Set!,* John Naisbitt warned that the right to run the world was up for grabs and that Europeans were poised to seize it. In the years since, as Europe has struggled with the social and financial repercussions of stagnation and what Naisbitt and his wife and coauthor, Doris Naisbitt, later described as the continent's "widespread exploitation of social welfare,"[6] China has ascended instead, accumulating not just massive power but also the self-awareness and confidence that precede it. That nation is not the only rising force, however, with new would-be masters including obscenely high-net-worth individuals and immense technology giants all working to create a future to their liking.

Hate in the ether(net): Hate is in the air, stirred up by two decades marked by increasing anxiety and stoked and distributed far and wide via new technology pathways. Worse, hate and hate speech have become normalized, with hostility and hate-drenched abuse spewed on social media by ordinary individuals emboldened by anonymity. The repercussions will extend well beyond the internet and are already linked to "a global increase in violence toward minorities, including mass shootings, lynchings, and ethnic cleansing," according to the Council on Foreign Relations.[7] Jihadist, white supremacist, and nationalist groups will get increasingly sophisticated in harnessing the climate of hate to their own purposes.

The missing middle: In these polarized times, *middle* and *center* have a bad rap. Up-and-at-'em types are fond of quoting the Iron Lady, British prime minister Margaret Thatcher: "Standing in the middle of the road is very dangerous; you get knocked down by the traffic from both sides." Those who style themselves as progressives point out that Dr. Martin Luther King, Jr., wrote of the "white moderate, who is more devoted to 'order' than to justice" as a great stumbling block in the way of Black freedom.[8] Today, hewing to the center is derided as indecisive at best, dangerous at worst, even though many people long for more moderate days and leaders. As sociopolitical dissatisfaction intensifies, more people will gravitate away from the middle ground in favor of the more radical ends.

Tribes: Tribes will become as important as national allegiances. Real tribes or virtual? Virtual is more likely. As democracy fragments in the Western urbanized world, it will be harder to identify physical tribes; beyond our immediate neighbors, relatives, and close friends, who is in our lifeboat? We will join various groups out of psychological need and will ultimately see them as key to our survival.

The end of privacy: As I write this, London is home to some 691,000 surveillance cameras—roughly seventy-three per thousand residents.[9] That is a massive number, but it is only enough to garner the English capital third place on the list of the top twenty most surveilled cities. The top two—and sixteen in total on the list—are in China, with the remaining three in India. Worldwide, we are using technology to perfect the art of digital control, and CCTV is just the start. Also on offer: AI algorithms, personal GPS, and on-body devices that track one's emotional state. In some countries, we see the trend of gadgets touted as "health devices" serving up user data to deep-pocketed bidders. In others, we can expect to see mandatory ID bracelets measuring reactions not only to commercial but also to political messages, to gauge attitudes and detect dissent. Is resistance possible? Yes (outside the most totalitarian societies). A digital detox—moving "off the grid" by turning off electronic devices and exiting the information superhighway, whether for a week or permanently—will be a status symbol, as in "the more disconnected I am, the more I am immune to digital control."

Science polarized: Through the first half of 2020, people worldwide longed for a vaccine that could protect them from COVID-19, expecting it would take quite a while. Yet within a year of the virus being identified and sequenced, scientists had the first of several vaccines ready for trial.[10] As of mid-October 2021, almost half the world's population had received at least one dose of vaccine. This astonishing scientific achievement has prompted admiration but has also stirred suspicion and fears, ranging from the expected (potential long-term side effects) to the extreme (the vaccinations are a cover for implanting microchips; the vaccines interfere with human DNA[11]). Ever since a flawed MMR (measles, mumps, and rubella) study in 1998 touched off a global anti-vaxxer movement, science has become a flashpoint for conspiracy theories, made worse by advances in gene intervention. Even the late Stephen Hawking expressed fear of the wealthy and otherwise advantaged using new scientific technologies to create a genetically enhanced elite.[12] Science, the great hope, is now also science, the great divider.

Population redistribution: Historically, cities have been the most expensive places to live. As more work is performed remotely and more retailers and cultural institutions go virtual, will people with money abandon urban landscapes for greener (literally) pastures? Already, the countryside and small towns are becoming more desirable—and more expensive. Rural areas will struggle to absorb this migration, with resentment taking hold among the natives.

The countertrend to the urban exodus in the United States and Europe will be huge growth in metropolitan areas in other parts of the world.[13] By 2025, there will be twenty-nine megacities—cities with a population greater than ten million—including Lahore, Jakarta, and Shenzhen in Asia, Bogotá and Lima in Latin America, and Kinshasa in Africa.[14] And we can expect to see new, highly planned cities emerge, such as the one proposed by ex-Walmart billionaire Marc Lore, who is planning to build his utopia, Telosa, somewhere in the American West.

Entertainment: Thanks to AI and ever more sophisticated algorithms, media and entertainment content will get better and better at hijacking our minds. We will succumb eagerly. This is in part because entertainment will become more adept at targeting our pleasure-generating brain receptors and at reaching us wherever we are, from standing in line at a grocery store to window shopping or soaking in the tub. And the psychological payoff will be more compelling, with entertainment delivering an escape from a reality that too often overwhelms.

Gender: One in six Gen Z adults in the United States identifies as LGBTQ+.[15] This reflects the new reality that gender is increasingly viewed as a social construct and as more malleable than people accepted in earlier eras. As a counterbalance to gender fluidity, some groups will "resuscitate" traditional gender characteristics and attempt a return to more rigid norms.

Money: A cashless economy is overdue. And with many permanently unemployed and underemployed people, a universal basic income (UBI) will no longer be quite so controversial; in some places, it will be deemed a necessity to ensure social stability. Cryptocurrency? NFTs (non-fungible tokens, which allow digital content to be bought and sold)? The latter is already spawning communities—Pudgy Penguins, anyone?[16]—and we can be sure the next fifteen years will bring events equally as astonishing as the $11.75 million selling price of the *CryptoPunk 7523* NFT sold at a Sotheby's auction in June 2021. With China already having announced a crackdown on cryptocurrencies,[17] efforts to regulate the sector globally will kick into high gear.

Climate: In the face of our looming climate catastrophe, we will see the phasing out of internal combustion engines, a reduction in air travel, and the development of renewable-energy technologies combine to create a new low(er)-impact normal. The Greta Thunberg generation will use smart technologies to achieve their ethical aspirations and live the less destructive lifestyles they demand of others. Entrepreneurs will find solutions that allow people to indulge while feeling good about being environmentally conscientious. For instance, the Midnight Trains service, expected to launch in 2024, will offer overnight rail trips from Paris to a dozen European cities, allowing travelers to save on hotel expenses and generating a far smaller carbon footprint than air travel.[18]

Shopping: The traditional mall will be extinct, with more of these massive properties converted to mixed-use campuses, work and education hubs, and complexes of tiny (also known as micro) apartments. Among the economically comfortable, the dominant consumer philosophy will be "less is better," with experiences more highly valued than products. Still, an intensified focus on feathering our nests and having fast access to the latest technologies will keep commerce flowing. And e-tailers will find ways to make online shopping more sociable and entertaining, ensuring that shopping as "sport" and "hobby" never quite goes away.

(Un)luxury goods: Luxury will be defined, as always, by what is unattainable by the masses, but the most valuable luxury items are changing. Increasingly, rather than things that glitter, we will be placing a premium on uncrowded spaces (e.g., business-class lounges at airports, large home lots); unscheduled time; natural settings and (relatively) uncontaminated water, air, and food; and quality concierge healthcare. Privileged people always want more, but in the future, their desires will be less about material possessions and more about quality of life. For dominant groups, add community living spaces marked by social order, government stability, uniform racial composition, and effective barriers to migrants.

Taken as a whole, the predictions above paint a picture of a future defined by uncertainty and unpredictability. And unintended consequences. Societies take longer to implode than people imagine, but when they do reach the point of collapse, they implode faster than anyone would ever have believed.

Throughout this book, I will touch on the issues and events that will shape our future and, I hope, start you thinking about potential answers to myriad questions. Among them: How will our perceptions of self change in a world where there is little to no privacy, where we might be monitored or surveilled in virtually every space we inhabit? What measures might we take to curb the power of Big Tech and return sociability to our increasingly antisocial social media platforms? Which aspects of our lives will we seek to shrink so that we may maintain more control over them? Will we trust credentialed experts or react to the chaos of modern life by retreating into ever more hermetically sealed echo chambers? Will the milestones and rituals our predecessors enjoyed—e.g., seeking higher education, working in an office, having children, buying a home—be deemed archaic or simply not feasible? How will the rise of far-right populism and the pandemic affect attitudes toward and faith in international institutions? Is capitalism capable of addressing, much less solving, our most complex challenges? Will we lose control over AI? Or have the manipulators *already* become the manipulated? Will cyberattacks replace physical warfare? And above all: As we are overwhelmed by news, as "history" means anything that happened yesterday and nothing from the day before, and as our lives become a nonstop blur, will we just tune out?

That is something none of us can afford.

PART ONE

The Big Picture

✳

Looking back over the past three centuries, one can imagine the enormous uncertainty that would have been kicked off by the Industrial Revolution, not to mention two world wars. Still, the chaos of today—even before COVID-19—seems somehow more pervasive and the contributing poisons (economic and racial injustices, inequity, nationalism, misogyny, extremism) more potent. Maybe that is because we are confronting the increasing probability that we have doomed our planet. Or maybe it's because, thanks to digital technology, we are far more aware of every horror that occurs around the world, no matter how distant or unlikely to impact us directly.

Underlying all this unrest and unease are two conflicting megatrends I call the Great Divide and the Great Reboot.

The Great Divide

Polarization is part and parcel of today's chaos. Even as new technologies make the world smaller, its citizens are growing further apart. In 2011, I wrote about people being "mad as hell"—a phenomenon I sensed mainly in the United States. Fast-forward ten years, and anger and frustration are erupting around the globe. In France, yellow vest protests over an unpopular fuel tax and immigration have given way to street clashes with police over a proposed vaccine passport. In Hong Kong, mass demonstrations have triggered increasingly hostile police responses and restrictive policies from the mainland. In Belarus, photographs of citizens being rounded up have evoked images of World War II. The list goes on—and we all know it will continue to expand.

Left versus right. Progressive versus conservative. Antifa versus Proud Boys. Young versus old. White versus nonwhite. Educated versus defiantly not. Male versus female. Feminist versus incel. Globocrat versus isolationist.

The inescapable truth is that sociopolitical, generational, and interpersonal divides are as much a part of modern society as are digital technologies. And intersections run like crosshatching between them, with overlaps among the various tribes.

The points of conflict are not always organic. There is profit (political and financial) to be made in manufacturing and exacerbating division. Public figures across the political spectrum understand the art of misdirection and the power of tribalism. Businesses, too, are mining profits from veins of conflict—in the process, creating commercial divides: Black Rifle Coffee Company and My Pillow on the right; Starbucks and Patagonia on the left. Our cash register receipts have become quasi-ballots.

At a time when we all face genuine existential threats, one might think people would come together to find solutions; instead, we focus on identifying convenient targets for our blame and condemnation. We live in an age of rage—an era of us versus them, writ large.

The Great Reboot

As is ever the case, countertrends have formed to balance the forces of division that have emerged. We saw a hunger for community and for a more fulfilling and equitable approach to life gain traction over much of the past decade, but this countertrend has taken on increased urgency in the age of the novel coronavirus. The pandemic-related disruptions upturned our lives and gave many of us our first opportunity in years—maybe ever—to pause and deeply consider the big questions: Are we living our best lives? Are we contributing to society? Are our personal and family relationships what we want them to be? Is society moving in the right direction—and, if not, what needs to be done to course-correct?

Some would argue that this period of introspection and demand for change is fleeting—that people will slip back into life as usual as soon as the threat of the pandemic recedes. I disagree. I am convinced that the virus and the circumstances surrounding it—from the "Great Pause" to heightened awareness of low-income workers and the spotlight shone on the fundamental inequities of many economic systems—will have an enduring impact. Many workers are no longer willing to accept conditions they deemed normal prior to the pandemic—whether they be long commutes, abusive work conditions, or inadequate benefits. This deadly virus has shown people their worth and revealed that the way things are is not necessarily how they need to be. People also are questioning their life choices, from personal relationships to career aspirations and location preferences. Amid all the chaos, more of us are contributing to upheaval, but in a controlled, positive way. We are insisting on change—both personal and systemic—and we are doing so with a level of certainty and clarity that was not available to many of us pre-pandemic.

As I consider the forces gathering to counterbalance the rise of hate, intolerance, and polarization, I perceive several impactful shifts that will remain and grow stronger. Among them:

The rise of allyship: Even in the face of societal rage, more people will make an effort not just to coexist with others but to throw their full support behind those least like them. This is a trend with roots that extend well into the past, but it gained strength in 2020 as more people tuned in—even outside the United States—to issues of bias and inequity in the wake of George Floyd's murder by a Minneapolis police officer. Though the initial burst of street demonstrations against racial injustices has subsided, nonmarginalized people will continue to seek opportunities to support the marginalized, including by shopping in their stores, promoting their causes, and finding ways large and small to counter institutionalized biases and discrimination.

The shift from *what* and *how* to *why*: This pandemic has pushed individuals, businesses, and governments to consider with greater rigor what is "essential." At its most basic level, this is a trend that encompasses the move toward more mindful consumption, downsizing, and minimalism, with more people rejecting excess. It extends beyond that, however, to incorporate the bigger picture of our personal and business choices. Why are we operating our businesses the way we are? What is the purpose of insisting workers be onsite five days a week? Is our salary structure geared toward motivating and retaining our best employees at all levels? Is the government's tax structure supporting the greater good or primarily benefiting those at the top? People will insist on examining more closely why we live and work the way we do—and what options exist for change.

A pushback against untruths: Would you ever have anticipated the extent to which facts are now open to interpretation? The possibility that "alternative facts" and "fake news" would be embraced by large swaths of citizens in some countries?[1] It is a situation worsened by social media and the misinformation it disseminates. In the United States, a study by NewsGuard found that social media users consumed twice as much news deemed "problematic, inaccurate, or suspicious" in 2020 as in 2019,[2] and Pew Research Center found that 80 percent of Americans reported being exposed to false news reports about COVID-19 in the early weeks of the pandemic.[3] The social media giants are beginning to corral and remove misinformation and disinformation, but they are moving slowly and not always with great effect. As external pressures continue to mount and more AI-enabled solutions are developed, we will see progress. Ultimately, though, it will be up to users to rise up against untruths and demand accountability among those complicit in the spread of disinformation.

On the radar:

By 2038, we will see far more proficient fact-checking in real time online thanks to crowdsourcing and AI—pop-up notices that contradict a page's content, question a site's bias, warn of potential scams, and recommend verified alternatives. Accusations of bias and censorship will abound.

An embrace of the authentic: This is the shift that may be the most far-reaching. Many people are desperately unhappy with their lives—and with the emptiness, artificiality, and vacuousness of modern life. We can see that in rising rates of depression, anxiety, alienation, and suicide, and we can see that in the rage so freely expressed both online and off. Happy, fulfilled people have little reason to lash out against others unless genuinely provoked, nor are they likely to derive satisfaction from operating as internet trolls. The Great Pause of the pandemic compelled many of us to confront the deficits in our lives. And it offered us a chance to reassess where we are against where we might prefer to be. The change that lies ahead will differ radically from person to person, but a common theme will be the retreat from the artificial to the real, from the digital to the natural, from the mindless to the mindful.

Arundhati Roy, author of *The Ministry of Utmost Happiness,* beautifully described the choice we now face:

> *Historically, pandemics have forced humans to break with the past and imagine their world anew. This one is no different. It is a portal, a gateway between one world and the next. We can choose to walk through it, dragging the carcasses of our prejudice and hatred, our avarice, our data banks and dead ideas, our dead rivers and smoky skies behind us. Or we can walk through lightly, with little luggage, ready to imagine another world. And ready to fight for it.*[4]

The Great Divide or the Great Reboot? Which future will you champion?

To help you consider that question within a broader context, I will ask you first to join me on a trip into the past, to a crisis of another time, albeit one that, happily, never realized its full potential: the Y2K bug that gripped imaginations, instilled fear, and sparked feverish preparations in the late 1990s. We emerged from that potential crisis almost entirely unscathed and never anticipated that it was merely an early shot over the global bow, warning us of the problems digital technology and systemic failures soon would bring. Will we feel the same sense of relief post-COVID-19, not quite grasping that the virus portends a future fraught with equally perilous threats? Even now, as we read of or experience food shortages in Britain, with the *Daily Mail* reporting that one in six shoppers is claiming to be unable to purchase essentials,[5] we struggle to imagine such shortages—and the panic-buying, supply chain disruptions, and employee shortfalls that cause them—as a permanent condition. We also cannot quite visualize the consequences of a mounting global energy crisis, despite Lebanon having run out of power, blackouts hitting China, and gas prices soaring in Europe and the United States.[6] It is over twenty years since Y2K, but we need to look backward to better prepare as we move forward into what comes next.

Also in this section: an examination of the most significant existential threat we face—climate change and continued ecological destruction—and the emergence of chaos as our new normal. I then will look at the forces reshaping the world's great superpowers: the United States and China, two countries whose cultural, economic, and political reach extends across the planet and will help determine what future we attain.

Chapter 1

The Bug and the Virus

The year was 1999. As the world prepared to welcome a new millennium, a torrent of alarming headlines threatened to extinguish the celebratory spirit.

At that time, half of households in the United States owned a computer, but most Americans (like other computer users worldwide, even today) had little idea what went on inside those bulky boxes. And the average user certainly did not understand the mechanics of what might go wrong with their Macs and PCs—and, possibly, every other digital device in an increasingly interconnected world—as the clock tolled midnight on December 31.

Y2K. The millennium bug. It sounded scary. But what was it?

Back in the 1960s—the Pleistocene of computing—storing information on mainframe computers was expensive, and providing storage space on popular commercial computers was an expense that manufacturers didn't want to absorb or pass on to customers. Their solution: minimal storage. If you bought an IBM computer in the early 1990s, that big box contained as little as two kilobytes of memory.[1] (To put this in perspective: Today's iPhone is thirty-two million times more powerful than that.) Beyond cost, there was the human factor. In the 1960s, what programmer was thinking ahead to the year 2000?

To conserve that precious computer memory, programmers compressed years from four to two digits. 1999 became 99. December 31, 1999, became 12/31/99.

That worked for a few decades, but what would happen at the

conclusion of Millennium Eve? The date setting on computers would roll over to 01/01/00. But would computers recognize 00 as 2000—or 1900?

The first recorded mention of a Year 2000 problem was in an internet newsgroup in 1985. No one in business or government seemed to take much notice. A 1993 warning in *Computerworld* has been described as "the information-age equivalent of the midnight ride of Paul Revere."[2] In that article, Peter de Jager, a South Africa–born Canadian, cautioned that a misreading of the year could cause catastrophe, disrupting financial markets, telephone systems, and more.[3] That alarm bell also went largely unheeded.

The general lack of concern didn't reverse course until 1997, when telecommunications giant AT&T announced it would devote "60 percent of the time and money" of its total compliance efforts to test source-code changes in preparation for Y2K. Even then, not everyone took the hint. A 1998 preparedness survey showed that among thirteen sectors studied in the United States, government was the least ready for the so-called millennium bug.[4]

By 1999, amelioration efforts had reached a fever pitch. Estimates of the combined public and private expenditures on Y2K preparation in the United States, the United Kingdom, Canada, Denmark, and the Netherlands range from $200 billion to $858 billion.[5] (All those countries took a proactive stance, unlike Italy, Russia, and South Korea, where little was done in preparation.)[6] Meanwhile, leaders sounded dire warnings. In the United Kingdom, Action 2000, a public-education initiative, was launched.[7] In Denmark, as reported on a family listserv, all households were sent a government brochure with pertinent information about the potential dangers.[8]

"This is not one of the summer movies where you can close your eyes during the scary parts," U.S. president Bill Clinton cautioned.[9] In a late nineties congressional hearing, Chris Dodd and Robert Bennett, U.S. senators representing Connecticut and Utah, respectively, painted a dark picture, saying (somewhat facetiously, Bennett later claimed) that the three places they wouldn't want to be on New Year's Eve 1999 were "in an elevator, an airplane, or a hospital."[10] Their Senate colleague Daniel Patrick Moynihan also raised the alarm: "I have no proof that the sun is about to rise on the apocalyptic millennium of which chapter 20 of the Book of Revelations predicts. Yet it is becoming apparent to all of us that a once seemingly innocuous computer glitch could wreak worldwide havoc."[11] Privately, Moynihan wrote to President Clinton: "You may wish to turn to the military to take command of dealing with the problem."[12]

Even in the midst of an impeachment trial, Congress took care to monitor the compliance efforts of the government and industry, devoting particular attention to the work being done to ensure that utilities, as well as the financial and healthcare sectors, would be ready. Clinton launched his own Council on Year 2000, headed by the Y2K czar, John Koskinen, to coordinate efforts in the United States, while the World Bank–backed International Y2K Cooperation Center helped other countries prepare.

Some evangelical leaders[13] proclaimed that Y2K was a divine judgment; secular society needed to be destroyed and replaced by Christ's realm. Rev. Jerry Falwell filmed and sold a video, *Y2K: A Christian's Survival Guide to the Millennium Bug*. Dr. James Dobson of Focus on the Family gave his staff larger than usual Christmas bonuses, suggesting they use the money to prepare for Y2K.[14]

Over the course of 1999, a perfect storm emerged, with doomsayers, evangelists, and media all painting a similarly dire picture. In the United States, fear was a popular business model: Americans learned to be afraid—and stay afraid. "Once you start warning people and scaring them," observed Koskinen, "it's a little hard to get them off the ledge."[15] Great Britain also had its fair share of fearmongering. Gwynneth Flower, the managing director of Action 2000, recalled a woman who had relocated her family to rural Scotland "because she thought it would be Armageddon."[16]

Gun sales spiked.[17] Late in 1999, FEMA and the American Red Cross suggested that citizens store food and a supply of water.[18] (Full disclosure: I stockpiled bottled water.) By then, Y2K alarmists were recommending keeping four to eight weeks' worth of essential supplies on hand. *The Complete Y2K Home Preparation Guide* suggested that, given the possibility of disruptions, six to twelve months' worth of food and water might be wiser.[19]

Then it was New Year's Eve. Millions braced for disaster.

News anchor Diane Sawyer and her husband, film director Mike Nichols, were guests of writer William Styron and his wife, Rose, on Martha's Vineyard. As they waited for computers to break down and the lights to go out, they created a list of their hopes for a better world. They placed that list in a container and buried it at the base of a tree.[20] And me? On December 31, 1999, this trendspotter and early tech adopter was snuggled up on the couch with her golden retriever, watching the news and calling friends in other countries. By the time Sydney and Tokyo had rung in a bug-free New Year and I had talked to friends in Amsterdam, where it was party hearty as usual, I understood that hiding and worrying had been a dumb move.

John Koskinen had said for more than a year that if the Y2K problem was solved, he would be airborne at midnight. True to his word, he had boarded a plane for New York, accompanied by reporters.[21] Koskinen landed safely. The ball dropped uneventfully in Times Square.

The best reports of that evening came not from oversupplied Y2K preppers or disappointed evangelical ministers but from citizens and organizations with comic tales to share.

At midnight, the Armed Forces Network cut its feed. "Five seconds later, the feed came back, and the newscaster shouted, 'Just kidding! Happy New Year!'"[22]

There is a lot of dawning-of-the-millennium lore. Consider these two anecdotes (neither of which I can substantiate but that are illustrative of the types of stories that circulated):

- The manager of the IT department in a state agency went to work on January 1, 2000, at dawn, checked the systems, and took his staff to IHOP for a celebratory breakfast. The date on their bill was printed as "32Dec1999."[23]
- A group of teenagers lived rent-free in a house in the woods owned by a software engineer on the condition that they undergo survivalist training by a high-ranking Marine officer at the engineer's expense. His hope:

> The teens would help him re-create society after the apocalypse. "New Year's came around, we sat by the fire, took some acid, and contemplated what was next for our lives."[24]

What had happened, for these kids, was a big fat nothing. For the world, the consequences of the not-to-be catastrophe appeared, at least initially, to be positive.

The Y2K effort required coordination and information-sharing between business and the government and among government agencies—including counterterrorist intelligence agencies—on a global level. As the 9/11 Commission reported a few years later, the last few weeks of 1999 were "the one period in which the government as a whole seemed to be acting in concert."[25]

Y2K gave organizations a rare opportunity to solve future problems rather than focus solely on the day-to-day. Budgets that were increased to address a narrow, specific problem allowed managers to test and upgrade all their technology. This paid dividends after the terrorist attack on the World Trade Center a year later. New York's stock exchanges might have been shut down for weeks after 9/11. Thanks in part to the work done for Y2K, they were open after just four days.[26]

The initial aftermath of Y2K was a productive glow of problem-solving. But the interagency coordination was not sustained; after the new millennium dawned with a whimper, governments relaxed. In the United States, a shortage of programmers led businesses to look elsewhere for personnel. When they found skilled programmers in India, they hired them—marking the start of the outsourcing trend that would erode the stability of many American jobs.

In a crisis, people generally respond with a shared concern for the common good. Looking back in 2017, technology journalist Farhad Manjoo reflected on what Y2K revealed about our motivations:

> *If you want to prompt expensive, collective global action, you need to tell people the absolute worst that could happen. We humans do not stir at the merely slightly uncomfortable.*

> *Only the worst case gets us going. . . . Y2K is one of the precious few examples where we mobilized to fight something looming on the horizon—the same kind of mobilization we now need for climate change.*[27]

And, I would add, the same kind of mobilization we would later need against COVID-19.

The threat humans mobilized against in 1999 never materialized—in large part because we mobilized to stop it from materializing. We did not plunge into turmoil because of a Y2K-created disaster, but neither did we ascend into a shiny new millennium in which spirited problem solvers would create guardrails for society. Instead, we slid into a two-decade period of economic and ecological downturns, terrorism, divisiveness, and extremism, all lived against a backdrop of newly digitized lifestyles.

No matter where you lived, how well prepared or economically secure you were, you were almost certainly uneasy or even frightened in 1999. That year was like an apocalyptic sci-fi movie come to life—and even though the ending turned out to be anticlimactic, it left us with the knowledge that technology could pose a threat to our way of life—and our lives.

Skip ahead two decades. By 2019, technology had become an even more pervasive and inescapable aspect of life, with an outsize influence not just on our behavior but on our opinions and beliefs.

In December of that year, Chinese experts were investigating an outbreak of a respiratory illness in the central city of Wuhan. This time the bug was real—a novel coronavirus that soon would begin its deadly spread around the globe. The emergence of such a menace should not have come as a surprise. "The single biggest threat to man's continued dominance on this planet is the virus," Nobel Prize–winning molecular biologist Joshua Lederberg had warned.

For years, Bill Gates had warned everyone who would listen—including through TED Talks and an address at the World Economic Forum in Davos—that the "greatest risk of global catastrophe" would come not from "missiles, but microbes."[28] He urged governments to develop rapid diagnostic tools and vaccines. Presidents George W. Bush[29] and Barack Obama[30] also urged action and infrastructure investment to prevent future deadly airborne disease, with the latter leaving his successor a plan entitled *Playbook for Early Response to High-Consequence Emerging Infectious Disease Threats and Biological Incidents*.[31] And yet, when COVID-19 struck, we all know the shambolic government response that followed.

In contrast to 1999, when well-deployed technological fixes helped avert a potential Y2K crisis, digital technology and the always-on mentality it brought were among the reasons we were ill-prepared to meet the threat of SARS-CoV-2. The insidious effects of constant connection, echo chambers, and the pervasive algorithms that had emerged over the intervening two decades had contributed to populations with little trust in institutions, an anti-expert mindset, and deep sociopolitical and ideological rifts that cast doubt on objective truths and provided fertile ground for conspiracy theories and obstructive behaviors. Almost two years into the virus, when the global population has been presented with clear evidence of the most effective methods of mitigation—namely, face masks and vaccines—we see millions of people refusing to accept either. Whereas Y2K was solved mainly by computer experts employed by governments and businesses, ending COVID-19 will require the active cooperation of the world's citizens. And many are balking.

In the United States, some have been quick to lay the blame for societal divisions and the pushback against global health authorities at the feet of Donald Trump. That's an oversimplification.[32] Trump was a conduit for divisiveness and a rejection of civil discourse, but he simply added water and other nutrients to seeds planted well prior to 2016. Where the former president stands out is in his mastery of social media platforms. He used them to great effect to appeal to a massive audience that had been waiting for someone to say publicly what they had been thinking privately for some time. And, in contrast to how government officials handled Y2K, Trump managed to politicize a crisis that should have been free of ideology.

The United States is far from the only country plagued by division and strife, of course (though the rapid pace of its descent into discord and dysfunction took much of the world by surprise). In South America, Brazil became a tinderbox under the leadership of President Jair Bolsonaro, another leader adept in the use of social media as a distraction and a bully pulpit.[33] Haiti reeled from the assassination of its president and yet another devastating earthquake. And the torturous process of Brexit and its aftermath continues to split the United Kingdom.

The traditional explanations for societal division are inequity, class resentment, racism, and lack of education.[34] Clearly, each of these defects factors into the torn social fabrics we see in much of the world. But there is another underlying reason for today's rage-fueled divides—and for the mass misery that has accompanied COVID-19. That is the ubiquity of technology and the sheer volume of media content. By the time the pandemic took hold in 2020, any theory, whether scientifically proven or a crackpot conspiracy, could potentially reach hundreds of millions of people.[35] Technology has allowed antisocial attitudes to manifest in more powerful ways.

If you were to walk down a street or ride a bus, train, or plane in most of the developed world, it would be rare to see anyone whose eyes are not glued to their phone. A *New Yorker* cartoon got it exactly right, depicting a father turning to his family and asking, "Where shall we go to look at our phones this weekend?" It's not just that we have become captives of our virtual lives, it's also that we do not share common virtual lives.

Our culture is atomized, and it is tribal. We each live in our own bubble, a bubble we populate with people who share our attitudes, beliefs, and values, creating an echo chamber in which we essentially talk to ourselves. Many of those bubbles get news and information from unreliable sources: podcasts, social media, and disinformation sponsored by bad actors domestically or in other countries. Is it any wonder many of us have trouble discerning fact from fiction?

As a society, we need metanarratives to bind us, to make us whole. The response to Y2K benefited from a shared narrative of a technological glitch with the potential to cause chaos if it wasn't addressed in time by experts in government and technology. Most people agreed on the threat, even if they interpreted it personally—for reasons I can't quite recall, I was obsessed with the potential demise of my blow-dryer—and most government and business leaders had been focused for months on preparing. We had a common goal: to get ahead of Y2K, to stop it in its tracks before it plunged civilization into chaos and maybe even darkness.

Contrast that with the response to the current pandemic. The absence of a shared narrative and the inability to agree on a single version of reality—*How did the virus start? Was it intentional? Were the vaccines developed to subjugate the population?*—turned a global health issue into a threat to social stability, forcing us to pay steep costs on all fronts. Nearly five million lives had been lost to COVID-19 as of late October 2021—more than 740,000 in the United States alone—and yet, there are still plenty of people who remain convinced the virus is a hyped-up hoax.[36] Global estimates of the financial damage run as high as $16 trillion,[37] and those costs will continue to mount. The managing director of the International Monetary Fund projected in December 2020 that the loss of global economic output as a result of the pandemic between 2020 and 2025 would total $28 trillion.[38]

Numbers aside, the pandemic has also taken a tremendous toll on people's mental health and sense of well-being. Humans crave stability and continuity. We grudgingly accept that we will experience reversals of fortune, illness, and death, but sustained chaos and uncertainty unhinge us. There is nothing more destabilizing than chaos, and the impact is exacerbated when people cling to conflicting narratives. Even in late 2021, there was broad disagreement about how and where the pandemic started and an abundance of conspiracy theories regarding who stands to benefit from it. And there continue to be global leaders, including Brazil's Bolsonaro, Belarus's Alexander Lukashenko, and India's Narendra Modi, who downplay the virus or refuse to institute measures to contain it adequately.

You might think our efforts to fight the transmission of the virus would have benefited from a critical survival tool most of us have at hand: our smartphones. Almost everyone uses one. Worldwide, there are around 14 billion mobile devices, a figure expected to increase to nearly 18 billion by 2024.[39] That is 18 billion devices for a projected global population of just over 8 billion. Surely, these devices might have proved vital conduits of information during the pandemic, in addition to facilitating contact tracing to mitigate the spread of the virus. No such luck. Instead, they have served as conduits of misinformation and disunity, with "news" from fringe groups and conspiracy theorists edging out mainstream sources.

Today, we do not set aside time to read the news. It follows us everywhere. And we are as likely to watch it as read it. Some five hundred hours of video are uploaded to YouTube every minute.[40] What percentage of the information conveyed do you think is well researched or accurate?

At some point in mid-2020, in the early weeks of the COVID lockdowns, it occurred to me that the twenty-first century had been operating on a two-decade delay. In 1999, we braced for cataclysmic disruption as the clock clicked past 11:59 P.M. on December 31. We didn't feel the anticipated impact until 2020, when the pandemic and a primal scream for racial justice upended the world.

Two decades ago, the primary problem posed by technology was both recognizable and addressable. Today, in contrast, technology in the form of digital images, social media, and citizen-as-news-bureau presents us with questions we cannot easily answer:

- Is technology a danger to democracy or its salvation? It can deliver a record of real events as they happen, but it can also be manipulated into propaganda. How can we tell the difference?
- Will technology enable us to confront inconvenient realities in time to save the planet, or will we be so mesmerized by our screens that we do not notice we are headed toward extinction?

One thing we can say with confidence: Post-2000, many of the most significant trends we are seeing—and will see—stem from the increasing centrality of digital technologies in our lives.

In the next chapter, I show how tech sneaked up on us over the course of decades—alongside violence, extremism, ecological mayhem, and a shaky approach to truth. Only once we understand how they took root can we find a way to dismantle them.

Chapter 2

2000–2019: A Slow Slide

Having spent much of 1999 waiting for the world to implode, we entered the new millennium feeling both relieved and a little foolish. Some people had stockpiled essential goods, weaponry, and cash to weather the coming storm.[1] The rest of us hadn't gone to extremes but still were expecting something big to happen. Instead, we entered two decades of what many would characterize as a steady decline—albeit with regular bursts of violence and calamity.

All of these factors have put us on the path to our current cultural climate, and it is by looking at them—going back to the source—that we can see how we will be propelled into the future.

Mass Shootings and Terrorism

For twenty years, we bobbed and weaved as life threw us one challenge after another. When the Columbine High School shooting occurred in Colorado in the spring of 1999, we had no inkling it would be the start of a horrible trend—with subsequent mass murders at Virginia Tech (2007), the Army Public School in Peshawar, Pakistan (2014), Garissa University in Kenya (2015), Marjory Stoneman Douglas High School in Florida (2018), and myriad other schools, including the horrific Sandy Hook Elementary School massacre in 2012. March 2020 was the first March in nearly two decades without a school shooting in the United States.

It isn't just schools that have been targeted over the past two decades, of course. In the years post-Y2K, mass shootings and terrorist attacks became an all-too-common occurrence around the world, hitting places of worship, nightclubs, shopping malls, concert arenas, restaurants and bars, and newsrooms, among other venues. Many of us can remember the smells and sounds of 9/11 in New York—as well as the sense of camaraderie we all felt in the days that followed. Downtown Manhattan had become ground zero in more ways than one, with ash and grief from the wreckage of the World Trade Center permeating every nook and cranny of that part of the city. It took residents years to realize the full emotional and physical impact of being attacked on our home turf. (I lost my middle-aged golden retriever in 2005 to a mouth cancer, which a Tribeca vet called "9/11 disease." So many people I know live with a range of healthcare challenges that are now termed the third wave of the 9/11 impact.)

Economic Booms and Busts

Economically, the period post-Y2K was boom and bust—heavy on bust—from the burst dot-com bubble in 2000 through to the subprime housing crisis and the global recession of 2007–9, as well as economic crises in Brazil, Greece, Venezuela, and elsewhere. In some ways, these events anticipated what we would experience in 2020; I remember talking with a friend about the Venezuelan toilet paper shortages of 2015–16 and us agreeing that, of all the commodities we would not want to have to live without, that would be very close to the top of the list.

Centers of economic power shifted between 2000 and 2019, too: China surpassed Japan to become the world's second-largest economy (more on this in chapter 6), and by 2018, seventy-one of the world's top one hundred revenue collectors were corporations, not countries.[2] Globally, as of 2019, the richest 1 percent of people owned 44 percent of the world's wealth, according to Credit Suisse.[3] Everyone assumed that Occupy Wall Street would have more of an impact than it has had thus far—although it did introduce much of the world to the notion of "the 1 percent" and made income inequality a talking point on campaign trails.

Extremism and Displacement

Politically and militarily, the first two decades of the new millennium saw the rise of extremist groups such as ISIS and Boko Haram. Around the globe, various forms of nationalism emerged or reemerged—right-wing, socialist, racial, even resource nationalism (governments exerting control over their countries' natural resources), with strongmen the likes of Brazil's Jair Bolsonaro and the Philippines's Rodrigo Duterte bulldozing their way through the opposition. The message was clear: In an era of increased globalization, many of the world's governments and citizens were looking to pull back and fiercely guard their goods and interests.

Meanwhile, wars raged around the world—in Iraq, Libya, Yemen, Afghanistan, Lebanon, Syria, Chad, Sudan, and Somalia, among numerous other places. By the end of 2016, according to the United Nations High Commissioner for Refugees, some 65.6 million people were forcibly displaced, adding a refugee crisis to the world's other woes. In the years since, we have seen the resettlement of refugees exacerbate nationalist tendencies and fuel cries for closed borders—as we have seen, too, during the corona crisis.

In 2016, in another rejection of globalism (or at least regionalism), the United Kingdom began its arduous and conflicted four-year journey of disentangling itself from the European Union. Talk about a dysfunctional process: Breaking up is hard to do.

Even outside of the U.K., anti-immigration sentiment started to run high, and people bemoaned the loss of the days when they had their countries "to themselves." We might have done better to focus on the falsehoods flowing freely across our borders rather than on the human beings. As the world's populations moved online, governments and other entities figured out ever more effective ways to sow disinformation and discord via the internet.

Ecological Mayhem

Environmentally, the twenty years leading up to 2020 were a nightmare (and a cautionary tale), with a profusion of devastating natural disasters and extreme weather events. In the Atlantic, category

4 and 5 hurricanes—most notably Maria, Katrina, Wilma, Irma, Matthew, and Harvey—tore apart areas of the Caribbean, Central America, and the United States. In the Pacific, tsunamis ravaged Indonesia, Japan, New Zealand, and other nations.

Those years also saw the escalation of extreme weather events, which scientists warn will continue to intensify if we don't get a handle on climate change.[4] Drought-fueled wildfires swept through countries from Greece and Australia to the United States, and floods and mudslides killed thousands in Asia. While some would explain away all this extreme weather as something that happens every several hundred years, subsequent storms, the ice melts in the Arctic, rising ocean temperatures, and other signs of an overheated planet have compelled all but the most die-hard climate skeptics to take heed. Let's face it: Mother Nature is angry.

A Global Crisis in Healthcare and the Ascension of Anti-Science

Healthwise, the two decades between Y2K and COVID-19 saw massive increases in obesity, diabetes, and mental health issues. In 2003, my team released a report on "globesity" (global obesity) and noted that the number of obese adults had climbed from 200 million worldwide in 1995 to 300 million in 2000, according to the World Health Organization (WHO). As of 2020, the WHO estimates the number of obese adults at 650 million.[5] Exacerbating the crisis is the fact that medical authorities have identified obesity as a major contributor to COVID-19 hospitalizations and deaths.[6]

Globally, healthcare has been in crisis throughout the past two decades, though some nations have fared far better than others.

Another big healthcare topic circa 2000–2020: the anti-vaxxer movement, sparked by British physician Andrew Wakefield and his since-debunked (yet still widely believed) 1998 study linking the rise of autism to the measles, mumps, and rubella (MMR) vaccine. A global survey conducted by U.K. research charity the Wellcome Trust found that one in three residents of France doesn't believe vaccines are safe, and only around half of Ukrainians believe vaccines are effective.[7] This was well before COVID-19 made vaccination an acutely political issue. UNICEF has cited the anti-vaxxer movement as a contributing factor in the spikes in measles cases in recent years[8]—which includes a 300 percent jump in the first three months of 2019 compared with the same period in 2018.[9]

The anti-vaxxer movement is part of a broader anti-science mindset that has taken hold in recent years. People are displaying a frightening tendency to dismiss scientific facts as being politically biased and just more #fakenews.

Social Progress and Antisocial Tendencies

Socially, we saw a monumental shift post-Y2K in attitudes toward LGBTQ+ acceptance, race, and the role of women in society. So many young people simply cannot fathom how recently homophobia was the default position for most. It was only in 2003 that the U.S. Supreme Court, in its landmark *Lawrence v. Texas* decision, struck down the remaining state laws banning sodomy. Until 2021, Switzerland, which prides itself on its tolerance, prohibited same-sex marriage, full joint adoption by same-sex couples, and access to in vitro fertilization (IVF) for lesbians. And it is telling how shocked many Americans were in 2020 by the U.S. Supreme Court's decision that transgender workers are protected against job discrimination under Title VII of the Civil Rights Act of 1964.[10] Many expected the conservative-leaning court to rule against such protections.

The discourse around race has been transformed by activism rather than the courts. In the 1990s, I watched from outside my home in Amsterdam-Zuid as the Netherlands celebrated Zwarte Piet (Black Pete) at the Sinterklass festival that takes place each year on St. Nicholas Eve in early December. In the summer of 2020, in the wake of the police killing of George Floyd in Minneapolis, I noted in images of the Black Lives Matter demonstration in Leeuwarden that signs protesting Zwarte Piet were out in force. Progress is coming—and perhaps finally at a less glacial pace.

The fight for women's equality and an end to gender harassment and violence also continued around the world during these two decades—most recently, with the rise of the #MeToo movement, which started in earnest in 2017. Behavior that in 2000 was considered normal—or was at least something women were expected to tolerate—would lead to sanctions in most workplaces today.

Simultaneously, these years—and particularly the last five—marked the beginning of the "age of rage." My 2011 trends report noted that anger was the color of the zeitgeist and that anyone who wasn't tapping it risked appearing out of touch. While Barack Obama's cool, calming rhetoric hit the spot for many Americans in panic-stricken 2008, this no-drama approach was way out of style at a time when everyday Americans were getting more and more incensed.

These last few years have seen a marked rise in not just anger but incivility, aggression, and hyperpartisanship. Sociopolitical divisions have intensified, spurred on by all manner of conspiracy theories, cries of "fake news," and the interference and rabble-rousing of social media bots.[11] It is astonishing how dissonant the news is on the different sides—and especially how irreconcilable the "facts" are. This disconnect has been playing out in real time during the pandemic, with some people still convinced it's all a hoax and others intending to go to ground for the long term.

Bye-Bye, Analog

As momentous as many of these happenings were, few would disagree that the most impactful shift we saw between 2000 and 2020 was the wholesale embrace of digital living. From general internet use to online shopping and social media, from GPS to e-finance, from streaming video to e-sports, from smartphones to smart speakers and smart homes, we gradually shifted our everyday activities into the digital realm.

The world is now divided not just by wealth and income but also by technology access. There is no better example of the digital divide than the two Koreas: In North Korea, internet access is essentially nonexistent among the general population. In South Korea, in sharp contrast, more than 95 percent of the population is online, and the country enjoys one of the world's fastest average internet connection speeds. There are also divides within nations. In the

United States, according to Pew Research, 92 percent of white Americans used the internet at least occasionally as of 2019, compared with just 85 percent of Blacks.[12] Moreover, internet use is prevalent among 94 percent of Americans living in suburbs and 91 percent in urban areas versus just 85 percent in rural localities.[13] This divide has tremendous implications for not only access to information but also the ability to influence. Those with full access to these digital tools can outcommunicate those without.

Virtual Is Vital—and Exhausting

As we all are aware by now, digital life increasingly *is* life for those plugged in to the internet. Nobody anticipated how the internet would change us as humans. Not just how we behave, but how we think. We have become less patient. Less accepting of delays and glitches. We are more anxious and competitive—scanning the pages and posts of others and fretting that we are missing out or not keeping up.

We have also managed to turn our new digital tools into life "wardens," using our smartwatches, apps, and fitness gadgets to track our every move (literally). Yet another way to measure our imperfect lives.

And then there is the sheer pace of life lived digitally. It is easy to fantasize about the old days, when a secretary would type a letter, mail it, and then wait for a reply to arrive a few days or weeks later. I never worked in that world—fax machines were already on the scene when I graduated from college—but the limited technology of the mid-1980s at least allowed us to leave work in the office from time to time.

A Dizzying Pace of Change

Without question, much happened over the first twenty years post-millennium—not least the move from analog to digital and the rise in extremism—but events never reached the level of catastrophe we expected from the Y2K bug. At no point did the world face a crisis as one. At no point did we all have a common enemy. At no point did people across the globe simultaneously wonder whether life would ever return to normal and realize that the answer was a resounding no. Which is not to say we weren't concerned. Many of us felt the world was moving in the wrong direction and that various elements of it—political, environmental, economic—were spinning out of control. We were living in a time of anxiety and animosity. A time of rapid, unpredictable, and often unwanted change. It was dizzying and exhausting. In December 2019, when I released my trends forecast for 2020, I wrote:

> *As we approach the new year, people everywhere are uncertain about the future and whether it's too late to change our present course. We're feeling emotionally out of touch with one another—and hungry for physical touch. We're fearful of the destruction we're collectively wreaking on the planet and clinging to the hope that our small acts of mindfulness will go some way toward reversing the damage. We're frantic to slow down the spiraling changes long enough to take a restorative breath and assess whether we're living our best life.*

Soon after, we would be forced to slow down—and the chaos would spiral. A few months into 2020, we were amid a global pandemic that wreaked havoc on a level that far exceeded what we expected from Y2K all those years ago.

2020: Kaboom! (Our New Anything-but-Normal)

By mid-September 2020, the world exceeded 28 million confirmed cases of COVID-19, and more than 900,000 people had died. By November 2021, those figures had risen dramatically, to 249 million confirmed cases and more than 5 million deaths. The numbers continue to rise even as more people are fully vaccinated and boosted.

This virus has touched each of us—some in debilitatingly painful ways; others more tangentially, but still with an enduring impact. Children experienced a vastly different world from what they had known at the start of 2020. Many schools shut down and moved online—for those students fortunate enough to have the required equipment and broadband access. Socializing with friends happened via social media, online gaming, or video chat. Adults in nonessential jobs spent the lockdowns at home, ordering supplies to be delivered or (reluctantly) venturing out clad in masks and gloves and clutching hand sanitizer (if they were lucky enough to find any in those early months). Financial markets were unsettled, and unemployment skyrocketed, with small businesses and retail workers feeling the greatest pain.

To one extent or another, this pandemic has forever altered our lives. And no one—not even the experts—knows the eventual extent of its toll.

The More Things Change . . .

One similarity between life during the pandemic and during the Y2K scare is the human tendency to obsess over the details rather than the looming existential threat. In March 2020, I flew from Zurich to Newark, New Jersey, settled into a six-hour car ride, and quarantined for two weeks in Rhode Island. (A barely winterized beach shack was our only available safe space in the United States, and so Jim and I moved in, both of us working practically around the clock, because we were living on COVID time, where time zones blended—as did the days and nights.) I had already become the de facto head of our family supply chain, organizing fresh produce and meat deliveries for a clan scattered across the country, ordering carrot cheesecakes as gifts to support a friend with a small bakery, sending dog pictures and videos (we have two goldens these days, Ben and Harley—both rescues) to cheer up friends around the planet, and working fourteen or fifteen hours a day, initially sequestered in a tiny guest room, following the strict quarantine rules I'd agreed to when I cleared customs. Thanks to warnings from a vigilant Polish friend in Switzerland who had been tracking COVID-19 for at least two months, I had ordered several bottles of sanitizer, a case of red sauce, a case of mushrooms, a large jar of grated Parmesan cheese, and sixteen rolls of toilet paper for the Rhode Island house, never imagining the eight weeks would be spent in a miasma of Zoom and Teams meetings, sustained by a single meal a day, oftentimes pasta or an omelet.

Many Americans were not taking the lockdowns and social distancing as seriously as Jim and I were. Both of us wore kitchen gloves and masks when we brought in boxes of canned goods from Amazon, one of the few deliveries we could arrange as supply shortages became more frequent. Believe me, our challenges were the epitome of first-world privilege, just as my ridiculously superficial worry about my blow-dryer failing to operate post-Y2K was, twenty years earlier, but this is how humans cope: We focus on what we can handle.

World, Interrupted

The twenty-first century is shaping up to be far different from what previous generations—and our younger selves—had imagined. Futurists looking ahead to the next century in the 1900s weren't forecasting a global pandemic, political extremism, terrorism, enduring poverty and misery for vast swaths of the world's people, and the wanton destruction of our planet. They anticipated progress—a world that would have managed to solve the big issues of the previous century and create life experiences that were heavy on convenience and light on strife.

Prognostications matter. Forecasts and fiction help to shape not just our expectations of the future but also our experience of the present. We use these inputs to establish notions of what the future will look like and are disappointed when reality fails to live up to what we envisioned, as it typically does. Sure, we can buy a hoverboard today, but it is nothing like what 1989's *Back to the Future Part II* (set in the far-off year of 2015) led us to expect. (On the flipside, *BttF PII* failed to anticipate the internet, so maybe we're ahead of the game.) It is hard to find a baby boomer who doesn't feel rooked to be living in a world devoid of the flying cars and robotic housekeepers promised by *The Jetsons*—even if that cartoon series was set in 2062.

We pretend to ourselves, too, that there is an orderliness to time—that one second flows into the next minute, the next hour, the next day/week/month/year/era—and yet no two people's perceptions of time are the same. In some respects, January 2020 feels like a lifetime ago. The weeks many of us spent in self-quarantine and lockdowns seemed at once cruelly slow and blazingly fast. What happened to April, to May?, people asked. Did we have spring?

Poet William Carlos Williams described time as "a storm in which we are all lost." In several ways, the two decades leading up to 2020 further distorted our sense of time. The once-shining beacon of the future dimmed during that period and, in some respects, darkened to the point of being menacing. In the United States, it was projected for the first time that young people would not enjoy a higher standard of living than their parents experienced.[14] Globally, we hurtled toward the catastrophic scenarios linked to climate change without having the first clue of how to change course. The gaping chasm between rich and poor, powerful and powerless, showed no signs of lessening. And even as the world embraced each new digital "solution," many of us were left feeling that the price paid—the loss of privacy, time with family, community-based activities, even boredom-induced creativity—was too high.

If we can point to a silver lining of the pandemic of 2020, it may be that it stopped the human population in its tracks, forcing us to assess our degree of satisfaction with the present and reshape our thinking about the future. In my lifetime, I cannot think of another period in which trendspotting and trends analysis have been more vital. Everything is up in the air.

One thing that has become apparent is that, even though time has passed in quantifiable segments—in years and decades and centuries, according to our calendars—so much has stood still or even regressed. Until the pandemic forced schools to shut their doors in the first few months of 2020, education was still a teacher standing in front of a classroom, much as it was three hundred years ago. For all the modern marvels of the high-tech workplace, in 2019, commuters in Los Angeles spent an average of a hundred hours stuck in traffic jams.[15] In Moscow and New York City, it was ninety-one hours. In São Paulo, eighty-six. Despite remarkable advances in medicine, half the world's population lacks access to essential health services, according to the WHO and the World Bank.[16] In what felt like the blink of an eye in March 2020, everything changed: We had new teaching styles, new commuting styles, and a new emphasis on wellness, including a greater appreciation of the importance of staying mentally and physically fit. There was a keen awareness of age—those of us aged sixty or older were warned we were especially vulnerable—and the word *comorbidity* suddenly popped up everywhere, further alarming those with preexisting conditions.

Collectively, the world has spent trillions of dollars over the past twenty or so years to avert (Y2K) or clean up and rebuild after disasters, to wage wars without clear-cut objectives (or resolutions), and to promote an economic model based on overconsumption—a model that has put us on a path to ecological catastrophe while rending the essential fabric of society in the process. What progress do we have to show for those trillions of dollars invested? Aside from basic advances in the standards of living of the people eking out an existence in the most impoverished places around the globe and some high-tech conveniences for the rest of us, how has daily life improved on planet Earth? Can most of us genuinely say we are better off—and more satisfied with the direction in which society is headed—than we were in 1999?

What might we accomplish if we were to allow the catastrophic events of 2020 to serve as a reset? If we took advantage of this unexpected crisis to reconsider what we want the future to look like? What if we took the time to consider deeply the lessons of the past twenty years and used that learning to conceive a better path forward? What if we created something meaningful out of the nothingness of the start of this millennium?

We have an opportunity to start the century anew. The pandemic gave us that. It is my intention that this book will help readers reset their societal GPS, showing them the urgency of rerouting ourselves toward a better destination than that toward which we were heading at the start of 2020.

Now that I've established the events that defined 2000 and 2020, I will unpack how that zeitgeist will impact the next two decades. First, we will turn to the existential threat of climate change and planetary destruction, both inextricably linked to the chaos that pervades our world. If we fail to solve the problem of climate change, how much will anything else we do matter?

Chapter 3

Climate Truths

Before we peer further into the crystal ball to divine the course of the next twenty years, we must first acknowledge one singularly inconvenient truth: Climate overhangs every aspect of our lives. Consequently, facets of the climate crisis will necessarily be woven into the forecasts throughout this book.

In one sense, humankind's reluctance to acknowledge and then act on climate change in a timely and effective fashion is an example of what happens when critical patterns and shifts are recognized but ignored. Alarm bells are only effective when they are heeded. We can place the first calls for climate action at least as far back as the late nineteenth century when Swedish scientist Svante Arrhenius suggested that fossil fuel combustion would lead to global warming.[1] Within my lifetime, calls to action have increased in frequency and urgency. In 1962, Rachel Carson planted a seed in the public consciousness with her seminal book *Silent Spring*, regarded as a catalyst for the modern environmental movement. Even with the book's impact on public perceptions, it took another fifteen years for a major global leader, U.S. president Jimmy Carter, to publicly recognize the problem of climate change and call for a reduction in carbon dioxide (CO_2) emissions. I was in college in 1979 when the World Meteorological Organization brought together experts on climate and "mankind" at the World Climate Conference in Geneva to find ways to "prevent potential man-made changes on climate that might be adverse to the well-being of humanity."[2] I can assure you that my classmates and I were paying far more attention to the anti-apartheid movement in South Africa than to anything having to do with global warming.

I had been out of college for a few years when, in 1988, Dr. James Hansen, then director of the NASA Goddard Institute for Space Studies, warned the U.S. Congress about the "greenhouse effect." He could say with "ninety-nine percent confidence" that greenhouse warming was happening—and accelerating.[3] *The New York Times* featured his testimony on its front page.[4] (That was also around the time many of us were introduced to the concept of acid rain, although the term had been coined a century earlier by Scottish chemist Robert Angus Smith.)[5]

Despite the media interest, Dr. Hansen's attempt to prod Congress into action on carbon emissions produced no widescale effort to slow global warming. After a brief flurry of concern following his testimony, the greenhouse effect had little presence in the national conversation, and most of the ensuing U.S. presidential administrations failed to energetically commit to protecting the environment. Other nations performed no better, although there were significant milestones the following decade, including the Earth Summit in Rio de Janeiro in 1992 and the Kyoto Protocol five years later.

The first hint of a movement-level wake-up call had to wait until the debut of former vice president Al Gore's 2006 documentary, *An Inconvenient Truth*—nearly two decades after Hansen's congressional testimony. Gore's movie became a staple of science classes in schools around the world. Many kids regarded it as they would an urgent group text. Their parents and grandparents? Not so much. The media? Only in the last couple of years has the climate finally been deemed worthy of significant coverage.[6]

Why is the biggest story of our lives not billboarded day and night? And how were government leaders and ordinary citizens blinkered on climate change for so long? The history of twenty-first-century media offers an explanation. Google launched in 1998, Facebook in 2004, YouTube in 2005, Twitter in 2006. Apple revolutionized portable phones with the iPhone in 2007. In the years in which coverage of the growing climate crisis should have been accelerating, local newspapers and television stations, network news, and investigative teams all shrank while interactive media that catered to interest groups and manufactured biased echo chambers thrived. Consequently, there has been no generally acknowledged "truth" about the climate crisis or even universal acknowledgment that there is a crisis, much less agreement on what has caused it.

A 2020 survey by the Yale Program on Climate Communication found that more than a quarter of Americans still do not accept that global warming is occurring.[7] And the UN's Peoples' Climate Vote survey of 1.2 million people in fifty countries found that less than two-thirds of respondents recognized climate change as a global emergency.[8] Even among those who do believe in climate change, not everyone supports radical action to slow it. A 2020 survey by the Open Society European Policy Institute found that while 80 percent of Spaniards agree that "we should do everything we can to stop climate change," agreement levels only reached as high as 57 percent in the United States and 58 percent in the U.K.[9] In the UN survey, one in ten respondents said society is already doing enough to combat the issue.[10]

Those of us already seeing the impact of climate change outside our windows are less likely to be in denial. In January 2021, the startup nonprofit Potential Energy Coalition launched a $10 million initiative called Science Moms. One of those moms, Dr. Joellen Russell, an oceanographer at the University of Arizona—yes, that seems strange to me as well—lives in Tucson, not far from me. Her experience in America's third-fastest-warming city mirrors what I have been seeing.

In a *New Yorker* profile of the Science Moms, Dr. Russell described a planet moving rapidly toward disaster in 2020: "We had one hundred and eight days above a hundred degrees—you can't quite get your head around just how long that is."[11] (Historically, the average number of hundred-degree days Tucson experiences in a year is sixty-two.) With COVID lockdowns in full effect and temperatures soaring, Russell's children, aged ten and fourteen, couldn't visit their friends' houses, and it was too hot to go to the playground—or even to play in the backyard. Cabin fever set in. Russell started waking the children before dawn to walk the dog. "I had to plan ahead for harsh conditions, like a general. I tried to make it fun. Like, we're on an adventure!" But she worried about their mental health. "They need to see the sky!"[12]

One hot day, she sent her children out for a bike ride in long sleeves and hats to protect them from the sun. An hour later, her daughter returned with what she described as a headache. It was heat exhaustion. Because of the potential COVID risk, Russell didn't take her daughter to the emergency room. She did what she could: In a darkened room, she covered the girl's head with cold washcloths. Dr. Russell was, she recalled, "scared to death."[13]

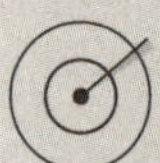

On the radar:

By 2038, rising temperatures will prevent many sporting matches from occurring outdoors, leading to the construction of high-tech indoor arenas and further boosting the rise—and profitability—of e-sports.

Take experiences like Russell's, add poverty and food scarcity, and you have a problem that promises to test the resolve and resources of governments globally: extreme weather exiles. In the last decade alone, according to a report by Euronews, some seven hundred thousand Europeans have been displaced because of extreme weather such as flooding and wildfires.[14] Climate events causing displacement on the continent more than doubled between 2016 and 2019, from forty-three to one hundred.[15] And experts are forecasting that the trend will not only continue but accelerate—in Europe and elsewhere. Gianmaria Sannino, who heads the Climate Modelling Laboratory at Italy's National Agency for New Technologies, Energy, and Sustainable Economic Development (ENEA), warns that events now classified as extreme will become normal.[16]

People in virtually all regions and at all income levels will be affected, with millions potentially forced to migrate or perish. Jola Ajibade, an assistant professor at Portland State University who studies climate migration, says "impermanence" will characterize the way we live in the future. She calls the recent tendency for families to live in one place for generations "a privilege" that no longer is feasible.[17]

Climate migration will bring its own troubles by 2038, as parts of the world deemed safe—or at least safer—feel the strain of newcomers their systems were not built to support. Conflicts will erupt, and legislation will be passed to ensure that life-enabling resources such as clean water and healthcare are inequitably distributed, prioritizing the wealthy, politically connected, and deep-rooted over the poor and more recently arrived.

In the coming years, "location, location, location" won't just be about gorgeous views and tony neighborhoods. It will be about tapping into housing and communities that offer high levels of preparation and resources. Exclusive enclaves will boast abundant supplies of water (perhaps through desalination), stockpiled rations for those emergencies bound to occur, and construction codes and land-management techniques designed to fortify the populace against floods, fire, drought, hurricanes, or whatever other phenomena are likely to come knocking. Think: six-foot "fire moats" surrounding homes and communities, as Christiana Figueres and Tom Rivett-Carnac have forecast in their book, *The Future We Choose: Surviving the Climate Crisis.*[18]

Philip Alston, UN Special Rapporteur on extreme poverty and human rights, speaks of an impending "climate apartheid" in which low-income households are priced out of areas less vulnerable to climate change. "Perversely," Alston says, "while people in poverty are responsible for just a fraction of global emissions, they will bear the brunt of climate change and have the least capacity to protect themselves."[19]

The good news: After decades of inaction, change is afoot—or at least hard conversations are afoot, and those can lead to change. In summer 2021, the world witnessed a series of extreme weather events, ranging from catastrophic flooding in Germany and Tennessee to wildfires that ravaged Greece and the American West. At long last, those unceasing and dramatic events made the climate crisis hard to ignore. There's even a growing awareness that, in addition to the more obvious impacts—rising seas threatening coastal communities, extended heat waves costing lives and destroying crops—climate change will make us sick.

The 2021 *Lancet* Countdown report cites geographic areas previously safe from diseases such as malaria, dengue virus, and Zika virus becoming susceptible because of changing environmental conditions. Climate change, the researchers conclude, "is threatening to reverse years of progress in public health and sustainable development."[20] Already in 2021, the World Bank pointed to a rise in infectious diseases and a decline in mental health in Bangladesh due to floodplains now occupying 80 percent of the country.[21]

How much direr will the situation be by 2038?

To a large extent, that depends on the actions the world's governments and businesses take over the next fifteen years. Current indicators are alarming—and that's putting it mildly. According to NASA research, the amount of heat that Earth traps each year has nearly doubled since 2005, outpacing predictions.[22] A report released by the UN in 2021 cites changes in rainfall patterns due to "climate breakdown" as a primary driver of droughts worldwide.[23] Mami Mizutori, the UN secretary-general's special representative for disaster risk reduction, warned: "Drought is on the verge of becoming the next pandemic, and there is no vaccine to cure it."[24] She noted that a majority of the global population will have to contend with water scarcity in the years to come.[25]

Asia and Africa have been hit particularly hard by drought, but many other regions are feeling the impact, too. As of the end of September 2021, severe to extreme drought affected more than a third of the United States as measured by the Palmer Drought Severity Index.[26] The American West has become a tinderbox.

This heat/drought issue is personal for me. I consider Tucson, Arizona, my principal residence, although admittedly, it may be years before I move "home" to Old Pueblo. In 2019, the region saw 197 fatalities attributable to long stretches of triple-digit temperatures—the highest number of heat-associated deaths on record.[27] Compounding the problem is the lack of water. Decades ago, the state and federal governments built an aqueduct to transport water from the Colorado River to Arizona's cities and fields. In mid-August 2021, U.S. officials declared the first-ever water shortage from the Colorado, triggering cuts to agricultural users.[28] Goodbye, crops.

It's equally bad in California. Fire season in Ventura County, near Los Angeles, used to last three months. Now, it's any time the wind blows. In 2020, wildfires burned 4.3 million acres across the state—the most ever—killing thirty-three people.[29] And worse lies ahead: At least one-quarter of California's population lives in a high-fire-risk zone.[30] A friend who lives in the Santa Cruz Mountains emailed me recently: "We are so doomed. Good thing I am only a few yards from the Pacific. When the fire comes, I will run west as fast as I can."

For sheer fire devastation, nothing tops Australia. The wildfire season that began in June 2019 killed at least thirty-three people and destroyed more than three thousand homes. More than a billion animals perished.[31] An additional 13.6 million acres burned during 2020's "Black Summer" wildfires. Early in 2021, it began to rain—but at volumes far exceeding what was needed to water the plants and retard flames. The east coast of Australia experienced the worst floods in more than half a century. "I don't know any time in our state's history where we've had these extreme weather conditions in such quick succession," New South Wales premier Gladys Berejiklian said.[32]

On the radar:

By 2038, the ranks of amateur meteorologists will have swelled, with individuals and communities banding together to collect and distribute data. They will be the ham radio operators of our new age.

The situation isn't going to get better anytime soon in Arizona, Australia, or elsewhere around the planet. It's a numbers game, and humans and animals—all living things, really—are losing. By 2038, watching and reading weather reports will not just be about planning outfits or determining whether to carry an umbrella. We will be closely monitoring these reports to prepare for possible trauma, calculating when to evacuate our homes or whether the air quality is poor enough that children should be kept indoors.

For life on Earth to avoid certain catastrophe, global average temperatures need to fall. They have not.

Anybody who has experienced long, hot summers knows it will not take much heat to disrupt human life. We are used to reports of hunger among the poor, but few people recognize the full extent of food insecurity among the not-so-poor. Researchers at Northwestern University found that nearly one in four Americans experienced food insecurity in 2020.[33] Globally that same year, according to the UN, as many as 811 million people were affected by hunger, an increase of 161 million over 2019, a rise attributable to the COVID-19 pandemic.[34]

Even the *prospect* of food shortages can be all it takes to trigger chaos in stores. Empty stomachs and bare supermarket shelves are a recipe for conflict. We have seen it in Venezuela, South Africa, and other parts of the world.

As the inhabitants of planet Earth begin to take the threat of climate change more seriously, many national governments are moving with unusual speed to legislate change. But will it be too little, too late? President Joe Biden has vowed to reduce U.S. emissions by at least 50 percent by 2030, compared with 2005, but he faces roadblocks in Congress.[35] The U.K. has committed to cut emissions 68 percent by 2030 compared with 1990.[36] Germany has passed legislation to close all its coal plants by 2038.[37] New Zealand has announced that it will generate all its energy from renewable sources by 2035 and will be carbon neutral by 2050.[38]

Business, too, is ramping up its efforts. In 2021, the World Business Council for Sustainable Development outlined nine "transformative pathways" that companies should take to address climate change and inequality, including providing reliable and affordable net-zero carbon energy for all and offering safe, accessible, clean, and efficient transportation.[39] Endorsers include 3M, Microsoft,

Ikea, Nestlé, Unilever, and Toyota.[40] In January 2021, General Motors announced that, by 2035, it would no longer sell gas-powered cars—it is transitioning completely to electric vehicles. Even the oil and gas industry is getting on board. At a 2021 White House meeting, ten of the world's largest oil companies announced support for the regulation of carbon prices to curb emissions.[41]

Individuals are also responding. In the face of devasting climate predictions, it would be all too easy for the average person to go from climate denial to climate fatalism—throwing up their hands at a problem that can seem insurmountable. How could any one person possibly make a difference? Instead, shoppers are beginning to change their habits.

Consider what is happening around meat. By some estimates, 30 percent of the calories consumed globally by humans in 2021 came from meat products, including beef, chicken, and pork.[42] Meat certainly was a staple on my dinner plates growing up. It's hard to imagine either of my parents embracing "meatless Mondays," much less veganism. And for a while, meat consumption only ramped up as portion sizes grew. According to the U.S. Department of Agriculture, Americans consumed a record 225 pounds of red meat and poultry per capita in 2020, up from 167 pounds in 1960.[43] But the trend is beginning to reverse: Grocery store sales of plant-based meat reached $1.4 billion in the United States in 2020, up 45 percent in a single year. Around one in five U.S. households purchased meat alternative products in 2020, and nearly two-thirds of purchasers were high-repeat customers.[44] In Europe, the plant-based meat-replacement industry ballooned 49 percent in 2018–20, to a total sales value of €3.6 billion.[45] In Asia, demand for plant-based alternatives to meat is expected to triple by 2026.[46]

The category shows every sign of continuing to grow. In 2020 and 2021, plant-based food startups such as Rebellyous Foods and Livekindly secured millions of dollars in funding, and demand for vegan "meat" spiked.[47] Proteins like algae, chickpeas, and insects are already the stuff of news reports, and, late-night television jokes aside, flour from crickets and mealworms could well become everyday ingredients over the next decade.

For those unwilling to forgo meat and poultry entirely, there is the trend of "reducetarianism," under which people simply limit their consumption of these products to help the planet. This shift away from beef burgers and steaks is a big deal, given that meat production accounts for between 14.5 percent and 18 percent of global greenhouse gas emissions.[48]

Other signs of a changing public mindset: Half of the respondents to PwC's June 2021 Global Consumer Insights pulse survey said they have become "more eco-friendly."[49] And nearly seven in ten respondents to a Getty Images survey, fielded in twenty-six countries in 2020, said they are doing everything they can to reduce their carbon footprints.[50] These people are putting their money where their ethics are: A study by the Economist Intelligence Unit found a 71 percent rise in online searches for sustainable goods globally between 2016 and 2021, with demand especially pronounced in Australia, Canada, Germany, the U.K., and the United States.[51] The global market for ethical fashion is forecast to grow from $4.67 billion in 2020 to $8.3 billion in 2025.[52] Meanwhile, global sales of electric vehicles skyrocketed 41 percent in 2020, led by Europe and China.[53] There is an excellent chance that the car you'll be driving in 2038—or perhaps the autonomous one that will be driving you—will be plugged in at night.

As you will see throughout this book, everything is connected—work, the economy, consumer trends, lifestyles, social status, health—and at the hub of it all is climate. Small actions we take every day contribute in ways we may not currently recognize. Consider a package from Amazon, just one click and a one-day delivery away. It can be challenging not to make that purchase. But how will that choice—multiplied by millions—impact our world in 2038? Is the convenience worth the price we will pay?

An Amazon ad—"Net-Zero Carbon by 2040"[54]—heralds the megaretailer's commitment to 187 renewable projects worldwide. The company has ordered a hundred thousand electric delivery vehicles. It is investing $2 billion in carbon-reducing technologies. And Jeff Bezos, Amazon's founder and face, has personally pledged $10 billion to help heal the climate.[55]

On the other hand, Amazon has tripled its number of warehouses in Southern California since 2020. Some are in areas with the highest rate of toxic emissions in the state; San Bernardino is ranked number one for toxic ozone in the country.[56] Eighty-five percent of residents within half a mile of warehouses serving Amazon and other companies are people of color. In those areas, 640 schools are within half a mile of a warehouse, and research shows that the severe truck pollution in the neighborhoods surrounding these facilities is correlated to poor air quality and related health conditions.[57] So, yes, kudos to Amazon for increasing its electric fleet. But will that be enough to offset the company's contributions to poor health conditions in San Bernardino and other locations?

Manufacturing and transportation have long contributed to pollution and their associated conditions. The new twist in the internet age is that, as consumers, we can no longer credibly pretend to be ignorant of the suffering in which we are complicit. That item you order from an online retailer makes you part of the climate story as a customer, enabler, co-conspirator. It may also compel you to ask yourself: How can we influence the e-commerce giants to hasten the reduction of their carbon footprints? Do Amazon, Jingdong, and their competitors have a role to play in the regeneration of planet Earth? As online shoppers, do we?

Looking ahead, we have reason to be afraid and reason to be hopeful. You will see both responses reflected in the trends I cover. How we respond to chaos—whether we retreat in fear or use that emotion to fuel our actions and commitment to change—is a crucial, if not the *most* crucial, factor in determining what kind of future we will have.

A decade or more ago, I forecasted sleep as the new sex; today, my forecast is bleaker: more sleepless nights worrying about all the negative news that drives us deeper and deeper into anxiety. If there is a cure for climate change and environmental destruction, it certainly won't be seen before 2038. The best we can hope for is to slow Earth's decline enough to buy time for scientific and technological solutions that have not yet been imagined—and to devise an economic approach along the way that doesn't depend on fossil fuels and overconsumption for its success.

Finding a more fulfilling, more sustainable alternative to consumerist societies will have an added benefit: injecting a sense of control into a world that seems permanently poised at the edge of chaos.

Chapter 4

The Chaos of Now

Chaos does not show up unannounced and knock loudly at your door like police at a predawn raid. It sneaks up on you gradually. That bruise on your toe seems unimportant, so you do nothing, and it turns out to be cancer, and then you lose your leg. The apartment complex built yards from the ocean has structural flaws, and the concrete degrades, and the problem is discussed without any meaningful action taken, and one night, in eleven seconds, the building collapses.

Chaos is nothing new. Humankind has always experienced disruption caused by food shortages and natural disasters, tribal and military conflicts, pandemics, and economic implosions. We need look no further back than the two world wars of the last century to recognize that much of history is a chronicle of uncertainty, instability, and fear.

Consider the chaos of a single year: 1968. Mass student protests rocked cities globally, from Paris and Warsaw to Washington, D.C., Mexico City, and Tokyo. In the United States, it was a year marked by political assassinations (Senator Robert F. Kennedy; Martin Luther King, Jr.), social strife, and violent riots. In France, May 1968 saw massive protests, occupations of university buildings and factories, and a general strike organized by students and workers. For French students, it was less a political movement than a cultural one—a fight against social restrictions and the beginning of the women's movement and sexual revolution. A popular motto of the time: "It is forbidden to forbid." In then-Czechoslovakia, 1968 saw a brief period of reform and liberalism—"Prague Spring"—that was swiftly extinguished by the Soviet Union's invasion and crackdown. In Mexico City, in what has become known as the Tlatelolco Massacre, troops opened fire on student demonstrators, killing a still-undetermined number possibly rising into the hundreds.[1]

And yet in the last two decades, the sense of chaos has escalated, with society experiencing what can best be described as free-floating anxiety and desolation as we face both existential threats (climate change, COVID-19, societal discord) and, for many, a deeply felt sense of dissatisfaction, unease, and even hopelessness. That anxiety and desolation make the current chaos feel different from that experienced in 1968 or earlier periods of strife. And it seems inescapable because it isn't tied to any one event or to a broad social movement. Nor are we receiving blows one at a time. Giuseppe Raviola, director of mental health at Partners In Health and an assistant professor at Harvard Medical School, points to a term that has emerged in this era of chaos: *syndemic.* As individuals, we face multiple traumas simultaneously. As S. I. Rosenbaum writes in *Harvard Public Health,* "The *syn* in *syndemic* stands for synergistic because each source of stress and trauma compounds and feeds off one another."[2] So a person struggling with the pandemic may be further endangered by an immigration status that makes them reluctant to seek medical care. A family fleeing a natural disaster may face racism when attempting to settle in a new spot.

By 2019, in many parts of the world we were experiencing a newfound flexibility and freedom to live differently from how we did in previous decades. That was exciting but could also be scary for those already feeling a bit untethered. With the onset of the pandemic, many people felt further unmoored because they lacked the grounding afforded by the traditional nuclear family of the twentieth century. We had already morphed into societies that take a mix-and-match approach to family and household composition, and this left some of us on our own or compelled to form survival pods with friends and neighbors. Five adults and two kids I know in Switzerland formed such a pod, eating meals together and watching out for one another. Their hastily assembled "family" was made up of a Dutch family of four, a single Dutch woman, an Englishman, and a Swiss American woman. They cooked together and even set up workstations in one of their homes—all within walking distance of one another—so that they would have companionship and support during a blur that lasted for many months.

In the United States, more than a quarter of households were single-person in 2020, according to census data, up from 13 percent in 1960.[3] And a third of adults aged fifteen and older had never been married, up from 23 percent in 1950.[4] Moreover, almost a quarter of U.S. children (23 percent) lived with just one parent and no other adult in 2019, compared with a global average of just 7 percent.[5] Marriage rates across the European Union have declined 50 percent in relative terms since 1965, while divorce rates have nearly doubled.[6] Economic factors intensify the household chaos. Across Europe, nearly half of single-parent households (47 percent) were at risk of poverty and social exclusion in 2017, according to Eurostat, compared with just 21 percent of two-parent households.[7]

Also contributing to our sense of disorder: We feel disconnected from nature and lack the sense of community that once anchored people. We spend countless hours interacting with strangers on social media and doomscrolling on our phones rather than having meaningful exchanges in person. We can't blame the pandemic for that. These behaviors were fully entrenched prior to 2020, although they have been exacerbated by social distancing and the move to remote work.

Perhaps more than anything else, the current sense of chaos and discontent stems from a pervasive feeling that, as a society, we are moving in the wrong direction. A 2021 Pew Research survey conducted across seventeen advanced economies found that 64 percent of respondents believe their children will be worse off financially than their own generation.[8] In only two markets—Singapore and Sweden—did an optimistic view win out. Where once the future promised progress, now it is cause for angst.

Compare predictions made at the turn of the twentieth century with what we anticipated in 2000. In 1900, a writer named Thomas F. Anderson interviewed several experts to anticipate what the city of Boston might look like in the year 2000.[9] Some of his predictions, published in *The Boston Globe,* were prescient, including wireless telegraphy, cooled liquid air (the forerunner of air conditioning), and nighttime baseball games played under the lights. Others—home deliveries via pneumatic tubes, moving sidewalks, the tides of Boston Harbor furnishing the city with heat and light—didn't come to pass. What is worth noting about these predictions is their optimism and steadfast faith that better times lay ahead. Anderson foresaw a Boston so pristine that the word *slum* would be removed from local dictionaries. He believed that universal education would uncover genius among the lower classes and that public health would benefit from the absence of soot and smoke.[10]

Contrast Anderson's rosy predictions with those made in the 1990s about 2020. *USA Today* put together a collection of these forecasts,[11] and while some were hopeful—rising life expectancy, hydrogen-fueled cars able to operate for months on a single fill-up—the majority were not. Experts predicted the death of books, the loss of privacy, the extension of the standard retirement age to seventy, a rise in global surface temperatures, and heart disease and depression replacing lower respiratory infections and diarrheal diseases as the leading causes of sickness, disability, and death.

Cheery.

This premillennial gloom and doom was in keeping with the zeitgeist of Y2K. Rather than dream of a brighter future, we anticipated crises and calamities aided and abetted by new and unfamiliar technologies.

A critical reason we perceive a higher degree of chaos today is that we don't feel up to the challenge of meeting current and future crises. When we're unable to draw strength from a belief in a better tomorrow, how can we find the fortitude to manage existential challenges? What is the point in fighting for change when we have little to no hope that it will make a difference?

This pervasive sense of pessimism is new. To a worrying degree, we wallow in uncertainty and fear—taking tentative steps in what we think might be a better direction but without the drive that comes from confidence. How can we fix this?

One thing we can count on by 2038: intensified and systematic efforts to instill in the younger generation the critical-thinking skills, agility, and resilience that will enable them to discern and combat misinformation and jump from crisis to crisis without succumbing to anxiety or depression. Already, we are seeing programs emerging for use in classrooms and at home. GoZen! offers tools to help parents "raise resilient, happy, inspired, thriving children."[12] Road to Resilience, launched by the Mayo Clinic in 2020, is a six-week virtual program to help youth combat the effects of adverse childhood experiences.[13] Also in 2020, Janet Borland, an assistant professor at the University of Hong Kong, published *Earthquake Children,* a book that considers how the aftermath of the Great Kanto Earthquake in 1923 helped to build modern Japan's infrastructure of resilience and its people's ability to maintain composure in times of emergency.[14]

We will also see simplicity and "happy time" emerge as luxury items as people seek to escape the chaos. Think: new variations on sensory-deprivation tanks, in-home salt therapy rooms, and sound-healing spas in suburban strip malls. How much would you be willing to pay to leave the chaos behind for sixty minutes?

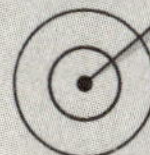

On the radar:

By 2038, look for more people to opt out of "real life" in favor of time spent in carefully constructed metaverses—virtual worlds in which they interact, play, shop, engage with art, and travel via avatar. This, finally, is a world over which one might feel some sense of control.

There is an old saying: Where it's tight, that's where it rips. In 2020, battered by one crisis—our changing climate and increasingly severe weather—we were treated to a second, the COVID-19 pandemic. Were we going to die? Were we going to live but watch loved ones die? What could we do to protect ourselves? Would there be a vaccine, and if so, would it be effective? Would it be safe? Would it be in sufficient supply to reach poorer nations and economically marginalized groups?

The medical issues alone were terrifying, with harrowing reports of death and morgues unable to cope with the overflow. Even the wealthiest countries faced shortages of ventilators and critical personal protective equipment. Then social media and opportunistic politicians and media personalities exploited our dread and confusion, spewing fear like exhaust from an old truck.

The lockdowns followed, and for those deemed nonessential or who were able to work remotely, an imposed sheltering in place began. The office and some factories closed, and with them went the social life of the workplace. Work relationships that felt like family—or closer—were put on indefinite pause. No post-work outings. No family events. No visits with sick or dying loved ones in the hospital. For those unable to return to work after the lockdown restrictions eased and unable to do their jobs remotely, it was a time of days, weeks, months on the couch, watching every series available to stream.

And those people were the lucky ones. Workers deemed essential and who didn't have the financial freedom to refuse to report to work found themselves acutely vulnerable to the virus, especially when their employers failed to offer adequate protection. Analysis by Amnesty International determined that in the first six months of the pandemic alone, at least seven thousand healthcare workers worldwide died after contracting COVID-19.[15] Race has played a role in both virus contraction and death, with white privilege glaringly apparent in the statistics: Researchers at the University of California found a 59 percent increase in mortality among Hispanic food/agriculture workers and a 40 percent increase among Asian healthcare workers. In comparison, excess mortality among white working-age Californians increased just 6 percent.[16] In part, that disparity can be attributed to minority groups being overrepresented in fields such as healthcare[17] and agriculture.[18]

In no time at all, a health crisis became an economic crisis, a food crisis, a housing crisis, a political crisis. A crisis of inequities. Everything collided.

With no end to the pandemic in sight in 2020, we internalized chaos. Despair, alcoholism, suicide, domestic abuse—the classic responses to chaos—all ramped up. In Australia, 4.6 percent of women surveyed said they had experienced physical or sexual violence from a current or former cohabiting partner in the three months leading to May 2020, with nearly two-thirds indicating that the violence had begun at or escalated since the start of the pandemic.[19] In the European Union, emergency calls about domestic violence in which alcohol consumption was a factor rose 60 percent during the COVID-19 lockdowns.[20]

No matter where on the planet we live, we all felt the impact of the events of 2020. The cumulative effect of everything that we endured that year and extending into and beyond 2021—globally, nationally, and locally—is crisis experienced on a personal level. We have become justifiably afraid and confused. And because fear and confusion threaten our emotional stability, we feel alternately paralyzed and frantic. Crisis unsolved leads to chaos, and chaos becomes our new normal.

On the radar:

Wealthier communities will tap into crisis concierge services, a new form of insurance that ensures that when a crisis hits—whether a natural disaster, a pandemic, riots, or something else—the residents are covered. Benefits might range from home deliveries of essential goods and onsite healthcare professionals and equipment to paramilitary forces and evacuations. The public-versus-private divide in healthcare and emergency management will widen further.

For Americans, the 2020 presidential election and its aftermath generated a fresh round of strife and polarization. In late October, with new COVID-19 cases nearing a hundred thousand a day, infections rising in thirty-two states, and hospitalizations up 46 percent,[21] President Trump held maskless rallies. Stock markets tumbled. The Chicago Board Options Exchange's Volatility Index—the stock market's fear gauge—jumped 20 percent.[22]

While there is truth to Sun Tzu's notion that in the midst of chaos, there is opportunity, that opportunity will go largely untapped if the chaos is not brought under control—or, worse, if it is encouraged to grow. Consider chaos in the political sphere. It is one thing when politicians twist established facts to suit the views of their supporters. It is quite another when politicians conclude that the chaos these mistruths generate offers a path to greater power.

The Atlantic has dubbed U.K. prime minister Boris Johnson "the minister of chaos"[23]—a label Johnson welcomes, according to one of his chief deputies: "Covid 'chaos' made him more popular."[24] *The Independent* reported that Johnson allegedly remarked: "Chaos isn't that bad; it means people have to look to me to see who is in charge."[25]

Chaos doesn't just offer avenues to consolidate political power; it also enables criminality. In our digital world, this often means cybercriminals. Cybersecurity researchers Comparitech found that, in the United States alone, ransomware attacks on healthcare organizations cost an estimated $20.8 billion in 2020.[26] In May 2021, an Asian division of European insurance company AXA was hacked. A presumed catalyst: The company had announced that it would stop reimbursing many clients for ransomware payments.[27]

This threat will grow between now and 2038. According to the World Economic Forum's Global Risks Report 2021, cyberattacks are the leading human-caused risk globally.[28] The authors warn of the failure of cybersecurity measures, which will mean "business, government and household cybersecurity infrastructure and/or measures are outstripped or rendered obsolete by increasingly sophisticated and frequent cybercrimes, resulting in economic disruption, financial loss, geopolitical tensions and/or social instability."[29]

Cybersecurity Ventures projects that the financial cost of global cybercrime will reach $10.5 trillion annually by 2025, up from $3 trillion in 2015 and $6 trillion in 2021.[30]

Chaos also is mounting in the analog world. Look at what happens when governments fail to get serious about infrastructure repair and upgrades. As Tropical Storm Elsa moved up the East Coast of the United States in July 2021, subway riders in New York City found themselves on platforms and in stairwells flooded with murky, waist-high water.[31] Several days later, in China, at least a dozen people drowned when record-breaking rainfalls inundated underground railway tunnels.[32] Then Tube stations in London flooded after what were described as "biblical" rainstorms.[33]

In the past couple of decades, we have seen structural failures of all sorts worldwide: bridge failures (including ones that killed 130 or more people in India in 2002 and forty-three in Italy in 2018[34]), dam failures, levee breaches (who can forget the gut-wrenching images of Hurricane Katrina in 2005?), and all manner of engineering disasters. In 2009, an electrical outage in India knocked out power to 9 percent of the world's population.[35] A report issued by U.S. federal regulators in 2011 warned that power plants in Texas would be unable to withstand temperatures lower than usual.[36] The warning went unheeded. Consequently, in 2021, severe winter storms left more than 4.5 million homes and businesses in Texas without power for days in brutal (for Texas) cold. Nearly two hundred people died.[37]

The situation will worsen in the face of a changing climate. Analysts forecast airport runways under water, bridges degraded years earlier than anticipated, and extreme heat damaging roads and rail lines, among other impacts.[38]

What entities are capable of preventing systemic collapse? Who is going to pay to keep people moving safely and systems in place? Who is going to tame the chaos when tens of millions of people in even the most advanced societies are unable to commute or travel safely, access electricity or clean water, or feel secure in their homes?

Even the slightest changes can create great consequences. They might not look like great consequences at first. They can seem orderly and incremental. Suddenly, without warning, they are not.

We have seen the economic impact of natural disasters. Hurricane Katrina is estimated to have cost $172.5 billion.[39] And reconstructing areas of Germany damaged by flooding in July 2021 carries an estimated price tag in excess of $7 billion.[40] We prepare for or respond to such disasters by lining the banks of rivers with sandbags. We open field hospitals. We give blood, donate money. In other words, we behave collectively, like members of a community, like citizens.

COVID-19 was not that kind of event. In the beginning, ignorance about the disease paralyzed us. Add political turmoil and misinformation, and we suddenly had a disease on top of a disease. CNN's Brianna Keilar got it right when she said, "Misinformation is a virus unto itself."[41] After a year of lockdowns (government-mandated or self-imposed) in the United States, enough of the population had been vaccinated to allow the country to begin to open up. International travel resumed. Families went on vacation. And people, being human, banished the memory of the plague year and pretended all was well, though they surely knew it wasn't and would not be for quite some time.

That brief party ground to a halt in summer 2021, when the Delta variant made its way to North America from Europe and Asia, and cases of COVID-19 surged anew. This new variant—which accounted for at least 93 percent of all new sequenced* cases in the United States at the start of August—was thought to be twice as contagious as the original COVID strain, and it ultimately was detected in every country in the world.[42]

The good news is that transmission of the Delta variant saw a sharp drop, including in the two countries in which it appeared early on: India and the United Kingdom. Even better news: As of mid-October 2021, 37 percent of the global population had been fully vaccinated, including more than a billion Chinese.[43] The bleak news—aside from the onslaught of the highly transmissible Omicron variant in fall 2021 and the knowledge that further variants are certain to emerge—is that some of those hungry for power have discovered that it can be very profitable to keep people in a heightened state of fear and confusion. As a consequence, we are battling far more than a novel coronavirus. We are battling disinformation and efforts to pit people against one another. We are battling the frustration that comes from global political divides and entrenched

* Scientists use genomic sequencing analysis to compare the virus sample taken from a diagnosed COVID-19 patient with that of other patients.

interest groups thwarting progress. And most of all, we are battling the chaos that threatens to overwhelm.

Perhaps nowhere do we see these forces of conflict and chaos more clearly than in the United States. It is increasingly hard to remember that for more than a century, the American national myth was defined by a sense of moral superiority and swagger.

Chapter 5

America Divided

Trends are increasingly global, so why devote a chapter of this book to the United States and the crisis of identity it is undergoing? It is for the simple reason that there is scarcely anyone on the planet today whose life has not in some way been touched by this young nation, which makes up just 4.25 percent of the world's population but has reigned essentially unchallenged as the leading global superpower and the epicenter of trends for nearly a century. Now the "Land of Opportunity" faces unprecedented challenges, including both external assaults on its power and destructive internal forces of polarization, upheaval, and stagnation. We can view the nation's decline through a variety of lenses, but perhaps nowhere is it more apparent than in its reputation as a welcoming port for immigrants.

The Statue of Liberty has been a dominant symbol of the United States of America since 1886, but the image of this émigré from France has been tarnished in recent years. The words on the pedestal—"Give me your tired, your poor / Your huddled masses yearning to breathe free"—was in theory the spirit of the young country in 1883, when Emma Lazarus penned her poem. It no longer is even close to a national mission statement.

The underlying truth is that America has never been as welcoming of immigrants as rhetoric and myth suggest. The last to come have always looked down on the next to come, and for all the talk of a "melting pot," the citizenry has shown a strong preference for newcomers who look and think like them. Still, the United States stands out for its multicultural composition. If you need proof of that, watch the procession of athletes at the opening ceremony of any Olympic Games. The relative "sameness" of other countries' surnames is obliterated when the announcers get to the U.S. team. Among the American athletes marching in Tokyo in 2021: Muagututia, Holland, Jha, Kumar, LeLeux, Capobianco, St. Pierre, O'Brien, Federowicz, Stewart, Kipyego, English, Iosefo, Zhang, Leibfarth, Loschiavo, Constien, Papadakis, Buckingham, Mucino-Fernandez, Morikawa, and Uptagrafft. . . . You get the idea.

However begrudging, America has had an unparalleled history of assimilating people from foreign shores. During a 1950 case before the Supreme Court, Justice Hugo Black described U.S. citizenship as not only a "high privilege" but a "priceless treasure."[1] And yet it's a treasure an increasing number of Americans have been willing to forgo. In the first decade of this century, fewer than a thousand Americans annually renounced their citizenship. In 2010, that figure jumped to 1,534.[2] In 2016, it was 5,411. In 2020, it reached 6,707, an all-time high.[3] Although many of these former U.S. citizens are high-net-worth individuals seeking to reduce their tax burdens, it seems likely that forces beyond finances factor in. Just prior to July 4, 2018, a Gallup survey of American patriotism marked its lowest numbers in eighteen years of polling. Only 47 percent of respondents said they were "extremely proud" to be American, down from 51 percent in 2017 and well below the post-9/11 peak of 70 percent in 2003.[4]

These statistics are consistent with a general sense of decline. In January 2021, barely half of Americans surveyed (54 percent) felt that America's best days were still to come. If you drill down into the data, partisan hues are clear. More than three-quarters of those self-identifying as Democrats (77 percent) thought the nation's best days were ahead of them as their party headed into the White House. Less than a third of Republicans (31 percent) agreed.[5]

Until very recently, Americans were known for their optimism, a trait that was both mocked, usually good-naturedly, and lauded. As recently as 2013, a Pew Research study found that 41 percent of

Americans said they were having a "particularly good day," in contrast to 27 percent of British, 21 percent of Germans, and only 8 percent of Japanese.[6]

"Anyone visiting America from Europe cannot fail to be struck by the energy, enthusiasm, and confidence in their country's future that he or she will meet among ordinary Americans—a pleasing contrast to the world-weary cynicism of much of Europe," wrote Irish philosopher Charles Handy in *Harvard Business Review* in 2001.[7] In the piece, he considered the extent to which Frenchman Alexis de Tocqueville's impressions of a young America in the 1830s had withstood the test of time. Tocqueville had been especially taken by the strength that America's political system was able to draw from the nation's physical communities.[8] In his eyes, the township was democracy's great advantage over the closed social and economic classes of Europe.

Nearly two centuries after Tocqueville set sail for home, few in the United States are alive who recall the experience of life in a township or even in a town. The percentage of Americans living in urban areas increased from less than 10 percent prior to 1830 to 60 percent in 1930[9] and 86 percent in 2020.[10] Of the 384 metro areas in the United States, 312 gained population in the decade leading to 2020.[11]

Americans have segued from shopping at the corner store to shopping at Walmart to shopping online. Towns across the country have been forced to consolidate their few remaining students into regional high schools.

And yet there still are towns. We find them in rural areas, where diminished populations enjoy the pleasures of small-town living and endure all its tribulations: too often, a shrinking economy, crumbling infrastructure, second-rate education, and high levels of drug use. The coastal elite dismissively call this "flyover" country, an attitude that has consequences. At a fundraiser two months before the 2016 U.S. presidential election, Hillary Clinton used the term *deplorables* to describe Trump supporters who held "racist, sexist, homophobic, xenophobic, Islamophobic" views.[12] Unsurprisingly, most of the targets of her remark voted instead for a presidential candidate who shared their sense of resentment.[13]

If you were to choose a handful of Americans at random today, the odds are that they would live in states boasting cities that have more residents than the entire population of states dotted with small towns. Only eleven states (not including New York) have populations greater than the number of people who live in New York City—8.8 million, according to the 2020 census.[14] And there were more people living in Los Angeles County (10 million plus) in 2021 than in each of twenty-three states. That's right: There are more Los Angelenos than there are people in Connecticut or Oklahoma or Nevada or Mississippi or nineteen other states.

The consolidation continues: As reported in *The New York Times* in 2021, around 40 percent of America's population growth since 1980 has taken place in just three megastates: California, Florida, and Texas.[15] If current trends continue, according to the Population Reference Bureau in Washington, D.C., the combined population of those states could exceed 100 million by 2030.[16] Already, a third of the U.S. population lives in those three states plus New York. That is more than the number of people who live in the smallest thirty-four states combined.[17]

This information isn't just useful for trivia night. It has profound implications for access to power and political representation. These four largest states are represented by eight senators. The thirty-four smallest states are represented by sixty-eight. Put another way: States that represent less than a third of the U.S. population now control more than two-thirds of the votes in the Senate.

This disproportion was not the intent of the framers of the Constitution. They never imagined that a person's address could effectively disenfranchise them. And they would also have been stunned by political columnist Noah Millman's observation that more populous states such as California and Texas wield far more influence than might be considered appropriate. "On issues like environmental regulation and education policy," Millman writes, "these behemoths can shape or frustrate national policy by their unilateral actions in ways that smaller states cannot easily dissent from" and "wield disproportionate influence in the national and state capitals."[18]

It is one division after another, isn't it? Small states versus big states. Red versus blue. Rural whites versus liberals, Blacks, and Hispanics. Professional and educated versus blue-collar. Solvent versus struggling. OAN versus Fox versus MSNBC. Tucker Carlson versus Rachel Maddow.

The truth is that sociopolitical, generational, and interpersonal divides are as much a part of modern America as digital technologies are. Consider the meme of the moment: the dreadful, dreaded, and much-derided "Karen."

Karen (Caryn, Karin, Karyn) was among the most popular girls' names in the United States in the 1950s and '60s—signaling that it is my generation being called out for bad behavior. As *The Atlantic* noted, "Amid the coronavirus pandemic, 'Karen' has been adopted as a shorthand to call out a vocal minority of middle-aged white women who are opposed to social distancing, out of either ignorance or ruthless self-interest. It's the latest evolution of a longstanding meme."[19]

Though there is truth to the anti-mask characterization, the prototypical Karen (or Chad) personifies much more than that. She is the quintessential slave to consumerism, a fierce protector of white privilege and the status quo, an implacably confident (and usually ill-informed) online troll, and proud owner of the nothingness that has kept so many frantically pedaling in place for more than twenty years.

No meme captures better than Karen the sound and fury, the ridiculousness and sublimity, of this era marked by unprecedented wealth and abject poverty, by simultaneous miracles of technology and the crippling of our home planet. At a time when we all face genuine existential threats, one might think people would come together to find solutions; instead, we focus on identifying convenient targets for our blame and condemnation. Boomers dismiss Gen Zers and millennials as "Peter Pan" idealists who refuse to grow up. Gen Zers and millennials, in turn, blame boomers for, well, pretty much everything—from climate change to systemic racism, gender and wealth inequities to global conflicts.

Perhaps the way Americans have looked at their fractured country over the last few decades is too streamlined for the reality they now experience. In his 2021 book, *Last Best Hope: America in Crisis and Renewal,* George Packer proposes that there are now multiple new subsectors of America:

- Free America, of Reaganism (committed to personal freedom and responsibility)
- Smart America, of Silicon Valley and other professional elites
- Real America, of Trumpist reaction: "These people didn't want to hear how good things were. They wanted to hear how bad things were."
- Equal America: "a deep, old American drive to be as good as anyone else, to have no one able to say, 'I'm better than you. I can do what you can't do.'"
- Just America: "a new generation of leftists"

The distinctions are interesting, but for Packer, they are not the point. As he writes, the origin of the splintering is the five million manufacturing jobs that the country lost in the beginning of the twenty-first century and the decline of working-class wages. It comes down to "two classes, rising professionals and sinking workers." Packer concludes: "Inequality undermined the common faith that Americans need to create a successful multi-everything democracy."[20]

What Packer identifies is that America is no longer a nation unified by commonly held attitudes, beliefs, and values, let alone the commitment to township that Tocqueville so admired. Instead, rising inequities have turned the country into a series of disparate groups wielding varying degrees of power and influence. The echo chambers I referenced earlier are a manifestation of multiple Americas.

Our shared notion of "America" in recent decades has revolved mainly around the middle class—the upwardly mobile people who once kept their lawns manicured, paid their taxes on time, sent their children to public schools, populated parades, and kept social clubs going. On television, that would be Richie Cunningham and his family on *Happy Days* at the upper end, the Winslow family of *Family Matters* at the midpoint, and the Heck family of *The Middle* at the lower end.

That middle class is shrinking. According to Pew Research, 61 percent of U.S. adults lived in middle-income households in 1971. By 2019, that figure had dropped to 51 percent.[21] In part, that is a positive trend, reflecting the movement of more Americans into the upper income bracket. What is worrisome—and what threatens social stability—is the movement of not people but wealth out of the middle and into the upper reaches of society. Between 1970 and 2018, the proportion of aggregate income earned by middle-class households fell nearly 20 percentage points, dipping from around two-thirds (62 percent) to less than half (43 percent).[22] And the wealth gap continues to grow: Between 2001 and 2016, the median net worth of middle-income families fell 20 percent. It was even worse for lower-income families, whose net worth nose-dived 45 percent. Upper-income earners? Totally different story: They saw a 33 percent increase in their net worth.[23]

The lack of bipartisan compromise in Congress doesn't inspire confidence that economic inequality will be significantly reduced anytime soon. Money tells the story. Between 1978 and 2019, compensation for the typical worker in the United States grew 14 percent, not enough to keep up with inflation. How much did it increase for CEOs during the same period? Maybe 20 percent? Or 100 percent? Try 1,167 percent.[24] Today, CEOs of big companies make, on average, 320 times the pay of their typical worker.[25]

By looking at the numbers, we can get a sense of where Americans are likely to find themselves in 2038.

There will be more Americans—probably 350 million by 2030, up from 331 million in 2021—and many will be seniors. (You may be surprised to learn what the fastest-growing metro area was between 2010 and 2020: The Villages, Florida—a retirement community for people aged fifty-five and up. It grew 39 percent during the decade.)[26] And those Americans will be much more diverse. In 1980, whites made up 80 percent of the U.S. population.[27] In 2020, they represented just under 60 percent. By 2030, non-Hispanic whites are projected to make up 55.8 percent of the population, while Hispanics will account for 21.1 percent.[28] The percentage of Black and Asian Americans will also increase, to 13.8 and 6.9 percent, respectively.

We are on our way to a historic moment: whites in the minority. By 2060, they are projected to make up just 44.3 percent of the U.S. population.[29]

The story of the generations will be an equally crucial demographic shift between now and 2038. A 2020 report by the U.S. Census Bureau, based on the 2010 census, indicates that by 2034, Americans aged sixty-five and older will outnumber those aged seventeen and under for the first time in history.[30] Not great news for the already beleaguered Social Security system. By 2060, Americans aged sixty-five and older will make up nearly a quarter of the population, up from around 15 percent today. And the number of Americans aged eighty-five and older will double by 2035 (to 11.8 million) and triple by 2060 (to 19 million).[31]

These demographic shifts will impact everything from housing to healthcare. For starters, we can anticipate more congregant living, "smart homes" geared to the needs of the aged—including robotic companions to monitor medication use and ease loneliness—and a part-gig and part-volunteer economy that harnesses the skills and aptitudes of the elderly. Two examples: The town of Greensburg, Indiana, is seeking to grow its population by luring young people who work remotely. Among the incentives offered: "grandparents on demand"—elderly volunteers willing to step in as needed to help young families adjust.[32] In upstate New York, an organization called Umbrella hires active retirees to provide services—from house-cleaning and lawn maintenance to errand-running and small repairs—to peers who can no longer perform the activities themselves.[33]

On the radar:

By 2038, we will be seeing a dichotomy in the approach to elder care: More nursing homes and assisted-living facilities will replace care staff with robotic assistants capable of handling routine tasks such as bed-changing and food preparation and delivery. At the other end of the spectrum, communities will work to integrate the elderly into society, including by creating campuses that co-house elder congregant living, schools, and family-oriented recreation areas.

The United States of America no longer resembles the country it was when the Founding Fathers were around, and so it should come as no surprise that the American myth is beginning to evaporate. Even though Americans still love to scream "We're number one!" at the top of their lungs, it is objectively untrue by many measures in the twenty-first century. The 2021 Index of Economic Freedom places the United States twentieth out of 178 countries[34] (the United States was eighth on that list in 2010[35]), and the United States placed sixth on *U.S. News & World Report*'s Best Countries ranking in 2021 (down from fourth place in 2010), behind Canada, Japan, Germany, Switzerland, and Australia.[36] According to other rankings, the United States is thirtieth in quality of healthcare,[37] fourteenth in the percentage of people aged twenty-five to thirty-four with higher-education credentials,[38] eighteenth on the list of best countries for women,[39] and forty-sixth in life expectancy.[40] On which measures does America still come out on top? Military spending, arms exports, beef production, and dog and cat ownership.[41] How non-Americans view the United States is changing, too. The nation's global standing took a huge hit in the first year of Donald Trump's presidency. A 2017 Pew Research Center survey of thirty-seven nations found that, on average, only 22 percent of respondents had confidence that President Trump would do a good job of handling international affairs, a sharp drop from the

64 percent who had expressed faith in Barack Obama in the final years of his presidency.[42]

In 2018, Pew found divergent attitudes toward the United States. In France, America's oldest ally, just 39 percent of respondents held a positive view of the United States, compared with 50 percent in the U.K. Favorability ratings were significantly higher in Asia, at 67 percent in Japan, 80 percent in South Korea, and 83 percent in the Philippines. And what of America's closest neighbors? Mexico returned a favorability rating of just 32 percent, while Canada came in at 39 percent.[43] Not a promising sign.

Despite mounting evidence of their nation's decline, many in the United States have fervently resisted the notion of national backsliding, because it runs counter to the myth of American exceptionalism—the widely held belief that the United States is inherently different from other nations by virtue of its values, political system, and history. Being exceptional is as integral to the country's narrative and sense of self as the American Dream.

Then the pandemic arrived, and it quickly became apparent to many Americans that their country was spectacularly ill-equipped to handle the crisis. Cholera, dengue, Ebola—for decades, Americans had watched as other nations grappled with deadly outbreaks. We were confident our healthcare authorities would protect us. In the words of Drew Gilpin Faust, a historian and former president of Harvard University, medical and societal achievements in the United States had caused many Americans to believe "we were ready for anything—that we had conquered nature. We had not thought this would ever happen to us."[44] Tent hospital wards in New York's Central Park in the early weeks of the pandemic? Refrigerated trucks as temporary morgues in hospital parking lots? Nurses improvising protective gear out of garbage bags? Unthinkable. "That sense of mastery over nature has been so seriously challenged by this pandemic," Faust concluded.[45]

While some Americans still believe passionately in our exceptionalism, we have also splintered into tribes based on how we have come to understand our role in the world. Let's face it: Americans are the undisputed world champions of cognitive dissonance. When we do not want to believe what our eyes tell us, we rely increasingly on our own narratives. And the narratives vary greatly by tribe. Today, there is no single American story, and there may not even be a shared dream. This forces us to consider what stories we will tell in the next two decades. We can be certain that many tales will center on a power rising rapidly in the East: the People's Republic of China.

Chapter 6

China Makes Its Move

The story of the Communist Party in China is the story of the Long March, which began in 1934 with a military defeat. As with much of history, there are markedly different perspectives—but the myth that has taken hold in China belongs to the ultimate victors of the Revolution of 1949: the Chinese Communist Party and Mao Zedong, who emerged from the March and ensuing military campaigns not simply as the founder of the People's Republic of China but as the country's savior.

The Long March is less a story of victory (only 4,000 of the original force of 86,000 survived[1]) than of tenacity and grit. To escape Nationalist leader Chiang Kai-shek's forces, the troops endured an unlikely-to-impossible trek of some six thousand miles to Shaanxi, a province in the north, where they regrouped and were able to continue their fight.

In *Red Star over China,* American journalist Edgar Snow describes soldiers marching over mountains and across narrow gorges by day and being lectured at night by political workers exhorting them to fight to the last breath. "Victory was life," said military leader P'eng Te-huai. "Defeat was certain death."[2]

In one night and day, Mao's soldiers covered eighty-five miles, entered a town in silence, and quietly disarmed the garrison. And then they did it again. And again—for a total of 368 days. Their journey took them across eighteen mountain ranges and two dozen rivers, a phenomenal feat for an army and its transport vehicles. In all, they occupied sixty-two cities, defeating both central-government troops and the armies of ten provincial warlords.[3]

But the numbers are not the story. The story, wrote Snow, lay in "the undimmed ardor and undying hope and amazing revolutionary optimism of those thousands of youths who would not admit defeat by man or nature or God or death."[4]

Where in Snow's accounts does history end and literary license and propaganda begin? That is for the reader to discern, but Snow's telling of Mao's trek sits within an ever-expanding trove of Chinese government–approved books, films, and television shows honoring Mao and his triumph and intended to infuse younger Chinese with reverence for their nation's founder and founding principles. In a piece in *Asia Times,* Martin Adams quoted documentary filmmaker Sun Shuyun, who speaks of generations of Chinese youth being indoctrinated in the "Long March spirit":[5] "If you find it hard, think of the Long March; if you feel tired, think of your revolutionary forbears."[6] From industrialization to space exploration, Sun says, the citizenry of China have been spurred to endure and triumph by the founding mythology of the march to Shaanxi.

In this decade, China is reaching an inflection point.

In the nearly half a century since Mao's death, the country has transitioned from communism to a uniquely Chinese form of capitalism to increasingly autocratic rule under Xi Jinping, the first head of state to be born after the Chinese revolution. President of the People's Republic of China (PRC) since 2013, Xi also holds positions within the Communist Party as both general secretary of the Central Committee and chairman of the Central Military Commission. In November 2021, his power was further strengthened by the passage of a landmark resolution[7] at a meeting of the Communist Party elite that places Xi at the same level as two party heroes: Mao and Deng Xiaoping, who masterminded China's transition into a global economic powerhouse. Among other impacts, it all but ensures that Xi will have a third term in office.

Xi has powerful tools at his disposal through which to steer his country away from Western values and practices in favor of a version of capitalism that rejects the unfettered rule of market forces. In a 2015 profile in *The New Yorker,* Evan Osnos pointed to Xi's "ultimate authority over every general, judge, editor, and state-company CEO"[8] and recalled this assessment of the ruler by a longtime Beijing editor: "[Xi is] not afraid of heaven or earth. And he is, as we say, round on the outside and square on the inside; he looks flexible, but inside he is very hard."[9] Xi has used that strength to tighten his grip on media, internet access and content, the political realm, and increasingly, the policies of both domestic and foreign companies.

My first visit to China was in 1996, when I was hired to support the commercial launch of China Online. Over twenty-five years, I have been back several times, and with each visit, I have been shocked and impressed by the country's progress, driven in large part by its shift to private ownership. From my first visit, when virtually no one I encountered spoke English, to a trip in 2007 when I was able to wave away my translator because the young women who had assembled to participate in my consumer research study were nearly fluent in English, I have seen firsthand improvements in efficiency and in the confidence of women's voices. Chairman Mao famously proclaimed that "women hold up half the sky"—a powerful manifesto for gender equality and a legacy of the Chinese Communist Party.[10]

Now the government seems to have tired of hearing those voices. In June 2021, the Australian Broadcasting Corporation reported on the pressure the Chinese are putting on feminists and the #MeToo movement, both seen as disruptive to the social order.[11] Many of their social media accounts have been canceled, and nationalistic trolls hound those who remain online.

But attempts to stifle Chinese women will not be without obstacles. On my 2007 trip to the country, one woman in her late twenties taught me a phrase that speaks to a global trend for women living under repressive regimes: "I am serene of face, wild of heart." She translated this as living her version of a free life, in which she played by the rules in public and rebelled in private. This is not an uncommon approach in China. Osnos's piece in *The New Yorker* referenced another local saying: "When a rule is imposed up high, there is a way to get around it below."[12]

Xi has his hands full. At the same time that his government is asserting itself around (and beyond) the globe—including through its Belt and Road global infrastructure initiatives, its push into Africa, and its ambitious plans to challenge U.S. dominance in space—the Chinese leader is cracking down on domestic behaviors he deems antisocial or counterproductive. This includes instituting limits on video-game playing (no more than three hours of gaming a week for minors[13]), a ban on cryptocurrency,[14] and harsh penalties for rogue CEOs and businesses.[15] As in other countries, authorities in China are increasingly concerned about a growing mental health crisis among youth and so are instituting policies to reduce pressures and ensure children have adequate time for rest and exercise.[16]

Far more difficult to control are the cracks appearing in China's once unstoppable economy. In 2021, the world watched a daily drama reminiscent of the Lehman Brothers collapse of 2008–9: the potential implosion of Evergrande Group, a massive real estate development company now drowning in more than $300 billion in debt. It is not yet clear whether Xi will deem Evergrande "too big to fail" and bail it out, as the U.S. government did with the auto industry, or whether he will allow the real estate group to collapse as a warning to other companies. One thing is increasingly clear to all large Chinese companies, however: The government is an active partner in their businesses.

The cracks in China's economic armor go beyond a spiraling real estate empire. As in other countries, the leadership is contending with a generation of youth unhappy with the direction in which their country has been moving. In China, the ideals of the revolution are at the fore of the dissatisfaction. Mao died in 1976, but legends live forever. Almost half a century later, young Chinese who were not yet born when Mao established an iron rule that saw millions jailed and killed invoke him as a counterpoint to all that angers them about their country's current leaders.

What are their grievances? Widening social and economic inequality: capitalists who make billions while 43 percent of the population earn a monthly income of around $150.[17] Expensive housing. Inadequate protections for workers. Workplaces so demanding that a new term has developed: *966*, meaning that employees are expected to work 9 A.M. to 6 P.M. six days a week.[18]

In other words, issues also at the forefront of youth grievances in almost every postindustrial society. The difference in the PRC is that the nation was founded on the notion of economic equality for all. Mao wrote bluntly about what he perceived as the core problem of society: the class struggle between the oppressed and their oppressors. So the young turn to Mao to support their fight for equity.

In 2019 and 2020, students at one Beijing university library borrowed *The Selected Works of Mao Zedong* more than any other book.[19] "Didn't the proletariat win the revolution?" a Chinese blogger asked after reading Mao. "Why are the masters of the country now at the bottom while the targets of the proletarian dictatorship are on top? What has gone wrong?"[20]

Just as Americans struggle with the disconnect between their nation's founding ideals (all created equal, immigrants embraced) and current realities, so, too, do young Chinese grapple with the failure of their leaders to live up to the ideals set forth by Mao and other revolutionaries in the last century.

Is youth pushback an inevitable response to China joining the global rat race and wanting something different—something more—than modern society affords? Or is something else going on?

One perspective on what has "gone wrong" in China is that the government has inserted itself in its citizens' lives in ways that Mao could never have envisioned. Consider the response to the COVID-19 pandemic. The outbreak started in Wuhan, the most populous city in Hubei Province in central China; almost immediately, the government declared a seventy-six-day lockdown. You might have seen a widely shared video taken near the start of the lockdown: An elderly woman walking outside is confronted by a drone on which a loudspeaker is mounted. As translated by China's state-owned *Global Times*, a voice from the sky warns her: "Yes, Auntie, this drone is speaking to you. You shouldn't walk about without wearing a mask. You'd better go home, and don't forget to wash your hands."[21]

For all the valid criticisms of China's heavy hand, the quick and seemingly effective countermeasures leaders took following the emergence of COVID-19 demonstrated its potential benefits. After just three cases of the novel coronavirus were identified in the coastal city of Qingdao in October 2020, the government tested 10.9 million people—almost the entire population of the city—in just five days.[22] And in rapid order, the country's scientists developed a handful of vaccines that could be stored at normal refrigerator temperatures—a significant advantage over most of the inoculations developed in the United States and Europe. Once the vaccines were introduced, China's government administered 20 million shots a day.[23] A lack of transparency has raised questions about the efficacy of these homegrown vaccines, but the logistical feat alone is worthy of admiration.

Saving lives was just one objective of the Chinese vaccination effort. International influence was another. The vaccine makers claimed they could produce 2.6 billion doses a year. With that, China pledged to send half a billion doses to fifty-three countries—a policy decision that stands in sharp contrast to those of Western nations, including the United States and the U.K., that only belatedly began to share their precious stores of vaccines with less wealthy nations. In just two generations, we seem to have moved from ping-pong diplomacy to vaccine diplomacy.[24] Score one for China.

The source code of the Chinese formula for world domination is simple: Bring every critical industry home, then export it. Along the way, make the rest of the world dependent on Chinese goods and services, leading to economic growth and better-paying jobs across the nation. And critically: Maintain a relatively high percentage of satisfied citizens.

You could see the success of that formula (boosted by government-mandated COVID measures) in 2020 during National Day Golden Week, a holiday celebrated in October. While most of the world was marooned by COVID and its related restrictions, more than half a billion Chinese traveled that week. They were not stuck at home, cowering from the virus. Instead, they rode on high-speed railways and sparkling new highways.[25] Could you imagine if half the population of France or Italy or the United States decided to travel at once during that first week of October 2020 (or really, during any week)? My brain tumor surgery at Harvard Medical School's Brigham and Women's Hospital in Boston was postponed from that fall to the following spring because the city's hospitals were at or over capacity from COVID patients.[26] This stark contrast between more than five hundred million Chinese traveling while on holiday and a major U.S. hospital postponing surgeries as it braced for a holiday spike in COVID transmissions has me questioning whether the Chinese way in 2021 is the more effective way. Will other governments be tempted to prioritize control in the name of safety? Is social cohesion by decree the key to instilling a sense of security in a world that seems to be spinning out of control? And if it is, how on earth can that be instituted amid polarization and discord?

One thing is certain at a time when many nations are struggling with crumbling infrastructures and a lack of political will to spend the money to fix them: Infrastructure advances in China in the past two decades—including the construction of tens of thousands of miles of highways and high-speed rail lines—have boosted not just industry but also quality of life. (For anyone interested in China's rapid automotive transformation, I recommend *Country Driving* by Peter Hessler.) Research by ETH Zürich found that the average travel time between an arbitrarily chosen pair of Chinese prefectures has fallen 13 percent for goods and 50 percent for people over the past fourteen years.[27] Such efficiency requires a total coordination of resources, businesses, and the citizenry. And so, we have seen heavy state control grow in tandem with housing developments and highway systems.

In the PRC, "know your place" is an immutable rule. The last thing anyone wants is to step out of line and get noticed. And given the expansion of the country's social credit system, it is harder than ever to stay under the government's radar. The general idea, according to *Insider,* is that people are ranked according to their behaviors and perceived trustworthiness.[28] Get a speeding ticket, fail to pay off a loan on time, or get caught walking a dog off-leash, and your score is docked. Penalties range from being barred from air travel to being denied loans or entry to university. Follow the rules, and your score goes up. First announced by an arm of the government in 2014, the system is currently made up of multiple state and commercial systems and entered into mostly voluntarily, but is intended to eventually be nationwide and mandatory.

There is also a government-controlled credit system for companies, which blacklists, penalizes, or rewards businesses based on their behaviors.[29] That system is even applied to foreign companies. In 2019, at least three U.S. airlines—American, Delta, and United—received letters threatening a hit to their social credit scores if their websites did not label Hong Kong, Macau, and Taiwan as part of China.[30] The consequences of lower scores, they were warned, might include frozen bank accounts and limitations on the movements of airline employees.[31]

As digital technologies advance, the prying eyes of the government are growing keener. Like many countries, China uses facial recognition software in its public surveillance; unlike other countries, it also uses more sophisticated tools such as emotion-recognition technology that records movements of facial muscles and changes in vocal tones to detect mood. Are you experiencing anger, sadness, happiness, boredom? In certain spots in China, the government might detect that instantly. It's no secret that Xi Jinping wants his citizens to display "positive energy." In essence, he wants to encourage some emotions and discourage others[32]—and tying the display of certain emotions to one's social credit score may prove an effective method of coercion. I'm betting we will see more acting classes on offer in Chinese cities by 2038.

Not only is this scrutiny increasing in sensitivity, it's also becoming harder to escape. Launched in 2013, China's Sharp Eyes program aims eventually to surveil 100 percent of public spaces in the country. Some residents have access to local security footage via special TV boxes equipped with a button they can push to report illegal activity or anything they deem untoward.[33]

Many Westerners would recoil from the idea of Project Sharp Eyes as horrific government overreach. In the United States, two major cities—Boston and San Francisco—have banned the use of facial surveillance technology by police within city limits, and Amnesty International's Ban the Scan campaign is working to add New York City to the list.[34] But the technology has found supporters in China. A Beijing research center has found that while 80 percent of Chinese surveyed are worried about the security of their personal information, two-thirds agree this technology makes them feel safer in public spaces.[35] The reliability of that data may be open to debate, but despite the obvious human rights and privacy implications, emotion-recognition technology is a global industry, growing 30 percent annually. Allied Market Research predicts the category will be worth $33.9 billion by 2023.[36] In other words, many of us will need to make similar calculations between privacy and safety, freedom and security in the coming years.

The Chinese government's appetite for control is not limited to surveillance—or the mainland. In 2019, Hong Kong residents protested an extradition bill that could have sent local defendants to mainland China for trial. Those pro-democracy protests led to more than ten thousand arrests and sparked placements of CCTV cameras throughout the special administrative region.[37] The latest move is to install cameras in schools to monitor teachers.[38]

The vise on Hong Kong tightened further in 2020 when a national security law laid out four new crimes: promotion of secession from China, subversion, terrorism, and collusion with foreign forces. Soon after the law was enacted, pro-democracy media mogul Jimmy Lai and his two sons were arrested for collusion.[39] More arrests followed—including those of fifty-five opposition leaders accused of displaying banners or organizing primary elections for seats in the legislature.[40]

For all the harsh measures imposed on Hong Kong, the circumstances are more draconian in the far-west Xinjiang region. Starting in 2017, under the guise of counterterrorism, China has carried out a sweeping crackdown on Uighur Muslims. About a million members of this ethnic minority group have been detained in "reeducation" camps for periods ranging from weeks to years. The U.S. State Department has declared that China's actions against the Uighurs constitute genocide. And the United States has banned imports of goods from Xinjiang.[41] As that region produces 20 percent of the world's cotton, this is more than a symbolic protest.[42] Neither time nor the glare of publicity has softened the Chinese government's determination to break the Uighurs, however. So much for Mao's professed belief in equality for all.

Even China's CEOs cannot escape the heavy hand of the government. This July 2021 *New York Times* headline is a blunt summary: "What China Expects from Businesses: Total Surrender."

In the decade prior to Xi Jinping's ascendance, China had given far more latitude to businesses—seemingly more interested in economic expansion than in imposing total control. Even prior to Xi, though, there was a core difference in how China regulates its businesses compared with most other countries: The nation's leaders prioritize not just consumer protection and economic growth, as other countries do, but also the reinforcement of Communist Party control. The private sector is expected to "firmly listen to the party and follow the party"[43] and support the prosperity of the people. And so, steps are taken to ensure that the masses are not excluded from the wealth accruing to titans of industry.

In 2015, Xi set a deadline of 2020 to eradicate extreme poverty in the country. Right on cue, in November 2020, the government announced that the goal had been achieved, with some 93 million Chinese removed from the poverty rolls.[44] Commenting on the announcement, Martin Raiser, the World Bank's country director for China, agreed that the country's eradication of "absolute poverty" in rural areas likely had been successful, but given the enormous resources it required—about 1 percent of annual economic output—he questioned whether it would be sustainable.[45] The redistribution of resources included cash transfers to the rural poor under a minimum-basic-living guarantee plan (*dibao*) first launched in the 1990s to support urban workers during a period of rapid economic reform.[46]

In other words, China has delivered on Mao's (and now Xi's) promise of economic prosperity, to an extent. The median per capita income of China's 1.4 billion people is $1,786. In India, the world's largest democracy, it is only around one-third as much: $616.[47] A stable job, a home with a good roof, a fully stocked kitchen all combine to make China's people willing to ignore a great deal of oppression and oversight.

For businesses, success—and the ability to operate with a minimum of roadblocks—comes at a price that includes both financial components and a pledge of loyalty.[48]

Cognizant of Xi's emphasis on poverty elimination, tech companies and other corporations go to extremes to curry favor and avoid backlash. After the government launched an antitrust investigation of on-demand delivery giant Meituan, its chairman and CEO donated $2.3 billion to his own foundation, which funds education and scientific research.[49] The founder of the Midea home-appliances empire donated some $975 million to poverty alleviation, medical care, and cultural programs.[50] And Tencent has raised and donated vast sums for Chinese charities through its annual 99 Giving Day campaign, during which it matches donations made by the public via its online platform.[51] In 2019 alone, the campaign raised an estimated $384 million.[52]

Domestic companies aren't the only businesses compelled to toe the Communist Party line. International corporations also are backpedaling on statements or altering their behavior. In 2019, Daryl Morey, general manager of the NBA's Houston Rockets, touched off a firestorm by tweeting, "Fight for Freedom, Stand with Hong Kong." Morey apologized for the tweet and tried to walk it back, but it was too late.[53] Chinese companies and the Chinese Basketball Association terminated ties with the Rockets. Worse for the NBA, the league's games were banned from China's airwaves for a year, a harsh penalty given that China is by far the NBA's most important international market.[54]

Perhaps most impacted has been Hollywood, whose studios have begun self-censoring to avoid displeasing this critical market. In 2020, *The Guardian* reported on a study by literary and human rights group PEN America, which found that filmmakers routinely make changes to "cast, plot, dialogue, and setting" to avoid antagonizing Chinese officials.[55] Among many other examples, the producers of *Star Trek Beyond* removed LGBTQ+ content, and a major character in *Doctor Strange* was changed from Tibetan to Celtic in order to, in the words of the screenwriter, avoid the risk of "alienating one billion people."[56]

Professor Erik Gordon of the University of Michigan's Ross School of Business noted that U.S. companies' concessions to Chinese mandates represent a change: "I think ten years ago, the American companies would have ignored China's demands. But today, they can't bow quickly enough or low enough."[57] Former U.S. secretary of state Condoleezza Rice termed the Chinese response to the NBA general manager's tweet "a violation of American sovereignty."[58]

Given the country's importance as both a manufacturing center and massive consumer market, China has many international businesses over a barrel. Now that the pandemic has revealed the extent to which so many vital goods—prescription drugs, electronics, and even the minerals needed for everything from wind turbines and aircraft engines to computer hard drives—are dependent on China, we can expect increasing efforts to resume domestic production of vital materials and goods in the United States and other markets. Will we see a measurable difference by 2038? For the first time in at least a couple of decades, it is beginning to seem feasible.

In its 2021 annual report, sourcing specialist Thomas reported that 83 percent of the companies it surveyed said they are "likely" or "extremely likely" to reshore all or some of their production in the near future, meaning that they will return it to their home countries.[59] This is up from 54 percent in 2020. Much will depend on government incentives, of course, and we are seeing more countries, including Japan, the U.K., and the United States, enact policies to encourage domestic companies that have set up shop in mainland China to return home.

A shift worth watching in China that speaks to its new position in the world is the rise of localism. Where all things foreign once carried a certain cachet, there is a growing pride among the Chinese in their unique culture of brands, media outlets, and platforms. And that is having an impact, unsurprisingly, on consumer-facing companies in other countries.

A 2021 report by search engine Baidu shows that the percentage of brand searches for domestic (rather than overseas) brands on Baidu rose from 38 percent in 2009 to 70 percent in 2019, spurred by consumers' growing preference for Chinese-made goods.[60] The predilection for Chinese brands is especially strong among younger consumers.[61] We can see this trend playing out in cinemas, too. Just 35.9 percent of the box-office earnings in China, the world's largest theatrical market, came from foreign films in 2019, down from 53 percent in 2012.[62] Hollywood movies have been taking a real hit as China's domestic studios grow in strength. In part, that has to do with a rising anti-American sentiment in the People's Republic. According to Chris Fenton, U.S. film producer and trustee of the US-Asia Institute, "Chinese consumer sentiment toward anything American is at an all-time modern-day low."[63]

This trend toward localism, dubbed "*guochao*,"* is leading domestic manufacturers to incorporate traditional Chinese symbols and retro designs into their products and packaging. "Made in China" is now a coveted label, speaking to the population's boosted sense of self.

Two centuries ago, French emperor Napoleon Bonaparte was said to have remarked, "China is a sleeping giant. Let her sleep, for when

* According to *Jing Daily*, *guochao* refers to a mix of contemporary design and nostalgic cues.

she wakes the world will tremble." Whether Napoleon actually uttered those words is up for debate,[64] but the quote itself has proved prescient. From a long historical perspective, China has always been a sizeable force—just not in the colonial mold. Unlike the European powers and the United States, China was interested only in dominating and controlling its immediate neighbors, not faraway places. That has changed. In this century, the once isolated nation has emerged as a leading influencer of global affairs.

In his first news conference as president, in 2021, Joe Biden addressed the emerging superpower, saying that Xi Jinping "doesn't have a democratic . . . bone in his body."[65] Biden went on to describe the next decade as more than a competition between nations, calling it "a battle between the utility of democracies in the twenty-first century and autocracies."[66] That battle will not involve military engagement (one prays). It will be fought on the field of technological and scientific innovation. The Chinese, Biden said, see autocracy as the way forward, and believe that democracy will founder amid the complexities of the modern world. To compete, America needs to make an unprecedented investment in infrastructure and research. "China is out-investing us by a long shot because their plan is to own that future."[67]

Owning the future starts with modernizing everything, including energy, technology, and diplomatic outreach. Writing in *Foreign Policy,* Zachery Tyson Brown describes the "impressive system of dependence and influence" that China has built, including by buying up controlling interests in ports, connecting fifth-generation telecommunications networks, financing the development of modernizing states, and creating a far-flung constellation of diplomatic posts, the most now of any country on Earth—all while the United States has cut its foreign service to the very bone.[68]

These practices have paid off. Amid the economic pressures of the pandemic, China emerged as the only major economy to record positive growth in 2020.[69] And analysts have begun to update their forecasts for when the People's Republic will surpass the United States as the world's largest economy. Working with International Monetary Fund projections, Nomura Holdings has shortened the timeline for that milestone from 2030 to as soon as 2026.[70] (Other economists argue that the United States will retain its lead for at least another decade due to China's eroding workforce demographics,[71] which I explore below.)

However the economic footrace turns out, the Asia Society refers to China rising as "the geopolitical equivalent of the melting polar ice caps: gradual change on a massive scale that can suddenly lead to dramatic turns of events"[72] and designates China's ascent as the defining trend of the twenty-first century. Already, looking at trends in China offers hints of global trends to come because of the immense influence the country wields on the world stage.

For all the country's economic progress and accumulation of power, China's road to global domination is beginning to show potholes, created internally by youth demanding the economic equitability Mao promised and externally as nations get more serious about combating Chinese influence and control.

The biggest wrench in China's plans for global domination, however, will potentially come neither from internal unrest nor competing nations but from demographics. Currently, there are more elderly in China than there are children aged fifteen and under. By 2050, the number of elderly (defined as aged sixty or above) will nearly double, from 254 million in 2021 to almost 500 million.[73] The birthrate will not soften this development. In 1950, some 46 million babies were delivered in China.[74] In 2020, China recorded just 12 million births, the lowest in six decades.[75]

Confronted by a future in which a shrinking workforce will be unable to support the aged—a situation also faced by the United States and Europe, though on a smaller scale—Chinese party leaders are scrambling to reverse the trend. In 1979, China famously implemented a one-child policy, which deterred couples from having more than one child. The campaign to reduce population growth also extended to mass sterilizations and the mandatory insertion of an intrauterine device (IUD) after a woman's first delivery.[76] (These sterilization and contraception efforts, together with forced abortions, reportedly are being used among the Uighurs.)[77] In 2016, as concerns about its aging population increased, China revised its policy, allowing two children. As of May 2021, married couples are permitted—even encouraged—to have three children.[78] The government has also imposed sweeping restrictions on the country's $100 billion private education industry, including tutors and online courses, partly out of concern that the expense was deterring some couples from having more than one child.[79]

Another looming impediment on the path to progress: climate change. China's economic ascendance has carried a steep ecological cost. China may have been the only major economy to grow in 2020, but it was also the only one in which greenhouse gas emissions increased. Currently, more than a quarter of the world's climate pollution originates in China,[80] a fact that spotlights the critical role the country will play in slowing climate change.[81] In September 2020, Xi Jinping announced that his nation is aiming to achieve carbon neutrality by 2060—a step in the right direction but far too slow in the minds of leading scientists. A 2018 report issued by the Intergovernmental Panel on Climate Change indicated that limiting global temperature rise to 1.5 degrees Celsius above preindustrial levels—the aim of the twenty-first Conference of the Parties of the United Nations Framework Convention on Climate Change in 2015—will require that all countries achieve carbon neutrality by 2050.[82]

Pressure will mount on China to act faster, especially as its citizenry experiences the intensified effects of extreme weather. The numbers are eye-opening. In a seventy-two-hour period in July 2021, rainstorms dropped the equivalent of a year's worth of water on Zhengzhou, a city in central China. The flood killed nearly 300 people and displaced 1.5 million.[83] Extreme weather in China, as elsewhere in the world, is a critical risk factor going forward.

The battle for global supremacy between the United States and China has two fronts: economic dominance and geopolitical influence. In his book *Has China Won?,* Singaporean diplomat and academic Kishore Mahbubani outlines critical differences between the two superpowers as they vie for supremacy, including America valuing freedom while China values freedom from chaos and China's patience versus America's strategic decisiveness.[84]

The stakes could not be higher, and tensions are rising, not least because of China's extraterrestrial ambitions. (China has announced plans to send its first crewed mission to Mars in 2033.)[85] To counter China's power, nations will seek to rethink geopolitical alignments and alliances, as happened with the Australia–U.K.–United States deal regarding nuclear-powered submarines in 2021—a deal that enraged France, which saw a separate submarine sales deal with Australia scuttled as a result. Global relations are a tricky matter, and the bigger the nation the louder the bang when deals are cut that reshape the balance of power.

Bottom line: China is fully awakened from its centuries-long slumber, and there are many who see reason to tremble.

In this first section, I have established some of the big-picture forces that will shape the next twenty years, including our ever-increasing reliance on technology, climate change, chaos as our new normal, and major shifts within and between this century's two dominant centers of power: China and the United States. Up next: an examination of the cultural shifts impacting our now and next, including emerging forms of tribalism, the blurring and shoring up of boundaries, the allure of small, and the new face of luxury.

PART TWO

How We Live

✳

The clock is ticking, and with every second, people around the planet seem more anxious. In 2017, the World Health Organization reported that 264 million adults suffered from anxiety.[1] Since then, circumstances have only grown tenser. Will the catastrophic events of 2020–21 serve as a reset, awakening society to the need for immediate, radical change? Or do they spell a point of no return, serving as indicators that the global situation is so grim we can no longer hope to resolve it? It is possible that both outcomes will prove true.

It is always instructive—albeit not always comforting—to consult the Doomsday Clock. The Bulletin of the Atomic Scientists conceived the metaphorical device in 1947 as a way to depict our proximity to a catastrophe that would end humanity. Today, it is managed by that organization's science and security board. (The group's board of sponsors includes thirteen Nobel laureates.) Over the seventy-plus years prior to January 2020, the closest the Doomsday Clock had been to midnight was in 1953, when it was set to 11:58 P.M. after both the United States and the Soviet Union carried out hydrogen bomb tests the previous year.[2] In 1991, at the end of the Cold War, when the Strategic Arms Reduction Treaty was signed, the clock was turned back a reassuring quarter-hour to 11:43 P.M.[3] On January 23, 2020—yes, *prior* to the COVID-19 pandemic and resulting economic meltdowns—the clock inched closer to midnight than at any other time in its history. Owing to the combined threat of nuclear weapons, inaction on climate change, and the rise of "cyber-enabled disinformation campaigns that undermine society's ability to act,"[4] the clock now stands at a mere 100 seconds to midnight.

We can do better. We have to do better. And I genuinely believe we will. The response to the question on so many of our minds—what's next?—is not beyond our control, *provided* we address the myriad challenges we face in a resolute and reasoned way. Most pressing: continued environmental devastation and rising temperatures, entrenched economic and racial inequities, the ascent of an authoritarian superpower, intensifying nationalism and sociopolitical polarization, cyberterrorism in a networked world, and—last but not least—a modern-day angst that is palpable and too often debilitating.

Each of these issues is being addressed (albeit inadequately) at the governmental level, but how the world's citizens, especially in wealthier countries, choose to live—what we prioritize, what we permit, what we fight for—will determine whether our world is moving in a more hopeful direction by 2038. The coming chapters explore social shifts pertaining to tribalism, the blurring and bolstering of boundaries, new definitions of luxury, and the pernicious inequities of wealth. In ways large and small, shifts in how we live and regard those around us will determine whether we are positioned to achieve a societal reset sufficient to save the day.

Chapter 7

Who's in Your Lifeboat?

The 1944 Alfred Hitchcock film *Lifeboat* is set in the Atlantic, during World War II, in a single location: on board a small vessel carrying the survivors of a ship torpedoed by a German submarine. A near-perfect metaphor for the human condition. Would the passengers ignore personality differences to survive? Would a leader emerge, or would they make decisions democratically? What would they do when food and water ran low or when someone fell ill? In short, all the problems and challenges of human society, in a location where no problem can be avoided or papered over.

There was only one set—a water tank inside a Hollywood studio—but the characters were more than sufficient sources of drama and conflict. It was a microcosm of a macrocosm. There was a striking diversity of characters for a movie shot in 1944. A rich and sociable woman, wearing privilege like perfume. An opportunistic tycoon. Two meek women, one clinging to her lifeless baby. Four men from the ship's crew—one Cockney, one Black. And a man no one has seen before, a German, who is pulled out of the icy waters. Though he denies it, the German is the captain of the U-boat, which has also sunk; quite a choice for a movie released when the outcome of the war was still uncertain.

In the film, the Americans are ineffectual. The sailors are competent but, by virtue of their class, are not considered leaders. The German had been a leader and is a good one now. A man needs to have a leg amputated. The others are squeamish; the German handles it. He also lies about the course they are on; they are not bound for Bermuda (*Spoiler alert!*) but for German-controlled waters. Ultimately, the passengers kill the Nazi captain—not because of his clever plan to alter their course but because he has been concealing a flask of water and food tablets.

Lifeboat has become a cult favorite, and not just for the director's innovative filming technique. Beyond its aesthetic merits, there is a powerful message in the script, delivered by the U-boat captain: "To survive, one must have a plan."

In the twenty-first century, we are all playing out both collective and individualized versions of the lifeboat. This vessel has become a metaphor that involves us all, whether we recognize it or not. A mass of people find themselves bound together in what promises to be a moment of imminent peril—if not from a pandemic, then from one of the other threats looming on our horizon. And so, more and more, we find ourselves gaming out our futures. When X happens, what do we do? Are we prepared for Y? And most crucially, who counts as "we"?

That "we" question is becoming extremely uncomfortable for many people. Who merits a place in our notional lifeboat, our survival play? On whom can we count when the tides of fate turn against us?

You might think that the obvious answer is based on genetics—our family members. That was Noah's rule of thumb for his ark. But ours is an era when family members have become estranged over political and cultural issues or simply geographic distance and a disinclination to stay in touch. And many people are without family, living solitary lives. A 2015 study found that an American woman aged sixty-five to seventy-five with at least two living adult children has an 11 percent chance of being estranged from at least one of them and a 62 percent chance of having contact less than once a month with at least one child.[1] An earlier study found that whereas more than 70 percent of the elderly in Japan and 20 percent of those in the United States lived with their children in the early 1980s, those figures had dropped to 52 percent and 12 percent, respectively, by 1996.[2] In Japan, it is forecast that more than 40 percent of people aged sixty-five and older will live alone in 2040.[3] In the United States, Harvard University's Joint Center for

Housing Studies projects that the number of people aged seventy-five and older living alone will jump from 6.9 million in 2015 to 13.4 million in 2035.[4]

Family bonds are fraying.

The family structures of old (extended/multigenerational and nuclear) have ceded ground to a new reality marked by cohabitation without marriage, single parents, divorce and remarriages, blended families, grandparents as primary caregivers, and smaller households.

The lifeboat calculations become infinitely more complex when you factor in these diverse ways people live. Several years ago, I was invited to a wonderful Thanksgiving meal, where guests included a married couple, a single woman with her teenage daughter, a widow and her nephew—who invited via FaceTime his sperm-donor dad for a piece of virtual pumpkin pie. It seemed perfectly normal. This past year, I hosted a holiday meal for twenty-two people, including my siblings, a brother-in-law, one sister's best friend, two nieces (one who brought a boyfriend), an Indian couple newly relocated to New York City from London, two Dutch friends, three of Jim's four children, one of his nieces (daughter of a brother who did not attend), and Jim's sister and her two children (one who came with his girlfriend).

We call this a family meal. But is this the family we would yank into our lifeboat? That was a topic of conversation at our dinner table.

In myth and media, many of us used to know who "we" were. In the United States, we were the citizens of Bedford Falls in *It's a Wonderful Life*—voted Britain's favorite Christmas movie.[5] (What does it say about Americans that our favorite Christmas movie is *Home Alone*?)[6] In this fanciful version of reality, we had known one another all our lives. We looked alike. We were friends, but really, more like family, however dysfunctional. We were not all the same color, ethnicity, or religion as the solid citizens of Bedford Falls, but we were at least of the same class: the middle class. Or at least we assumed we were.

In Bedford Falls, the lifeboat presumably would welcome as many neighbors as could fit without sinking the boat—first come, first served.

In reality, our schisms and petty differences would likely make for a far less harmonious picture. Would a banker who forecloses on a widow's house be hauled into the boat by the widow's son? Would the mechanic who was let go for a minor infraction save the woman who fired him? And how many churchgoing Christians would reach into the water for the town drunk—or ardent atheist?

Let's say you had room for ten in your lifeboat. Or room for twenty. Or five hundred. Or a billion. Whom would you invite? Whom would you leave to their doom? The smallest boat would likely be the hardest to fill. Does a beloved but aged grandma take precedence over your despised brother's third wife? What if there is a chance she is pregnant? Are you willing to be stuck in a small space with your perpetually bickering divorced parents? If not, which parent do you prioritize? Are you going to subject your best friend to your homophobic uncle?

The largest boat, too, would present complicated decisions. Do you choose your billion on the basis of age? Race? Ethnicity? Religion? Attractiveness? Intelligence? Country of origin? Diversity? Body mass? Survival skills? If you choose to prioritize those linked most closely to you by genetics, how will you recognize them? Not, as you may assume, by their skin color. A hundred years ago, Britain's oldest complete skeleton was discovered in a cave. Dubbed Cheddar Man—a nod to his location in Cheddar Gorge, near the village of Cheddar, Somerset—he is thought to have had blue eyes. He definitely had dark skin and dark, curly hair.[7] And what of Jesus? The real Jesus of Nazareth would have looked nothing like the fair-skinned northern European familiar from centuries of religious images. As a Jewish Galilean, Jesus is highly likely to have had brown eyes, dark brown to black hair, and olive-brown skin.[8] Would he count as "one of us" among conservative white Christians doling out spaces on their lifeboat?

As the world becomes less settled and homogenous, people are looking for ways to isolate and to find security in the familiar. But who truly belongs to our extended tribe?

The rise of at-home DNA test kits is adding to our understanding of who we are. According to *MIT Technology Review*, more than twenty-six million people had submitted their DNA for analysis by one of the four leading databases (Ancestry, 23andMe, FamilyTreeDNA, MyHeritage) by the start of 2019, and that number was expected to quadruple by 2022.[9] I know someone who found out about the existence of a brother thanks to the test. And the internet is rife with stories of people who discover that the families they have always known are not, in fact, blood relations.

Craig Cobb is an avowed white supremacist whose test results—unveiled to him on TV—showed his DNA reflected 14 percent sub-Saharan African heritage.[10] Conversely, Sigrid Johnson, a woman who had always identified as Black, discovered not just that she was adopted but that she was less than 3 percent African. Her primary heritage: Hispanic, Middle Eastern, and European.[11]

The shock people like Cobb and Johnson feel when they take a DNA test—though Cobb was quick to dismiss the findings as "statistical noise"[12]—speaks to the depth of human identity and the power of belonging to a defined tribe. These identity markers signal more than just percentages of ethnic and cultural heritage. They are about who we are at the most personal level. It is commonplace in America to attribute love of drink or a poetic soul to one's Irish ancestry, one's hot temper to Greek or Italian origins, one's stinginess to Scottish genes, one's stellar organizational skills to a Swiss background.

What happens when those innate "truths" turn out to be false? Who are we, really, when we are stripped of those identity markers?

On the radar:

By 2038, one-size-fits-all approaches to modern medicine will have given way to more customized approaches based on DNA. As advances in nutrigenomics continue, don't be surprised if food manufacturers adopt packaging symbols to indicate for which DNA "types" a product is recommended.

In secure and settled times of calm and plenty, most people feel there is no need to look too closely into who counts as "one of us." Lines of ethnicity, affinity, and allegiance can be fuzzy, and people can move between identities without much judgment. In times of chaos and uncertainty? Not so much.

All it takes to upset our comfortable sense of belonging is the prospect of insecurity or shortages (think: mobs of frantic shoppers on Black Friday, people tussling over toilet paper rolls and disinfectant at the start of the pandemic). All it takes are political opportunists willing to reopen the wounds of old grievances, to play on "us versus them" and demand that people make "with us or against us" decisions. Hence, the spike in white supremacy and far-right nationalism in the past decade as globalization, European unification, and the refugee crisis made it more likely someone of a different color, language, or religion (often all three) would move in next door.

Some parts of the world embrace the concept of multiculturalism (at least in theory), but the reality for immigrants is often more stratified and less accommodating than many natives assume. Berlin is home to the largest population of Turks outside Turkey, with many having arrived as guest workers in the latter half of the twentieth century. In early 2001, many Germans were stunned when a study uncovered that 42 percent of these immigrant populations were registered as unemployed.[13] The reality was that most Germans lived largely separate lives from immigrants, seeing them only when ordering a meal at an ethnic restaurant or when passing through certain neighborhoods.[14] They had little concept of how these people live.

In the last century, we saw an embrace of multiculturalism—a recognition of and appreciation for cultural differences. In this century, support has waned as more people question whether diversity has eroded the common culture in some countries.[15] There is a generational difference at play here. A 2017 study in Germany found, for instance, that most respondents under age twenty-five would like to see a merger of cultures, with components taken from both the dominant culture and the cultures of newcomers.[16] In contrast, two-thirds of those over age seventy wanted immigrants to shed their cultures and adopt Germany's.

The debate over multiculturalism versus a common culture will intensify as global conflicts, economic hardship, and climate change combine to push even more people across borders. At any moment of the day, some eighty-two million human beings are on the move[17]—as refugees, sometimes in actual lifeboats. In the countries to which they are fleeing, millions of people are turning against the large-scale influx. They are questioning who "belongs" where and who "belongs" with whom. At its most extreme, this manifests as nativism—the ideology that only those born in a country or born of long-established ethnicity have the right to live there. This raises deep and disturbing questions of history and ancestry, now further elucidated (and complicated) by DNA analysis.

History, anthropology, and sociology give us countless examples of in-group/out-group thinking—people banding together in tribes, clubs, associations, political parties, and other assemblies. For a social species, it is normal and indeed necessary. And now digital technologies have made it possible for millions to divvy themselves up in new ways: grouping according to opinions, building bonds around shared interests. Some of these groupings have socially beneficial effects; others, less so.

On the radar:

By 2038, generation- and interest-based congregant living will be much more common, for reasons related to sustainability, affordability, and the modern-day crisis of loneliness. The living-and-learning communities so popular on college campuses these days will extend into the wider world.

The novel coronavirus that put half of humanity in lockdown in 2020 redefined many people's notion of community. In a phenomenon I call "zooming in" and "zooming out," people are simultaneously zeroing in on those people and businesses closest to them by geography or emotional bonds and taking care to notice, perhaps for the first time, those people "unlike them" who helped them get through a frightening time. In July 2021, New York City threw its first ticker-tape parade since 2019. Those honored? Not a victorious sports team, astronauts, or a political titan but rather, essential workers—aka hometown heroes: the doctors and nurses, sanitation workers, bus drivers, and others who put their lives at risk to protect the rest of us. Our tribe expanded.

For the first time since World War II, the pandemic gave people worldwide a collective experience, a sense of unity unfamiliar in the digital age. We had a common enemy, a common focus, a common fear—and a common goal: survival. That shared experience offered a sense not just of community but of solidarity.

"We before me" is the default way of thinking in societies that prize collectivism over the individual. That is why it was not uncommon—long before COVID-19—to see people in Japan wearing face masks out in public. In that culture, if you feel a cold coming on or are ill, it is customary to don a face covering to protect those around you. It is common courtesy. In contrast, in cultures such as those of Great Britain and the United States, rugged individualism takes center stage, and "me first" has been a longtime mantra.

The question is how our experience of coming together during the pandemic while staying physically apart will color our attitudes and actions in the future. Have we genuinely learned how to work together, or will we continue to see one another as rivals for limited resources? In 2013, I talked about the rise of *co-* words (*co-create, co-parent, co-preneur*) as an antidote to all the anger swirling around the world. It is reassuring to see fresh evidence of this trend: that New York City ticker-tape parade and the many selfless acts we saw during the first few months of the pandemic. One extreme: A New York City sculptor, Rhonda Roland Shearer, racked up $600,000 in debt procuring personal protective equipment for city healthcare workers.[18]

Many of us have a stronger sense than we did pre-pandemic of how our decisions impact others, whether it relates to the choice to get vaccinated, pay our fair share of taxes, or allow casual racism or sexism to go unchallenged. We have always been in this world together; we just have not always felt or acted like it. Now that more of us recognize we are all in the same boat, we can see that collaboration and cooperation will be vital to weathering the storms currently raging—and those just beginning to take shape on the horizon.

As so many of us spend more time on Zoom and Google Meet and in remote classrooms, we can begin to envisage the role of cooperatives in the future. Imagine digital platforms that connect not only individuals but communities. Cooperative housing developments that cater to multigenerational families. Collective "ghost kitchens" that focus on takeout and delivery versus in-restaurant dining, offering convenience to people pressed for time and opportunities for would-be entrepreneurs with children at home or other pressing household responsibilities. (Some people regard ghost kitchens as an antisocial trend wherein people sacrifice the traditional shared-meal experiences of restaurants for efficiency and privacy—even anonymity—but it seems to me that they encourage family meals and work cooperatives.)

Looking ahead, perhaps the silver lining of these times will be a return to a sense of true community and shared responsibility. Our "me" culture has not been cutting it.

In June 2020, already reeling from the virus, much of the world united around a second shared experience: witnessing via video the brutal police murder of George Floyd in Minneapolis. Many unarmed Black men (and women and children) have been killed by the police in recent years for "offenses" as minor as jaywalking, passing a fake $20 bill (knowingly or not), or playing in a park with a toy gun.

What made the Floyd killing different? It wasn't just the video. We had footage of the killings of Philando Castile, Sean Reed, Eric Garner, and others. It was the pandemic. It was the fact that we had been cooped up inside for months on end, more attuned to the inequities of the world as showcased by far higher rates of COVID-19 infection and death among people of color.[19] It was also the fact that we were more keenly aware of all the Black and brown and low-income people who had kept our countries' motors running while the more fortunate among us had the option of sheltering in place.

In earlier years, many of us were heartbroken and angry about the deaths of Tamir Rice, Michael Brown, and so many others. In the case of Floyd, we felt another emotion: a heightened sense of solidarity with all people subjected to centuries of institutionalized racism and abuse. As is so often the case, there is also a tribe gathering around a rejection of this notion. Still, compared with before the pandemic, fewer of us are willing to let others bear sole responsibility for fixing the system. People took to the streets en masse—and not just in Minneapolis and the United States but in Japan, Mexico, Britain, Bulgaria, Bermuda, Denmark, Iceland, and elsewhere around the world.[20] This sense of solidarity is impacting our notions of allegiance and belonging. More of us than ever before are standing taller as allies, which incites an opposite reaction: building taller walls.

As we grapple with chaos as the new normal and our collective loss of certainty and control, people are responding in unique, personal ways. I work with a man whose wife made it her mission to keep neighbors supplied with essential goods at the start of the lockdowns in Switzerland. I did the same for far-flung family in the United States. I needed the sense of control that came from knowing my loved ones were fed. And I also wanted to support small retailers, who were at acute risk during the lockdowns, and to cheer up people with a surprise delivery of something sweet, knowing full well that so much of the joy had been sucked out of our socially distanced lives. During Christmas 2020, we opted to forgo most family gifts; instead, we worked with local charity 4-CT to donate directly to a struggling local family.

A friend of a friend has responded to today's chaos quite differently. I would place his attitude toward the opposite extreme of the community–self-protection spectrum. He lives in the hills above

Los Angeles and has a small arsenal of guns. He is not a violent or aggressive man. He would consider himself practical. As he explained to our mutual friend in an email:

> *If the city fails and there is hunger and the supermarkets have been looted, desperate people will come up here looking for food. I have a shotgun to discourage them when they're at the edge of my property. If they get closer, I may have to shoot them with a rifle. And if it's them or me, I have a handgun. I regret all of this, but I'd be a fool to think that all they want from me is what's in my refrigerator and freezer.*

That man knows who is in his lifeboat: his family, period. Who's in yours?

In one possible version of a movie in the survivalist genre of Hitchcock's *Lifeboat,* you missed the memo, and now you are scrambling. You are not like the man in the hills above Los Angeles—a man who believes he is fully prepared for this moment, or at least better prepared than most. You are not like the ultrarich, with a private island or a well-fortified retreat. You have the gut-churning realization that, should civil society crumble, no one from the government will ride to your rescue. So, on whom can you count? Who will have your back when the hordes arrive at the front gate?

That moment in this imagined movie is when we will be forced to confront a bitter reality: We are increasingly isolated from one another in the real world. Those virtual communities we spent the last couple of decades building? The distant friends and acquaintances we found and connected with on Facebook or Instagram? Those hundreds of connections on LinkedIn? Meaningless; there is little safety in virtual relationships.

So, who really matters? We can ask that question not just of individuals but of governments. Who belongs in our national lifeboat? Who is owed a spot in the planet's lifeboat? The clock is ticking.

Unlike another disaster at sea with which we are all familiar, the greatest threat we face in the post-pandemic era is not an iceberg looming unseen in the dark, poised to gouge a fatal hole in our vessel. Rather, the iceberg is in plain sight, and we have already made contact in a slow-motion collision that is being felt more sharply in some places than others. No surprise here: It is the increasingly chaotic climate. The greenhouse effect that is contributing to record-high temperatures year after year, the melting ice that raises sea levels, the wind that drives the fire that burns homes and crops.

And it is also divisiveness. Our increasing inability to communicate calmly, constructively, and civilly with those we deem unlike us—those we would leave off our lifeboat manifest. And the persistent inequities that give some people more than they could possibly use while denying others the most essential goods.

In some ways, our collision course with catastrophe may be our saving grace. There may not be separate lifeboats—just one large enough for the entire planet. All eight billion of us. Some would say we are already seated in it—or maybe clinging to its sides.

We cannot choose to leave this lifeboat, but we do have choices. We can drift, terrified, waiting for the next headline tragedy. Or we can summon our courage and intelligence and do what is required to make our joint survival more likely, prioritizing not just the members of our tribe but everyone. Based on our human history of resilience, I am betting on the latter.

What we all do—our collective intent and actions over the next two decades—is consequential and will determine whether chaos will be allowed to prevail. If starlings can develop the instinctual means to move in concert to such a massive degree as described earlier in this book, then surely we can work in unison to quell the chaos that threatens us all.

Chapter 8

Crossing Lines, Resetting Boundaries

Boundaries shift. They always have and always will. The issue is: How fast, how far, and in which direction? To get a sense of time travel, look at documents, periodicals, and images from half a century ago and ask yourself where the boundaries were back then. On an old map, you will see countries that no longer exist and countries that didn't exist until a new line was drawn. Look at photos of people in popular magazines, and you will get an inkling of invisible boundaries—the demarcations that determined which individuals and groups were deemed to "matter." And, more than that, which classifications of people—by race, gender, geography, and more—were considered worthy of chronicling. Now consider what maps, periodicals, and other documents might look like half a century forward. Which boundaries will have softened or disappeared? Which new ones will have emerged?

There are all sorts of boundaries: physical, psychological, social/cultural, intellectual, sexual, temporal, and more. Virtually all of them are in near-constant transition, and perhaps never more so than today. We have entered into a period of hybridization, affecting where and how we work, how we dress, what we eat, with whom we partner, how we express ourselves, and more. A century ago, one could visit a hospital nursery and have a pretty good idea of the life a swaddled infant would lead based on gender, geography, religion, and the family's socioeconomic status. We would have a pretty good idea of the demographics of the person the baby would go on to marry based on all of the aforementioned variables.

Lines were drawn with bold strokes, and only the brave and strong-willed crossed them. Now consider a baby born today. We cannot even assume that the gender assigned at birth is accurate. A century ago, we could make an educated guess about what career (if any) the female infant would eventually pursue. Now, how would you even begin to guess? It's an impossibility. More choices. Fewer boundaries. No sense of certainty.

Historically, the most enduring boundaries have been cultural. You could find them almost everywhere people lived in communities with a population of ten or more. A long history of class and caste tells us those boundaries are just as neatly drawn as the physical borders between Egypt and Libya or Canada and the United States. For centuries, these unwritten boundaries have provided inspiration to comedians, dramatists, and novelists. It is not just that social boundaries are an easy access point to stories about characters we all recognize. It is because those boundaries seemed immutable in some parts of the world. Even today in England, for example, the landed aristocracy is at the apex of society; around a third of the nation's property is owned by aristocrats and traditional landed gentry.[1]

Social boundaries were learned early, and when rank derived from lineage and venerable fortunes, the excluded might as well have been physically branded. Charles Dickens is a classic example. When his father was sentenced to a stint in a debtor's prison, twelve-year-old Charles spent twelve-hour days at a blacking factory to support his family. He became the most famous writer of his time in Britain, but he never felt fully cleansed of the stain.[2]

It is not just Britain. The caste system in India, the hierarchy of the French court, the *von* in a German name—something in our DNA seems to require social boundaries. Us and them. Higher and lower. The exalted and the reviled. Stars upon thars or the Plain-Belly sort.[3] Except, with notable exceptions, in the United States. At least, that is how it was intended.

A young country, with half a continent of undeveloped land—this was the greatest possible invitation to the adventurous and ambitious. In his essay "The Significance of the Frontier in American History," Frederick Jackson Turner identified the West as the most significant incubator of democracy; he contended that, starting in the 1840s, with every mile the settlers moved west, they left a bit of European values behind. In 1868, Horatio Alger published *Ragged Dick,* a novel for young adults about a teenage boy who rises above his class at birth through virtue and merit. It was an appealing and inspiring message, easy to turn into cultural shorthand. Although the frontier was soon erased, the myth of social mobility and fortunes for the taking persisted. In California, you could reinvent yourself. All you needed was intelligence and ambition. A Jew could own a movie studio.

By the mid-twentieth century, boundaries seemed to dissolve even further in America. Maybe it started with the presidency of John F. Kennedy and the breeze of liberalism that blew away the staid "man in a gray flannel suit" values of the 1950s. Maybe it was the sex, drugs, and rock 'n' roll youth culture of the late 1960s. The Civil Rights and antiwar movements. And the Pill. And feminism. And women moving beyond the traditional occupations of nursing and teaching. Maybe it was the rise of soft power and new paths of influence.

Whatever the cause, I grew up feeling largely unencumbered by boundaries. People traveled freely. There was more money around, and it came to matter more than birthright. Increasingly, we began to speak of boundaries in purely psychological terms. By the 1990s, women who consulted therapists because they no longer wished to be oppressed in relationships learned to create—and enforce—"healthy boundaries." For arguably the first time, boundaries were something we set for ourselves, not something imposed upon us.

With the new millennium, societal boundaries continued to dissolve. The internet boom and the fortunes made in finance contributed to a culture that was more expansive, more laissez-faire. Gays married. Interracial couples no longer drew stares—at least in urban settings. A Black man became president.

Then Newton's third law—for every action, there is an equal and opposite reaction—kicked in. In June 2015, Donald Trump rode down an escalator to announce his candidacy for U.S. president, and the hopes of millions of adherents rode with him. His message was direct: Mexicans who come to our country, he said, "have lots of problems, and they're bringing those problems with [them]. They're bringing drugs. They're bringing crime. They're rapists." He added: "And some, I assume, are good people."[4]

Anti-immigrant sentiment is nothing new in the United States. What was different about Trump's campaign rhetoric was the language he used—no subtlety there—and the fact that the desire for impenetrable boundaries was spoken out loud by a national figure. The call to build a wall—to create a physical border between us and them—was a masterstroke. Its construction would establish a clear boundary, eighteen to twenty-seven feet high. Implicit in it: the repugnant notion that whites, especially white men, are the only true Americans. Somehow they had been swindled out of their birthright; they were now victims. It was a fitting underscore of the Trump administration's messaging when Secretary of State Mike Pompeo, two days before Trump left office, condemned "wokeism, multiculturalism, all the -isms—they're not who America is."[5]

In truth, these and other "-isms" are now integral to the American experience. For all the exertion of those who wish to return America to their idealized version of earlier times, it is impossible to stuff the genie back into the bottle. The racial and ethnic makeup of the country has forever changed, and so have attitudes toward everything from racial equality to sexuality and gender. Sexual lines have blurred, and "she" can be "they" or "them." Or "he" could be. Boundaries grow less distinct by the moment, supplanted by a gender-fluid culture in which exploring roles is an exercise in discovering one's authentic self.

A secondary force has emerged, too: a drawing of new boundaries, this time by women. For decades, sex with an underage girl was a premise that could produce a literary classic, as evidenced by Vladimir Nabokov's *Lolita*. Hit movies such as *Election* and *American Beauty* were built on this theme. In *Manhattan,* Woody Allen played a forty-two-year-old writer dating a seventeen-year-old high school student. When they first viewed the movie, few critics noted what many would consider the predatory nature of the relationship; it was considered one of Allen's best films.

Then Jeffrey Epstein and Harvey Weinstein ruined misogyny as an acceptable attitude and sexual violence and predation as simply "the way men are." Weinstein, once considered a tasteful if tyrannical producer of arty films, had a dark side much blacker than the traditional casting couch. That widespread gossip failed to become headlines for so many years speaks to the nature of power. And then, with #MeToo, everything changed. Bolstered by a level of societal support that did not exist a decade earlier, emboldened victims began to speak out. Filmmakers, studio executives, advertising execs, and others toppled like dominoes. Al Franken, who had, in comparison with others, committed at most a sexual misdemeanor, resigned from the U.S. Senate. Woody Allen—who began dating his former partner's daughter when she was twenty-one and he was fifty-six[6]—lost film deals. New York governor Andrew Cuomo, once seemingly invincible, lost his political base—and, ultimately, his job. Behaviors that would have been overlooked within even the last decade could now get a man cast into the wilderness—or a prison cell.

As so many cultural boundaries related to gender and social standing continue to melt away, new boundaries are emerging—and some are defined by the people once classified as victims.

Then there was the reapplication of political boundaries. In the waning years of the decade leading up to 2020, the obliteration of personal freedom and reinstitution of rigid ideology abounded. Autocrats in Turkey, North Korea, Russia, and China crushed dissent. Right-wing activists called for armed insurrection, the assassination of elected officials, the conversion of heads of state into virtual dictators.

Perhaps the most astonishing development was the redrawing of boundaries in Europe. Britain's withdrawal from the European Union turned the English Channel into the equivalent of Trump's wall. Brexit was sold to voters with a campaign that promised sunlit uplands[7] and did not shy away from propaganda and fabrication.[8] By most accounts, reality has fallen far short of the promise.[9] The same folks eager to see fewer Black and brown people in the

British Isles are feeling the consequences now that so many immigrants have moved out. In London alone, according to the Economic Statistics Centre of Excellence, almost 700,000 foreign-born residents left in 2020, creating an 8 percent drop in the capital city's population.[10] Nationwide, their departure has contributed to a shortfall of some 1.2 million workers, including critically needed truck drivers.[11] Product shortages have led to empty shelves, long lines, and panic buying.[12] Soldiers have been deployed to distribute fuel across the country.

Scotland's fishing industry has been decimated. Fishermen used to deliver fresh langoustines and scallops to European markets a day after harvest. Thanks to Brexit, health certificates, customs declarations, and other paperwork cost them more and have slowed delivery. A trade group has advised: Stop fishing for exported stocks.[13]

One British wine merchant complained to *The Guardian* that he was suddenly unable to import wine from the EU owing to post-Brexit customs rules. "We were a pretty good little business, we were doing quite well, until Brexit came along," he said. "While we knew Brexit would be a car crash, we did not know it was going to be a multiple pile-up in the fog with fatalities."[14]

On the other side of the channel, Dutch port officials reportedly confiscated a "small mountain" of items after Brexit rules came into effect on January 1, 2021, including chicken fillets, Tropicana orange juice, Spanish oranges, and even muesli, as they warned, "You can't just bring in food from the U.K."[15]

The real issue isn't about muesli, chicken fillets, or wine, of course. It is about a drawing inward of nations, with debates over who deserves a spot in the lifeboat. It can be a vicious circle. Even as the loss of immigrants in the U.K. has led to supply chain issues and critical jobs left unfilled, the economic upheaval is likely to fortify the sense of nationalism that paved the way for Brexit in the first place. Our world is increasingly globalized, but most of us want what's "ours" to remain sacrosanct.

Another example of once blurred boundaries being solidified comes in the form of Halloween. This favorite holiday of so many childhoods has become an occasion rife with accusations of cultural appropriation and insensitivity. The holiday has its origins in Samhain, the ancient Celtic festival, which provided an annual opportunity to blur the boundary between this world and the next. Leave it to the new-worlders to muck it up. By the early 1900s, Americans had begun donning costumes "to portray themselves as other cultures and races than their own, wearing blackface to imitate African Americans or donning turbans and other symbols of what was once referred to as the 'Far East' and other 'exotic' destinations."[16] By mid-century, there was a rise in "cowboy and Indian" costumes, with the latter modeled after Native American ceremonial garb.[17] A perverted celebration of the Wild West indeed.

I'm embarrassed to admit, it didn't occur to me as a child that dressing up as an Indian chief or a geisha was offensive. Thanks to campaigns such as We're a Culture, Not a Costume, today's youth know better—or at least should know better. They are much more apt to be aware that promoting stereotypes is a form of degradation, affecting members of the groups depicted. I consider costumes sexually objectifying Native women especially harmful given that these girls and women are victims of sexual violence at crisis levels.

Dr. Mia Moody-Ramirez, coauthor of *From Blackface to Black Twitter: Reflections on Black Humor, Race, Politics, and Gender,* told *The Washington Post:*

> *People need to consider how the costumes may be perceived by the community whose culture is being represented. . . . Ask yourself the question, does the culture you're imitating have a history of oppression? Are you benefiting from borrowing from the culture? Are you able to remove something when you get tired of it and return to a privileged culture when others can't?*[18]

As the debate around cultural appropriation intensifies, more public figures are paying the price. As one example, *Bon Appétit* editor in chief Adam Rapoport was forced to resign after a picture of him in brownface and dressed as a "Puerto Rican" at a Halloween party surfaced.[19]

While there is room to disagree with where to draw the line between appreciation and appropriation, it comes down to cultural knowledge and respect. Singer and actress Zendaya explains the distinction this way: "Some things are really sacred and important to other cultures, so you have to be aware, politically, about those things before you just adopt them."[20] Actress Amandla Stenberg explained that "appropriation occurs when the appropriator is not aware of the deep significance of the culture that they are partaking in."[21] Or, as she put it succinctly in a YouTube video, "Don't cash crop my cornrows."[22]

There is plenty of opportunity for confusion in terms of the appropriateness of cultural fusion. Where does one draw the line when it comes to blending cultures?

Shifting boundaries related to cultural fusion can also be seen in food, where the line between cultural appreciation and cultural appropriation is hugely subjective. Self-described "sculptor, comicmaker, and Hufflepuff" Shing Yin Khor created a comic, *Just Eat It,* to tackle "the tendency of people to easily co-opt 'ethnic' cuisine as their own while simultaneously obsessing over the 'authenticity' of food." Her advice-cum-plea:

> *Eat, but don't ask for a gold star for your gastronomical bravery. Eat, but don't pretend that the food lends you cultural insight into our "exotic" ways. Eat, but recognize that we've been eating too, and what is our sustenance isn't your adventure story. Just eat.*[23]

There will continue to be missteps and public censure for sure as people navigate these waters. Importantly, it is no longer just the power class that gets to determine the rules.

At the employee level, there are different boundary issues. Every white-collar worker whose job survived the pandemic is familiar with the initials WFH, shorthand for "work/working from home." For some, the parameters of the standard workday were obliterated as less enlightened employers and managers felt there was no longer a need to respect employees' evenings, weekends, and holidays. What else did employees have to do with their time?

And yet there is good news in the obliteration of the regulation workday within the regulation workweek. Now that the pandemic has upended traditional approaches to work, more employees are exerting agency over their workdays, no longer considering themselves at the mercy of the industrial clock. The nine-to-five is but one option. (Ironically, that schedule was a concession to unions, first instituted by the Ford Motor Company to protect workers from exploitation and ensure they had sufficient time to spend with family.)[24] The clock is different now. The minutes, hours, and days still tick by—but, crucially, more of us are not letting them drift by. The pandemic has taught us the simple art of savoring time.

For those who can scratch out the freedom to do so, that means we can pick up a book and keep reading, enjoy quality moments with our families, and abandon our laptops (without guilt) for a recharging stroll, swim, soak, or Spotify playlist.

The Swedes and Norwegians have a term for this: *lagom*—"just the right amount." Lagom encourages us to savor a moment—such as that first cup of coffee in the morning or slipping between freshly ironed bed linens. In an era that has introduced us to the simple pleasure of owning time, many of us have embraced lagom living without even being conscious of it.

Of course, the world post pandemic is difficult to predict. Will we revert to our old ways—hurrying the kids out of the house, impatiently shopping for essentials, ruing the lack of "me time," feeling frazzled from the constant hustle, drowning ourselves in oversized coffees? I am hopeful we will not. As I see it, the potency of "me time"—owned time—will prove too formidable a force for pre-pandemic norms to reckon with.

The Swedes know something else: escapes. Americans are notorious for not getting—or not using—vacation days; in 2019, for instance, a Bankrate survey found that more than four in ten Americans opted not to travel for a vacation in the previous year because of the cost.[25] Contrast that with Sweden, where one in five people owns a summer house—and more than 50 percent of the population has access to one.[26] When it is warm, they go there—and not just for a few days. As explained by Anna Wiklund, a teacher:

> *It helps you to escape the daily obligations you have back home. And because you spend such a long time here, you feel that you live here. If you travel abroad for two weeks, there are so many things to experience and do; it's not necessarily that relaxing. After a week or two here, I begin to slow down, and I think that's what I'm looking for: a gradual winding down.*[27]

In our heads, we are all Swedes and Norwegians, hungry to establish boundaries between work and chores and find respite from the frantic pace of modern life. We want to, in the immortal words of U.S. Representative Maxine Waters, "reclaim" our time. And, more and more, we want to control the chaos that whirls around us by instituting boundaries that discourage bad behaviors while knocking down boundaries that pigeonhole and constrain us in ways we are no longer willing to tolerate.

Another way in which we will seek to tame the chaos: reducing complexity by breaking our world into smaller component parts; rejecting the enormous and amorphous in favor of the intimate and discrete.

Chapter 9

Small Is the New Big

Vincent Van Gogh proclaimed, "Great things are done by a series of small things brought together." He understood the value of narrowing down complexities by focusing instead on individual elements of a challenge. In our modern world marked by flux and chaos, the human tendency is to retreat or make things more manageable: navigating day by day, focusing on hyperlocal activism, taking tiny steps onto a better life path rather than attempting to tackle widescale change in one fell swoop. It is a mechanism that helps keep us sane.

Psychologist Barry Schwartz coined the phrase "paradox of choice" in the early 2000s to describe what happens when humans face too many options, too many potential paths. They feel anxious and unhappy, and ultimately may be too paralyzed to make a decision. Schwartz argues that while the absence of choice is "almost unbearable," an abundance of options leads to overload. "At this point," he warns, "choice no longer liberates, but debilitates. It might even be said to tyrannize."[1]

We fight decision paralysis and feelings of inundation by compartmentalizing and reducing decisions to binary choices. If you've watched any of the zillion seasons of *House Hunters* on HGTV (shown around the world), you know how each episode ends: The homebuyers eliminate one of the three options from consideration and then choose between the remaining two homes. It's a production device, but it is also how the human mind is inclined to work.

Similarly, in times of strife, we narrow our focus to things that give us comfort or that we can control. I may not be able to reduce global temperature rises, but at least I can purchase an electric vehicle or buy sustainably made clothing. I couldn't hug faraway family during the lockdowns, but at least I could express my love by shipping them baked goods. We saw throughout the pandemic the focus people put on outfitting their homes to make them more comfortable, Zoom-background-worthy, and technologically sophisticated. It was about comfort, convenience, and capability, of course, but it was also about asserting control when the world felt off-kilter.

Small is where it's at right now—and where it will be for the next several decades. We derive comfort from indulging in the little things in life and embracing all things local, authentic, and intimate.

But how do we define *small*? That is subjective and far more about feelings than meters or feet.

In the late 1980s, a fabulously rich young man decided that maybe two paintings by Matisse were more than he needed, so he sold one for $18 million. This was enough spare cash for him to be generous, so he ordered a dozen cases of French wine to share with friends. The label was Petrus, a status wine produced from grapes grown on just twenty-eight acres in Bordeaux. In the late eighties, when he bought the 1973 vintage, it was selling for less than $100 a bottle. A bargain for such a highly regarded vintage.

He sent each friend three bottles. Some drank them straightaway, toasting his generosity. Some stored them so that age would deepen their excellence. When one of my friends showed me the bottles in his wine cabinet, he said it was entirely possible the gift would outlive him—it was unthinkable that he would drink wine this expensive. Then, a few years ago, he had a costly divorce. To cushion the blow, he sold the Petrus to a wine merchant for $1,000 a bottle. He did not understand why the merchant asked no questions about its storage for the forty-five years prior. Later he looked online—and found out. A vendor in Hong Kong was selling 1973 Petrus for $1,800 a bottle.

What happened here? To the wealthy young American in 1988, the Matisse was a small thing, not even a rounding error in his net worth. The gifts of wine were thus even more negligible. To the recipients, who were mostly wealthy, the Petrus was a small but thoughtful gesture. For the wine merchant, the purchase also was small, a minor piece of business—he probably had a buyer lined up in Hong Kong before he took delivery of my friend's bottles. For the Hong Kong buyer, the Petrus was perhaps a small cost that aligned with grandiose dreams. Or a sweeping gesture by a successful man who feels small and wants to look big to his friends. As for my friend—he seems to be the outlier. The Petrus, to him, was no small thing. It was a symbol of luxury. It was expensive and grew more valuable every year. For him, the gift of wine was large and memorable—an event, maybe even a burden.

The significance of things depends on who you are, what you have, where you are in your life, and how you feel about all of that. It is all relative.

Our universe is hypermega. Precisely how big is that? In the view of astronomer Pete Edwards of England's Durham University, it is hardly worth trying to fathom. "Don't go there. . . . There's no way a human mind can actually comprehend the true immensity of the universe."[2]

There is no way to relate to size that massive. So here is what I mean by *small:* human scale. Relatable. Something we can understand, that we can wrap our arms around, that we can control.

Why do we want human scale right now?

As with so many things, start with a pandemic that has redrawn our boundaries. Less radius. Less ambition. Less spending. The pandemic forced us to focus inward, to the point that our home became our entire galaxy. For many people, "going out" meant walking in the neighborhood, not driving any distance. Not going to a bar or restaurant or to a sporting or cultural event. And definitely not flying on an airplane.

This drawing in does something to the mindset regarding proportions—the relative value of the things around us. It is no coincidence that sales of home goods increased 51.8 percent in the United States in 2020.[3] Globally, the online market for home décor is forecast to grow almost 13 percent between 2020 and 2040, led by increases in Europe.[4] People who could afford to do so during the pandemic zeroed in on items to enhance the microworld of their confinement. They started potting plants, fixing things, purchasing items they normally would not consider, as spending moved into a space of healing, distraction, catch-up projects, and upskilling. There were several weeks in spring 2020 when many people's social media feeds were flooded with images of freshly baked loaves of sourdough bread. No wonder it became nearly impossible to score packets of dry yeast.[5]

This trend toward small and intimate started well before the pandemic, however. Even as Instagram showcases the lavish lifestyles of the rich and famous (and the photoshopped versions of those desperate to be seen as rich and famous), the past twenty years have witnessed a broad rejection of ostentation, of homes built to absurd scale, of tacky demonstrations of wealth. I'm sure I'm not the only fan of Kate Wagner's fierce architectural and décor critiques on her blog, *McMansion Hell*.[6]

Not that any of this pushback has discouraged a select few from amassing head-spinning fortunes that—like the universe—are immense beyond the limits of the imaginations of most people. In 2021, *Forbes*'s thirty-fifth annual list of the world's billionaires exploded to an unprecedented 2,755—that's 660 more than in 2020.[7] And what are they doing with all that money? Three of the world's best-known billionaires—Amazon's Jeff Bezos, Virgin's Sir Richard Branson, and Tesla's Elon Musk—have devoted a chunk of change to a space race. On July 12, 2021, Branson won that three-way race, making it to the edge of space aboard the Virgin Galactic spacecraft.[8] Bezos was not far behind, traveling on July 20 aboard New Shepard, a spacecraft created by his company Blue Origin. A Change.org petition asking that Bezos not be permitted back into Earth's atmosphere racked up nearly two hundred thousand signatures.[9] Ouch.

In earlier times, we celebrated the success of the entrepreneur. Pulling oneself up by one's bootstraps was an American ideal that resonated across cultures. Now, increased sensitivity to wealth inequity has led to campaigns against excessive personal wealth. That was almost certainly a factor when Bezos announced he would leave his spot as Amazon CEO.[10] Before Elon Musk hosted *Saturday Night*

Live, boss and creator Lorne Michaels assured the public that he would not force any cast member to work with the Tesla and SpaceX founder.[11] But even Musk seems to have balked—at least for the moment—at some of the trappings of wealth. He reportedly ditched his mansions to live in a tiny prefabricated house,[12] embracing the "living with less" concept that is exploding in the United States. According to a poll conducted by a Fidelity National Financial subsidiary in late 2020, 56 percent of Americans would consider living in a tiny house, despite many having spent months cooped up at home during the early months of the pandemic.[13]

In some respects, Americans are catching up to the European tendency to be critical of scales too far off balance. The boards of General Electric and AT&T formally voted to reject oversized CEO pay packages, setting a precedent for applying at least slight pressure to the brakes of this runaway train and giving boards more confidence in . . . well, smaller approaches.[14] Of course, this must all be considered with a grain of upscale, organic Himalayan salt—in the United States, we are looking at a level of wealth inequality greater than at any other time in the country's history.[15]

Humans are impressed by large scale and grandeur (hence, the never-ending competition to build the tallest tower[16] and the most massive dump truck[17]), but it is small that wins our hearts. We seem hardwired to find tiny creatures cute (see: babies, puppies, kittens),[18] and we marvel at the craftsmanship of miniature paintings, dollhouses, and verses etched into a grain of rice. Now, in a world where everything is inflating to massive, mega, and trillions (populations, pixels, bytes, debt, etc.), small is even more appealing. It makes life and the world feel less overwhelming and perhaps even slightly more manageable. Small is a welcome counterweight to bloat and sprawl.

We see this dramatically in entertainment. There will always be massive, action-driven spectacles. Now we also see smaller, folksier programming, like *The Pioneer Woman,* a television series featured on Food Network globally. Ree Drummond of Pawhuska, Oklahoma, is a phenomenon created in her kitchen: a top web celebrity.

We know her as the wife of Ladd, mother of Alex, Paige, Bryce, and Todd. And I know her because she is my companion when I cannot sleep late at night in Switzerland, even if I am unlikely ever to make one of her meals. She is someone to whom "regular" people can relate.

Drummond is part of the manifestation of the "small is the new big" trend, the anti-celebrity who rises to the top of the popularity charts. She is representative of those seemingly everyday people who become style-makers because they have excellent skills and set exceedingly high standards for doing everyday tasks. There are others, many in the home-and-lifestyle segment: Chip and Joanna Gaines, whose Magnolia empire has blossomed; Britain's popular gardening host Alan Titchmarsh; and relative newcomers Erin and Ben Napier, whose hometown folksiness has proved to be on-trend.

We also see the desire for the small—for the authentic and intimate—in the popularity of shopping sites such as Etsy, Artfire, Aftcra, and Folksy. Etsy, home to millions of artisans peddling their wares, reported a surge in shoppers and sales during the pandemic. Some sixty-one million new or reactivated shoppers joined in 2020, and their wallets were open. Not including face masks and coverings (a big draw), Etsy's independent sellers sold $3.3 billion worth of goods between October and December.[19] That is a lot of scented candles, handcrafted jewelry, and tchotchkes. The point for many shoppers, of course, is that the items are not mass-produced with plastic and other artificial materials in far-off factories. They are made one at a time by artisans (or at least individuals). And the purchases can feel like a point scored against the commodification—and what some think of as the Chinafication—of everything. Priceless.

The allure of shopping on artisan sites lies not just in the products we purchase but in how we feel about those purchases. People feel good about themselves when they support small businesses, perhaps especially when those businesses are struggling. A friend recently told me about Mary O'Halloran, a New York City bar owner who had struggled to get by with six children, a closed business, and a husband trapped for nine months in the Aleutian Islands during the pandemic shutdowns. A story on the Humans of

New York Facebook page noted that one of the ways O'Halloran got by was selling homemade soda bread scones made with a recipe from her mother in Ireland. Brandon Stanton, the creator of Humans of New York, persuaded O'Halloran to put together a limited-edition package at a premium price: six homemade scones, handmade blackberry jam, a "taste" of Kerry Gold Irish butter, and an original drawing by the youngest O'Halloran child, eight-year-old Erinn—all for thirty dollars.

Sure, my friend thought. Why not support Mary and her family? So she placed an order. It turns out she was not the only one. Overnight (literally), Mary sold $1 million worth of scones.[20]

Though it may seem that people in business have always internalized the "bigger is better" mindset, there have been exceptions. In the 1950s, when growth was the mantra and big was the goal, Switzerland-born Ernest Bader went the other way. Thirty years after he founded Scott Bader, a chemical company in England, he gave it away. To whom did he give the company? The Scott Bader Commonwealth, a Quaker-principled trusteeship founded on the belief that "a socially responsible undertaking cannot exist merely in its own interests."[21] Of course, the company understood the need to be profitable, but its ambition was equally to serve its people, its community, and society. If Ernest Bader had to choose, he would say that people came first. He did not see employees as labor units to be exploited; for him, they were valuable individuals who could, in a collaborative culture, develop their potential.

Consider how radical that was in 1951. When Bader converted the company to a trusteeship, the corporate language completely changed. Leadership was now founded "on approval rather than dictation."[22] Leaders and the 131 workers became mutually responsible. Everyone was encouraged to participate in charitable causes. A quarter of all profits could be used for bonuses; another quarter, for charity. And because of its new structure, Scott Bader could not be taken over.[23] That ruled out the possibility—or temptation—of a sale to a big corporation or private equity opportunists who would strip the assets.

By its standards, the Scott Bader Commonwealth is relatively successful, with profits of about $8 million a year.[24] By the founder's standard, it is even more successful because it remains aligned to his philanthropic ethos. When Ernest Bader died in 1982, aged ninety-one, he had amassed no personal fortune—he owned no personal business assets, private house, or even a car.[25]

E. F. Schumacher would cheer the Scott Bader Commonwealth as the model of a virtuous commercial enterprise.[26] In Schumacher's 1973 collection of essays, *Small Is Beautiful: A Study of Economics As If People Mattered,* he rejected capitalism's single-minded focus on growth and profit and the emerging gospel of globalization. His book became a bestseller and then a classic; in 1995, *The Times Literary Supplement* ranked *Small Is Beautiful* among the hundred most influential books published in the half a century prior.

Schumacher's message was way out of line with the greed-is-good, maximize-shareholder-value decades that followed, but it is resonating now in an era in which people are taking comfort in a more intimate scale. He taught that the right size for a business is one that respects the individual. A job is not a set of tasks. It is not something that can be coldly eliminated, with people laid off or "made redundant" to maximize profit. Rather, a job is a self-actualization project that should bring satisfaction, knowledge, even joy. In a phrase, the mission of the business and workers should be the same: "right livelihood."[27] In Schumacher's view, "Spiritual health and material well-being are not enemies: They are natural allies."[28] The aim of the business should be "to obtain the maximum of well-being with the minimum of consumption."[29]

Schumacher's idea of a big city was a population of five hundred thousand. In that city, ecology mattered. Neighborhoods were communities. He understood the impulse for more and more, but he stood with the Roman poet Virgil, who purportedly advised: "Admire a large vineyard, cultivate a small one." This ancient maxim is echoed in the twenty-first-century notion of the fifteen-minute city[30] that is being implemented in some of the world's most sprawling urban areas. The idea is that a guiding principle of urban development should be that city residents be able to meet most of their needs within a short walk or bicycle ride from their homes. This is a big pivot even for the old cities and towns of Europe, let alone those in countries where urban planners have carved multilane highways through city centers to appease proponents of capitalism and commerce.

The concept of the fifteen-minute city was popularized by Mayor Anne Hidalgo of Paris, who had been inspired by French-Colombian scientist Carlos Moreno. Across the Atlantic, Janette Sadik-Khan,[31] formerly New York City transportation commissioner, is the most visible of a growing group of leaders and influencers who advocate bringing a more human scale into urban development. Seoul is even more ambitious than New York and Paris, with plans in place for a high-tech, ten-minute city to be built on an old industrial site.[32] This creation of cities within cities is not about flower-child idealism or old-world quaintness; it is about developing metropolitan areas that work for everyone who lives in them—living and working spaces that are safer, healthier, and more inclusive.

As the world trends toward a desire for human scale, there are places from which we can draw valuable lessons. Geography shapes perceptions, and a human-scale mindset comes more naturally to those who live in smaller, more densely populated countries, where people live no more than a chip shot from one another.

Consider the difference between Europe and the United States. They are roughly the same size, but Europe is home to more than twice as many people.[33] To add a bit more perspective: Geographically, the state of Texas is larger than France, but there are 29.1 million people living in Texas versus 63.5 million in France. The higher population density in Europe and diversity of languages and cultures exert a powerful force on social behavior (not to mention being a more ecologically sound approach than suburban sprawl, in the view of many scientists and urban planners). Unlike in North America, it is not possible in Europe for a religious sect or other group to pull up stakes and head off to live on their own in a sparsely inhabited area, as the Mormons did in the United States in the early 1800s. Space is too tight and is likely to belong to other people—people who may well speak a different dialect or even a different language. After centuries of deadly strife, Europeans have managed over the past seventy years to find ways of sharing their crowded space in peace and mutual tolerance—with the notable exceptions of the Balkans and Northern Ireland.

In Europe, arguably no country has engineered a more tolerant culture than the Netherlands, and size is most definitely a factor. If you exclude tiny countries such as Monaco, Vatican City, and Malta, the Netherlands, with 1,316 residents per square mile, has the highest population density in Europe.[34] That is more dense than any U.S. state. With the country contained within just sixteen thousand square miles (roughly twice the size of New Jersey), you can cycle between its two most populous cities, Amsterdam and Rotterdam, in less than four hours. And Amsterdam is just a third the size of New York City and an eighth the size of London. How is that for human scale?

The Netherlands holds a special place in my heart because of my experiences living and working there in the mid-1990s. Coming from the churning pressure cooker of New York City, I arrived in Amsterdam with a combination of an American's disbelief that things could be so different (bicycling to a bar at *midnight*?) and an ethnographer's curiosity.

I learned that for social stability, two principles are central in the Netherlands: *verzuiling* and *gezelligheid*. *Verzuiling* ("pillarization") is a social order built on silos. Each religion and political party has its own institutions: separate radio stations, newspapers, unions, sports clubs, even bakeries. As a result, no one goes unrepresented. Still, the country is too condensed and the culture too pragmatic for people to stay in their little bubbles. *Gezelligheid* ("coziness" or "conviviality") cuts across these silos. Sit in a café for a few minutes, and someone is guaranteed to start a conversation—because it is key to know, if not love, your neighbor.[35]

It follows that tolerance is the social policy on all significant issues. The Netherlands was the first country to memorialize homosexuals killed and persecuted in World War II.[36] In 2001, it was the first country to legalize same-sex marriage.[37] Euthanasia is legal.[38] The Dutch parliament decriminalized possession of small amounts of marijuana (less than five grams) as far back as 1976.[39]

Does this culture of tolerance sound too good to be true? Apparently, it is. The Dutch love to gripe, especially about the weather—and this was the case long before the climate crisis reached what a Dutch official is calling "code red" status. (The low-lying nation faces a sea-level rise of nearly four feet by the end of the century if greenhouse gases are not sufficiently reduced.)[40]

The Japanese are even more tightly packed than the Dutch because so much of their country is mountainous. The average home in Tokyo, the most populated city in the world, is 710 square feet. And that's a house. Apartments are smaller. A quarter of Tokyo's population lives in spaces no bigger than 220 square feet. (In the United States, it is not unusual for bathrooms to be 120 square feet.)[41] No wonder the Japanese are big on bonsai, the carefully manicured miniature versions of full-grown trees. And no wonder more than 40 percent of Tokyo's population live alone.[42] More solitude.

Japan has traditionally been a collectivist culture, prizing the group over the individual. "We need to focus on living together in harmony, which is why peer pressure [to do things in a group] has been high," a Japanese economics researcher commented about his densely populated nation.[43] A recent trend counters that impulse. It is called *ohitorisama,* which loosely translates to "party of one."[44] Whereas the Dutch find ways to tolerate one another, the Japanese seek solitude as refuge from their tightly packed quarters—and that no longer carries much of a stigma. Just a decade ago, a solo diner would likely choose a *benjo meshi,* a "toilet lunch"[45]—a trend started by socially awkward high school and university students that migrated into the workplace. Now, more restaurants welcome single diners and drinkers, and there is little shame in being alone.

And then there are the cultural attitudes spawned by space and solitude. We can learn from those, too, as we reconfigure our approach to scale.

With just forty-nine inhabitants per square mile, Finland is the third most sparsely populated country in Europe, after Iceland and Norway. In Finland, if you want to know a person's salary, all you have to do is call the tax office; that is public information.[46] That is the case in no other country. And yet reticence is central to Finland's culture. The average Finn is private and notoriously taciturn.[47] Their stereotypical response to a social moment is to recoil. The more Finns are around other people, the more they crave personal space. *Finnish Nightmares: An Irreverent Guide to Life's Awkward Moments*[48] creates a new genre—Finnish comedy—by cataloging the Finns' penchant for absolute boundaries. "An introverted Finn looks at his shoes when talking to you. An extroverted Finn looks at your shoes." A Finn wants to leave his apartment—but a neighbor is in the hallway. The bus shelter is crowded—there is one person standing there. A Finnish nightmare? Giving a speech. Being trapped in a room with a loud person.

I'll bet a lot more of us can relate to the Finns post pandemic. Even extroverted friends have confided in me their hesitancy to resume life among the throngs—and as much due to a newfound social anxiety or shyness as to fear of the virus. Our social skills are rusty.

Also shaped by low population density: the people of New Zealand. The country is physically larger than the United Kingdom but has a population of just five million people, compared with some sixty-eight million in the U.K. There are nine sheep for each person, the highest ratio of sheep to humans in the world.[49]

For many in the United States, New Zealand is America as seen through rose-colored glasses—a place thought to be populated by hardworking, independent-minded people living self-sufficient, rugged lives while surrounded by stunning natural beauty. What we think we used to be except more perfect and far, far away. It says a lot about American fantasies of New Zealand that on election night 2020, Google searches for "how to move to New Zealand" skyrocketed.[50] Those were presumably made by folks who wanted to emigrate to a country with values like theirs—all part of the new tribalism that says hunker down with "my own kind" and keep a distance from those who aren't like me. Peter Thiel, a cofounder of PayPal and member of Donald Trump's 2016 transition team, was awarded New Zealand citizenship in 2011. He bought a mansion.

Then, in 2015, he bought another worth $10 million on the shore of a lake.[51] Trying to invest in property there now? You're late.

Thiel and countless disaster preppers moved to a New Zealand that is changing dramatically. The European population is decreasing. The Māori population is expected to grow by 25 percent. There will soon be 70 percent more Asians.[52] New Zealand will still be small, but it will be diverse.

Our approach to scale is informed by geography and urban density, as we have seen in the Netherlands and Japan at one extreme and in Finland and New Zealand at the other; but it also draws on perspectives related to ambition and the definition of success. We can see competing viewpoints at work in the mixed reception to E. F. Schumacher's collection of essays in 1973. His pushback against what he termed "gigantism" was hailed as visionary by some but faced a less welcoming audience in the corporate world—perhaps especially in the United States, where the post–World War II boom spawned "go big or go home" as the prevailing gospel. By the start of the new millennium in 2000, Schumacher's concept of "small is beautiful" was admired by some on the fringes but largely ignored by regular folk. His book was a cult classic beloved by progressives and assigned in universities but made a broader splash only in the public embrace of two slogans: "buy local" and "fair trade."

In the last few decades, a handful of large companies adopted Schumacher's philosophy of "enoughness," among them the Body Shop in the United Kingdom and Ben & Jerry's ice cream in the United States. But, at a certain point of success, both companies were offered more money than a sane business leader could refuse, and they were subsumed by large corporations that promised not to modify their DNA. The Body Shop was purchased by L'Oréal (and subsequently resold to Brazil's Natura & Co); Ben & Jerry's went to Unilever.

Most companies went fast and far in the direction that bigger was not only better; it was best—provided it referred to the bottom line and not the head count. Investment banks played accounting tricks. Employees became "consultants" to reduce the cost of pensions and health benefits. Could robots perform complicated tasks? Could drones replace delivery drivers?

Will we see the pendulum move in the opposite direction? Don't hold your breath waiting for big companies to downsize (at least voluntarily), but we can expect a stronger commitment to employee wellness and some semblance of life balance. Pre-pandemic, workplaces were the center of the universe for many employees, but that attitude is losing ground now that many workers have gained perspective born of both physical and emotional distance.

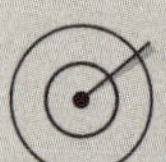

On the radar:

Companies may not get smaller, but they will become increasingly transparent (whether they like it or not). By 2038, rates of pay will be easily accessed and compared, increasing pressure on the C-suite to address inequities.

"Bigger is better" may have been the prevailing ethos of the United States for its first two centuries, but history is never a straight line. Under the surface of increasingly unregulated capitalism in the late twentieth century was a murmur of conversation about a warmer, softer way of living. In the 1980s, Ross Chapin, an architect who lives in a town of one thousand on Washington State's Whidbey Island, started thinking about a more human-centric way to live.

His solution was not, as he writes, new:

> *Humans are gregarious—we like to live around others. We also have a desire—and perhaps a need—for personal space. Sometime in the last generation, however, we became so charmed with the dream of a "house of one's own" that we overshot our desire for privacy, leaving us marooned on our own personal island in a sea of houses. . . . A picture began formulating in my mind that was like the Russian nesting dolls: pocket neighborhoods.*[53]

In 1996, Chapin built his first pocket neighborhood. You might think of a pocket neighborhood as a Schumacher community with Scott Bader Commonwealth aspects. Just a sprinkling of homes, not mini-McMansions but one-and-a-half-story cottages—most about 650 square feet, with lofts up to 200 square feet. All have that much-loved feature of nineteenth-century houses: a front porch with low railings so passersby can stop and chat. For anyone who dreams of living in a French village or an Italian hill town, this community on an island within commuting distance of Seattle has a powerful appeal.

In the first decade of the new millennium, business profits grew to levels beyond anyone's wildest dreams. But most individuals had a different experience, especially once the financial crisis of 2008 decimated their incomes, home equity, and savings. More and more Americans wanted to scale down, and some didn't have a choice. Land prices were soaring in the suburbs; you couldn't really drop a house with an oversized great room on a quarter-acre lot. Prices were even more inflated in cities. The size of new rental apartments in the United States shrank more than 5 percent from 2010 to 2020. And the smallest apartments got even smaller; the average new studio is 10 percent smaller than in 2008.[54] In Providence, Rhode Island, Westminster Arcade, the first enclosed shopping mall in the United States (c. 1828), has found new life as a collection of "micro-apartments," most smaller than three hundred square feet.[55]

Small spaces are not just for millennials starting out, couples stalled on the ladder to the executive suite, and boomers living longer with only underfunded 401(k)s and Social Security benefits to see them through. In Eugene, Oregon, "Conestoga huts" provide shelter to some of the city's homeless. Each hut is just sixty square feet. For $10,000—equivalent to the cost of a single tiny home—a community group can build eight huts. And sixty square feet is a foundation for a future. "When you have a place to keep your possessions dry and safe instead of hauling them around," a resident says, "then you can start stabilizing your life and figuring out what the next step is."[56]

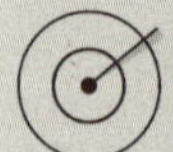

On the radar:

Off-the-grid tiny homes in remote locations will be the new "country home" for many city dwellers and suburbanites, offering not just nature and a respite from modern life but a place to escape natural disasters, civil unrest, or contagions.

Small is like the grass that grows between the cracks in the sidewalk—the will to live finds a way. And so it is with new trends in housing. Tiny homes have gone mobile, with some long-haul truckers kitting out the alcoves in the backs of their cabs with toilets, showers, kitchens, and TVs.[57] Weekends in the Hamptons? Unaffordable for most. A weekend in a tiny house is accessible to many more.

Janna Harris rented a five-hundred-square-foot house in a rambling wooded compound near LaRue, Texas. Her new landlord: Getaway, which operates tiny-home rental complexes within a two-hour drive of eleven major cities.[58] Occupancy rates during the 2020 pandemic never dropped below 96 percent. The homes are safe and socially distant: keyless doors and no communal spaces. Just kitchen, private bath, outdoor fire pit, and Wi-Fi in a stylishly designed house, with rates that start at $99 a night. "I didn't encounter another guest the entire time I was there," Harris says. "You can't get more distanced or safer than that."[59]

Others had tiny houses delivered to them during the pandemic. Rather than invite friends or relatives to stay in the main house, users of the Room + Wheel service in Oregon saw a tiny house placed on their property for a few days or weeks—allowing for sociability with social distancing.[60] Also a smart solution for health-care and other essential workers not wanting to risk bringing the virus home to loved ones.

Small has, until recently, often been a synonym for cute. Or it has signaled forced downsizing, a reduction in status. No longer. Timex is the new Rolex. Tesla has plans to build a $25,000 hatchback by 2024.[61]

The COVID-19 pandemic led many to reconsider how much stuff they need. Elizabeth Chai of Portland, Oregon, decided to fix things or borrow them instead of purchasing new ones and to get rid of possessions she already had, with a goal of 2,020 items sold, donated, or tossed. She met her goal.[62] (The notion that any of us owns two-thousand-plus items for which we have no need should give us pause.)

After nearly a century of unquestioning adoption of "mass," "massive," and "global," we will now create ways to reap the benefits of large scale while better meeting our hunger for human scale. Entrepreneur and New York University professor Scott Galloway talks of this as part of the Great Dispersion[63]—i.e., "the distribution of products and services over a wider area where and when they're needed most, bypassing gatekeepers and removing unnecessary friction and cost."[64]

It is likely we will face more pandemics in the coming decades, as it is far from certain that scientists will figure out how to nip mass infections in the bud. In part due to that uncertainty, I see the taste for smaller and human scale prevailing. So expect more working pods rather than big offices. Expect small cities to thrive. Expect a new iteration of the simplicity movement that blends smaller and fewer with state-of-the-art. Expect people to aspire to reduced environmental footprints.

Above all, expect that instead of asking the old question "Will it scale?" we will ask: "Will it human-scale?"

Chapter 10

The Luxury of Freedom and Time

Rising Sun, the 454-foot, $590 million yacht owned by entertainment mogul and DreamWorks cofounder David Geffen, can accommodate eighteen guests, seen to by a staff of forty-five. Over the years, those guests have inclined toward boldfaced names: Oprah Winfrey, Bradley Cooper, Orlando Bloom, Katy Perry, Chris Rock, Bruce Springsteen, Mariah Carey, Leonardo DiCaprio, Jeff Bezos, the Obamas, Tom Hanks.

You likely have never seen a photo of those celebrities—or any other—on that vessel. But we do know about the yacht. In late March 2020, when most of us were stuck at home in a panic in the first weeks of the COVID-19 pandemic, Geffen shared a photograph of the *Rising Sun,* likely taken from a drone, with his 87,000 Instagram followers: "Sunset last night. Isolated in the Grenadines avoiding the virus. I hope everybody is staying safe."[1]

Geffen posted this update on a day when there were more than 189,000 confirmed cases of the novel coronavirus in the United States and more than 3,900 American deaths.[2] (Globally, more than 39,500 deaths had been reported.)[3] Reaction was swift. Twitter: "Is anyone shocked . . . that David Geffen posted such an out of touch photo? He might as well have taken a picture flipping everyone in America off."[4]

Forbes estimates Geffen's wealth at $10 billion, which makes him the richest person in the entertainment industry.[5] His supersized yacht is right in America's Gatsby tradition: If you've got it, flaunt it. But is that tradition falling out of style?

It has been said that "luxury, like beauty, is in the eye of the beholder."[6] To pay $100 million for a painting at a high-profile public auction expresses more than one's love of the art; reading the breathless news item, most of us only record that X had a spare $100 million to spend. By that logic, a good part of the pleasure of owning a $168,000 Bentley SUV is the look on people's faces when they see you drive by. And heads are certain to turn when you walk into a restaurant clutching a $68,000 alligator Birkin—which the maître d' will set on a low stool next to your chair so the handbag doesn't make contact with the {{shudder}} floor.

And then, suddenly, everything changed, and like so much else in 2020 and 2021, our long-held assumptions about luxury were upended. Class resentment flourished. "Eat the rich" became a popular catchphrase on social media. The wealthy—for the most part—dialed down the latest additions to their good fortune. That Bentley? Now parked in the five-car garage of a gated $30 million East Hampton "cottage." That Birkin? Sleeping in its velvet bag in a closet as big as some New York City apartments. And David Geffen? In response to the immense backlash to his post, he took his Instagram account private.[7]

There is much more to luxury than the items themselves. Emotions are at play. "There is nothing more satisfying," a woman told me in 2020, before the shops closed and their windows were boarded up, "than slapping your Platinum card on the counter at Tiffany's and walking out with a luxury item in that distinctive blue box." I understood that, even if it is the antithesis to my thinking style. Many people would. And they would understand why this shopper took an almost indecent pleasure in her purchases; she was accomplished and successful, but love was in short supply in her life. She needed the comfort and reassurance that a status object provides.

Her pleasure would be fleeting. We know that. She knew it, too. And she knew that she would soon make another trip to a pricey boutique and buy something else she didn't need. High-end retail therapy.

With our new post-pandemic mindset, though, that Tiffany's

bauble does not qualify as a luxury purchase. Really, it never did. The impulse item she bought may be superior to the wares you'd find in outlet stores, but that mid-price Tiffany's prize lives in the suburbs of luxury. The mid-price zone has long been the sweet spot for upscale brands; these are objects that are not quite mass-produced but that don't require long hours of labor by an experienced artisan, either. These expensive but not unique items give shoppers a taste of the sense of exclusivity offered by their ultra-high-end offerings. And they stimulate desire. One more career promotion and she might slap her card down for a big-ticket treasure.

That is all over for most. Luxury has changed, even for those once accustomed to sipping champagne in velvet-lined private rooms while inspecting the merch selected by their personal shoppers. This is especially true among younger generations. It's now less about status and more about authenticity and feeling. As Switzerland's EHL Insights put it, "More introspective concepts such as health, happiness and mindfulness are fast becoming the new luxury commodities."[8]

What is increasingly relevant to customers is a more individually attuned luxury. It goes deeper than "comfort consumerism," incorporating well-being. In an era when a great deal of wealth has been generated, luxury has moved away from *things* and toward *experiences*.

Ian Schrager made his name as the co-creator of Studio 54, the legendary Manhattan disco that thrived by keeping one crowd out and shoehorning another in. Later, he created hotels that redefined expectations of luxury: small bathrooms with sinks that might be found in prison cells, art postcards over the bed.[9] In 2017, he went in a different direction, opening Public, a hotel built on the concept of "luxury for all."

Schrager's explanation: Whereas the "old and outdated idea of luxury was defined by how rich you were, where you lived, what car you drove and what fashion brands you wore," the new luxury is "the freedom of time."[10]

In Schrager's new worldview, luxury is centered on "comfort, ease, convenience, as well as being freed from distractions and hassles."[11] No pointless services or amenities. A comfortable bed, which he says has nothing to do with thread count. Great coffee, preferably brewed with a healthy dose of values (e.g., fair trade, Black-owned). Interactions that are easy, swift, and effective.

Like Baby Bear in "Goldilocks and the Three Bears," the new luxury consumer wants "just right."

This shift is major. No matter our age, we have been conditioned to believe that luxury is defined by wealthy, high-status people. That means mansions, fine art, tasteful furnishings, impeccable tailoring, elite schools, exclusive neighborhoods, clubs that discriminate—all the visible expressions of conservative, traditional values. Old-world values. Eurocentric values.

In that world, luxury is not sold. It is purchased or—even better—inherited. The item is not overtly marketed. It exists behind an invisible velvet rope, available only to the ultrasophisticated. The old acid test applies: If you have to ask the price, it really is not for you.

A lot of luxuries are now widely available and financially accessible to those with discretionary funds. A Peloton, the popular souped-up exercise bike, was once a $1,990 status object; now it's advertised on television and costs "as low as $39 a month."[12] (Granted, with interest accruing, "as low as $39 a month" adds up—and may go some way toward explaining why Gen Xers, on average, carry more than $7,000 in credit card debt.)[13] During the pandemic, millions learned to bake and discovered their bread was just as tasty as what a professional baker could produce. A suburbanite with a green thumb can grow vegetables as gorgeous and nutrient-rich as those sold by an upscale shop. Movies in a home theater do not look any better than those shown on a large flat-screen TV.

Yes, there are still high-priced luxury items, but now they are more apt to be treated as treasured collectibles—items to display on a closet tour, not flaunt on public streets. The Birkin bag, for example. Everything about it announces its elite status. It is relatively rare: Hermès makes no more than ten thousand of these $11,000+

bags a year. And until recently, the bag has been almost impossible to buy. If you were not a significant Hermès customer, your name went on a waiting list. It could take as long as two years for your number to come up, at which time you bought whatever bag the luxury-goods brand was willing to sell you.

You might think the pandemic produced a significant decline in Birkin sales, because what is the point of having a Birkin if you can't show it off? That's old luxury thinking. The new mindset is to acquire, savor, protect, and even manage a luxury item as part of one's investment portfolio. In recent years, a Birkin has proved a better investment than gold or most stocks. In 2019, Birkins had the highest return of any luxury investment, gaining 13 percent over the year.[14] In 2020, Birkin's attractiveness as an investment inspired a company called Rally to let those who could not afford a bag get in on the action; it offered two thousand shares in twenty Birkins at $26.25 a share, with no minimum investment.[15] It promises to be a worthwhile investment: A Christie's online auction of vintage handbags in July 2020 brought in $2,266,750, including $300,000 for a crocodile Hermès Diamond Himalaya Birkin 25.[16]

If you buy a Birkin now, you leave it in the box and store it in a cool, dry place. This is almost a French response. The French operate on the theory that the low profile is the one best seen. They downplay their money. Unless you know an affluent French family well, you will never be invited inside their home.

The French, you see, have sound economic reasons to be discreet. During the French Revolution, aristocrats were guillotined, and taxes were calculated based on the appearance of wealth, including the number of windows and doors in homes.[17] That continues to influence attitudes toward wealth and ostentation. As *The New York Times* noted, "Parisiennes rarely walk around wearing the giant diamonds that are de rigueur in certain New York neighborhoods."[18]

In 2020, when more people came to regard luxury items as smart investments versus goods for showing and strutting (plus, who had anywhere to strut?), they also discovered something more valuable:

privacy and seclusion. The ability to live safely ensconced, away from what used to be described as the unwashed masses—though we all know those masses were slathered in hand sanitizer by that time.

The wealthy already had privacy and a buffer from the "real world." They just did not recognize quite how precious that was. Then the world became a horror movie, and they traded their city residences for country compounds surrounded by many acres of manicured nature. The less privileged spent the pandemic on their couches, bingeing on streaming dramas, and when they ventured outside, they wore masks and feared close encounters with the unmasked. Meanwhile, the rich breathed fresh air and exercised in state-of-the-art home gyms. The rich did not live with a soundtrack of ambulance sirens; they enjoyed blessed silence. Everyone else's children had Zoom school; the rich hired private tutors who, like chefs and nannies, often "lived in."

And at a time when hospital workers were wearing garbage bags for protection against the virus, the rich made the single best luxury investment: health. "Concierge doctors" who charge as much as $20,000 a year to clients who feel the need to be at the front of every line—that was a story of the last decade. The update in 2021: cutting the line to get the vaccine first. In New Jersey, when only frontline healthcare workers and residents of long-term-care facilities were eligible for the vaccine, two longtime donors to the Hunterdon Medical Center and at least seven spouses and two adult children of medical directors, administrators, and executives—some in their twenties—got the vaccine "when eligible recipients couldn't be located rather than have the vaccine doses go to waste."[19] This also happened in at least three South Florida hospital systems.

And in New York? You might assume the rich were not just cutting the line in Manhattan and the Hamptons but getting in-home vaccinations from hospitals that were the recipients of their philanthropy. Why didn't that happen? Because then-governor Andrew Cuomo threatened sanctions of up to $1 million (and the revocation of the right to practice) against doctors, nurses, urgent-care providers, and others who delivered the vaccine unethically—which, in this case, can be translated as *inequitably*. And in case anyone thought he was bluffing, he proposed a law that would criminalize the administration of the vaccine to anyone trying to jump ahead of healthcare workers. For some, there is delicious hypocrisy in reports that Cuomo's family got COVID tests early in the pandemic, when they were in scarce supply, often administered in their homes by New York state employees.[20]

We were all reminded of the value of good health during the early stages of the pandemic, but we were reminded, too, of the value of time. In this frenetic era, Ian Schrager was right to call time the ultimate luxury. In his now legendary commencement address at Stanford University in 2005, Steve Jobs exhorted graduates to accord time its full value: "Your time is limited, so don't waste it living someone else's life."[21] Now time is not just valuable but a privilege. Young women freezing their eggs to buy a longer fertility window—they are buying time. Older people going on health retreats and practicing qigong to regain their flexibility—they are buying time. Households buying groceries on automatic redeliver—they are buying time. Even the parent who sends a son or daughter for an elite postgraduate year to postpone university admissions and get a leg up on the competition is buying time. These people understand its worth full well.

Luxury also is different today because of its new demographic makeup.

The planet tilted, and in the last few years, the center of gravity in the luxury-goods market shifted from Europe to China and other Asian locales, where new millionaires are minted daily. In 2000, Chinese buyers accounted for just 1 percent of purchases of high-priced luxury items. By 2019, according to consultancy Bain, that figure had jumped to 33 percent.[22] But most of those purchases, perhaps 70 percent, were made overseas—often on jaunts to Europe, reports McKinsey, another consultancy.[23]

If you have seen *Crazy Rich Asians*—the sixth-highest-grossing romantic comedy of all time[24]—you may know a bit about the Asian luxury market. Set in Singapore, the film speaks to wealthy

Asians' fondness for conspicuous consumption and high-end labels. The producers reflected the times by using a smart mix of internationally recognized (Prada, Bottega, Dior) and Southeast Asian designers (Carven Ong, Michael Cinco, Lord's 1974).

In the remainder of this decade, European luxury firms hope that shopping sprees will simply migrate from Paris to Shanghai, allowing them to still sell their high-priced goods, just at a distance from their famous ateliers. In the short run, this might boost margins: The likes of Louis Vuitton (part of LVMH, the biggest luxury group) and Gucci (part of Kering, another French giant) charge a third more in China than in Europe for the same products.

In the United States, luxury traffic now tends toward the understated: designer clothes that are expensive versions of simpler clothes, which are all the more status-wielding because they are recognized only by those in the know. Miuccia Prada got it right when she said, "These are polar times. Everything is opposite."[25] The current trend: the quasi-democratization of luxury. A vintage Chanel T-shirt can sell for $2,000.[26] Neiman Marcus sells a Balenciaga T-shirt for $495 and a $2,000 purse that is a cousin to a $1 blue Ikea shopping bag.[27] You can find examples in dining, too. Carlo Cracco, a Michelin star–winning Italian chef, uses commercial potato chips in his dishes.

This is not to say the rich have become self-effacing. "Vanity, vanity, all is vanity"—they skipped that passage from Ecclesiastes. Some commission ghostwriters to produce self-published memoirs to be circulated among family and friends. The latest vanity project is the private documentary—perhaps of greater appeal now that life feels more uncertain and potentially fleeting. In England, filmmaker Andrew Gemmell has created a business doing this. He interviews a client's friends and family and then creates a flattering portrait. The client pays up to $50,000 for a compilation film. With new footage shot on location, the cost can top $100,000.[28]

Because extreme wealth is often inherited, we tend to underestimate how much of it results from the careful preservation of a family's status rather than investment accounts that never lose value.

Some fail to recognize, for instance, how great a priority the rich place on education—their own and their children's, as the 2019 U.S. college admissions scandal showed. Let others dismiss credentials, condemn experts to second-class citizenship, and beat their chests in praise of intelligence that starts in the gut. The rich know better.

The rich know that the greatest advantage of a quality education is the ability to think critically. To make distinctions. To uncover truth. They know this empirically via their own experience. It is how they made decisions that made money. It is why they want their children to go to top-rated colleges where they will meet the children of other top-rated families and make connections that will help them after they graduate—a dream rapidly disappearing as colleges prioritize diversity and equitability. In 2021, Amherst College joined Johns Hopkins University, Massachusetts Institute of Technology, and other top-tier schools in banning preferential admissions for the children of alumni. That's a game changer. For context, consider that between 2014 and 2019, a third of "legacy" applicants to Harvard were accepted, compared with an overall acceptance rate of just 6 percent.[29]

Thomas Jefferson wrote, "Knowledge is power, knowledge is safety, knowledge is happiness."[30]

To be rich is to be able to invest in that proposition.

Wealth bestows another luxury: choice in some of the most crucial areas of life. Women who can afford to live independently can opt out of marriage. In South Korea, the "old miss" has become the "gold miss."

Another choice: parenthood. A young friend announced that his wife conceived early in the pandemic—in the same month as half a dozen other couples they knew. What did they have in common? Their families are all wealthy. Outside of bubbles like that, the pandemic produced no baby boom. Despite the closing of offices and the rise of households in which both partners now work from home, the Brookings Institution predicted the pandemic would produce a "large, lasting baby bust" in the United States, with a birth decline of three hundred thousand just in 2020. Nine months after the imposition of stay-at-home orders, hospitals reported lower birth rates compared with 2019: down 7 percent in Ohio, 8 percent in Florida, and 5 percent in Arizona.[31]

On the radar:

When the pandemic led to border closures, the gestational surrogacy business was turned upside down, and parents found their biological children stranded far away. By 2038, this industry will be more accepted, better regulated, and localized. Already there is pressure in Australia, Italy, and the United Kingdom to legalize commercial surrogacy.

It has been written to the point of banality that the pandemic taught us to slow down, to look inward, to excavate our "authenticity." The very rich may have done all that. But it is more to the point that they secured their dominance by coming to terms with what luxury means now—and how they might use it to best advantage.

What is happening now around luxury reflects a shift in attitudes regarding materialism and also a heightened desire among some of the well-heeled to protect their children from the disease of abundance known as "affluenza"—an addiction to overconsumption that has an inverse correlation to happiness. The term had been around for a while, but it exploded in the public consciousness in 2013, when a young man named Ethan Couch was sentenced to probation rather than prison for killing four people while driving drunk. Testifying in his defense, a psychologist argued that the then sixteen-year-old should not be held fully accountable for his actions because he was "a victim of 'affluenza,' a product of wealthy, privileged parents who never set limits for him."[32] Affluenza is more often linked to life dissatisfaction than vehicular homicide, of course. As *The Sydney Morning Herald* reported several years ago, "Having more—the McMansion, two-car garage, European appliances in the kitchen and labradoodle in a designer dog collar—than any previous generation, we are unhappy with our lot."[33]

Unhappiness with our lot—and stress beyond measure—make

buying and savoring time the holy grail of our age. This is especially the case for millennials and Gen Zers, who reject the outdated "he who dies with the most toys wins" perspective of their parents and grandparents. The antimaterialist tendencies of so many Gen Zers have led Daniel Langer, CEO of global brand strategy firm Équité, to forecast that as many as 50 percent of luxury brands in operation in 2021 will not survive the decade.[34] For a growing number of young people, the freedom afforded by time is worth far more than any high-priced fashion item.

Like all luxuries, however, time is not something everyone can afford, as we will explore next. You can't afford to buy time if you are struggling to make ends meet.

Chapter 11

The Inequity of Wealth

Luxury is but one aspect of wealth, a way for the haves to express what they have, whether possessions or freedom or the time to savor a great experience. Another aspect of wealth, with more profound implications, is inequity. As we examine the forces and trends of the past twenty years that have contributed to how we live, think, and experience our lives today, we cannot ignore the impact of the widening chasm between rich and poor, privileged and not.

Since the turn of the millennium, even as the middle classes have grown in some developing nations, so too has inequity and our awareness of it. While the wealthy dine on oscietra caviar and foie gras and truffle dumplings at the Ithaa Undersea Restaurant, situated five meters below the surface of the Indian Ocean in the Maldives, more than a billion people live on $2.50 a day or less, 800 million of whom do not have adequate food.[1] While the wealthy retreat to second and third homes, 1.6 billion people worldwide live in inadequate housing conditions and millions are homeless.[2] While investment accounts skyrocketed for many during the pandemic, some 1.7 billion of the world's citizens have neither a bank account nor access to basic financial services.[3]

The profoundly unbalanced distribution of resources globally and even within communities affects everyone to varying degrees, from the moment we are born till we draw our last breath.

We often talk about inequity as a challenging condition, deeply present in the now. But in the business of envisioning what comes next, inequity—of wealth, of resources, of clean air and water, of education, of opportunity—is perhaps the single most significant determinant of the future. Economic disparity has been a cultural constant, with roots that extend back nearly to the beginning of human history. In this century, it is starting to garner more attention for the simple reasons that inequity is no longer quite so easy to hide and is growing exponentially, with little indication the pattern will change.

Before we can begin to address the issue, we first must ask, what is wealth?

Wealth is tricky to define. What counts as wealthy where you live? Among your family and friends? Among factory workers in rural areas? Among homeowners in high-prestige zip codes? The *Oxford English Dictionary* defines wealth as "an abundance of valuable possessions or money." But what constitutes an abundance? That is very much in the eye of the beholder (and asset holder) and is influenced by an array of factors, including socioeconomic background, income source, age, and lifestyle. The perceived and actual value of $1 million in assets depends on the neighborhood in which one lives, the circles in which one runs. As Texas oilman Nelson Bunker Hunt famously shrugged after taking a massive loss: "A billion dollars just ain't what it used to be."[4]

For me, like many, wealth is measured by the security and freedom it affords: the security of knowing you can handle (financially, at least) whatever life throws at you and the freedom to do things you find fulfilling. As far as I'm concerned, Henry David Thoreau got it right when he defined wealth as "the ability to fully experience life."

Wealth's polar opposite, poverty, can be measured more precisely. The universal standard for measuring poverty is the international poverty line. As of 2015, that has been set at $1.90 a day, based on the average poverty lines of fifteen of the world's most impoverished countries.[5] The wealthier the country, the higher the poverty line. In the United States as of 2021, the poverty threshold—the minimum level of resources required to meet "basic human needs"—is set at $26,500 in annual income for two adults and two children in the forty-eight contiguous states.[6] (The threshold is higher in Alaska and Hawaii due to their higher costs of living.)

Wealth is easier to understand in relation to poverty—the contrast is dazzling. In 2021, there were 2,755 billionaires in the world, according to *Forbes*.[7] Their total worth: $13.1 trillion, up from $8 trillion in 2020. Of those billionaires, just over a quarter (724) live in the United States, the most of any country, but, with 698 billionaires, China is rapidly catching up.[8] If the spate of U.S. billionaires were testimony to hard work, original ideas, a healthy economy, and good fortune, it would be one thing. But much of this wealth is inherited—as evidenced by the sprinkling of people named Walton and Mars on the list—and supported by tax laws that favor the rich. After all, people with big money can afford to spend big to back friendly politicians.[9] And those tax codes are boosted by a survival-of-the-fittest, reverse–Robin Hood ethic that arguably is at its most extreme in the United States.

Thanks in part to favorable tax policies, the top 20 percent of Americans have managed to grab hold of 90 percent of the country's wealth.[10] The average real annual income of the top 1 percent has more than tripled since 1970. The income of the top .01 percent has risen nearly sevenfold.[11] Are you sensing a pattern? Meanwhile, the average pretax income of the bottom half of Americans has hardly budged.[12]

Other nations have equal or even more striking wealth imbalances. In the Netherlands, the top 10 percent control 60 percent of the country's net wealth.[13] In Russia, the richest 10 percent own 87 percent of the nation's wealth.[14] In Brazil, according to Oxfam, the six richest individuals—all men—have accumulated as much wealth as the poorest 50 percent of the population of 213 million combined. And the richest 5 percent have an income equivalent to that of the remaining 95 percent.[15] In Asia, the twenty most affluent families control an astonishing $463 billion.[16]

The pandemic made existing disparities more acute. In earlier recessions, billionaires were hit alongside the rest of us; after the 2008 recession in the United States, it took just under three years for *Forbes*'s four hundred richest people to recover their losses. But during the COVID-19 pandemic—which sparked the worst economic crisis since the Great Depression of the 1930s—the wealth of American billionaires did not decline. It grew by a third.[17] Perhaps it is time to rebrand the "1 Percent." The Invulnerable? The Impervious? Or maybe simply the Diamonds—the hardest substance on Earth.

What does it say about the nature of wealth that those who hold the most of it are seemingly immune to economic crises that force others into lines at food banks and onto unemployment rolls? While millions were scrambling to feed their children or risking a deadly contagion to earn a minimum wage, those in the upper echelons sat back and watched their fortunes balloon.

Especially worrisome in these pandemic times is that income inequality becomes health inequality. A study in the United States and the United Kingdom, released before the pandemic fully took hold, found that wealthier people are living about nine years longer than the poorest citizens.[18] (It speaks volumes that I find it surprising the gap is not larger.) Part of this is down to inequitable standards of care. I have seen firsthand disparities in healthcare—even within the same medical facility, where patients in private rooms are housed in separate units with more staff and on-demand menus that rival the finest hotel room service. The wealthy have physicians who make house calls while the poor languish for hours in understaffed hospital emergency waiting rooms.

More evidence of the impact of inequities in healthcare and other aspects of life: The average life expectancy in the United States decreased by 1.8 years between 2018 and 2020, primarily due to the pandemic. Not for African Americans and Hispanic Americans, though: Their life expectancy decreased 3.3 and 3.9 years, respectively.[19]

Numbers, in the form of economic and health-related statistics, are one reality. Dreams and aspirations and feelings of contentment and security are another. In a 1962 film, Elvis Presley crooned the words "A poor man wants to be a rich man / A rich man wants to be king."[20] Sixteen years later, Bruce Springsteen recorded a version of those lines and added a third in his hit song "Badlands": "And a king ain't satisfied till he rules everything."[21]

It seems endemic to human nature to want more. Mark Twain

fixed upon mankind's tendency toward greed as our point of separation from other animals. In his satirical essay "The Lowest Animal," he wrote about an experiment:

> *I was aware that many men who have accumulated more millions of money than they can ever use have shown a rabid hunger for more, and have not scrupled to cheat the ignorant and the helpless out of their poor servings in order to partially appease that appetite. I furnished a hundred different kinds of wild and tame animals the opportunity to accumulate vast stores of food, but none of them would do it. . . . These experiments convinced me that there is this difference between man and the higher animals: he is avaricious and miserly; they are not.*[22]

Princeton analysts Daniel Kahneman and Angus Deaton define the financial sweet spot as $75,000 in annual income per person.[23] After that point, their research shows, happiness levels off. Even knowing this, given the opportunity to earn more, would most people turn it down? Would you?

Much of the world derives its notions of wealth from popular culture—from the movies, television shows, and books that transport people to a world outside their direct experience. These windows into the worlds of others give us a sense of our position on the wealth pecking order in a way that was not available in previous centuries—and maybe that was a good thing for those earlier generations. Ignorance can be bliss, whereas comparisons facilitated by the media—traditional or social—can be painful. Today, evidence of excess is everywhere, emphasizing our shortfalls. As Teddy Roosevelt wisely noted, "Comparison is the thief of joy."

American novelist F. Scott Fitzgerald wrote about the very rich being "different from you and me."[24] He got that right. My own experience studying in the Ivy League reinforced my sense of that gap. While the rich and middle class and poor studied together and shared communal meals on campus, there was a gap between those who had been to public high school and those who had prepped. Some of us cooled off in city or town pools, while others summered in East Hampton or the Adirondacks or Martha's Vineyard. What some of us considered a summer cottage was something entirely different from those who conjured (or lived in) a ten-thousand-square-foot second home in Newport, Rhode Island, or in Bar Harbor, Maine. Those of us from more modest backgrounds didn't even know what we didn't know when we first encountered big money.

Once avoided in polite conversation, such disparities of wealth and experience are now part of a cultural conversation.

In 2019, Abigail Disney, Walt's niece, spoke out against what she saw as the naked greed of families such as hers in an opinion piece in *The Washington Post*. She mourned that the United States has become a "lopsided, barbell nation," where the majority have little while "the super-rich have invested heavily in politicians, policies and social messaging to pad their already grotesque advantages."[25]

Just how different are the lives of the wealthy in this century? Let's look at two extreme examples of the so-called 1 percent.

Wealth of Jeff Bezos in 2009: $6.8 billion[26]
Wealth of Jeff Bezos in 2020: $187 billion[27]

Wealth of Mark Zuckerberg in 2009: $2 billion[28]
Wealth of Mark Zuckerberg in 2020: $105 billion[29]

If you were to convert $1 billion into one-dollar bills and stack them, you would have to look up 67.9 miles to see the top. Sitting on Earth's surface, that stack would reach into the lower portion of the troposphere.[30] Now multiply that by 187 (Bezos) or 105 (Zuckerberg) . . . you get the idea. It is unimaginable wealth.

At a certain point, you wonder: What can one do with all that money? You can only eat so many gourmet meals a day, sleep in so many beds, buy so many companies, own so many yachts and planes. You cannot purchase extra hours in the day. You cannot cheat death (as Steve Jobs poignantly reminded us in his final months). And, as Ebenezer Scrooge discovered, you do not get credit just for being rich. At a certain point, what the world remembers is how you used your money to justify your possession of it.

In 2020, while much of the global population struggled to pay the rent and keep food on the table, America's wealthiest amassed around $1 trillion. Robert Reich, former U.S. secretary of labor and outspoken advocate of wealth equity, noted that America's wealthy elite could have sent a $3,000 check to every person in the United States during the pandemic without making even the slightest dent in their wealth.[31]

Instead of sharing in the spoils, those further down the food chain must pay the price for the excesses of the rich. A study by British charity Oxfam found, for instance, that the wealthiest 10 percent of people worldwide are responsible for half of all carbon emissions, having an average carbon footprint sixty times higher than that of the poorest 10 percent.[32] And yet it is the poorest among us who bear the brunt of climate change, even to the point of becoming climate refugees as they flee their homelands in search of safety and sustenance.

At the COP26 climate conference in Glasgow, French president Emmanuel Macron acknowledged that those most impacted by climate change have not benefited from the development models that cause it. "Small islands, vulnerable territories, Indigenous people are the first victims of the consequences of climate disturbances," he said.[33] Seychelles president Wavel Ramkalawan did not mince words: "We are already gasping for survival. Tomorrow is not an option, for it will be too late."[34]

The problem of the haves taking from the have-nots is hardly new. In the eighth century, Indian philosopher and poet Shantideva summed up the situation bluntly: "All the joy the world contains has come through wishing happiness for others. All the misery the world contains has come from wanting pleasure for oneself."[35]

Or, as Chance the Rapper has expressed: "Some people are so poor, all they have is money."[36]

A big question is, how could all those riches be put to better use? How could they be spread around to improve the lots of those with precious little? Happily, we are finding out—at least to an extent. Just as businesses are under pressure to pursue a purpose beyond profits, the wealthiest magnates are being coaxed to give back to people and the planet. In that spirit in 2010, Bill Gates and Warren Buffett launched the Giving Pledge,[37] committing to give away more than half of their wealth during their lifetimes or in their wills. Mark Zuckerberg, Richard Branson, and Elon Musk have signed on.

You will note a commonality among these billionaire philanthropists: They are white. It is not that Black billionaires lack the generosity gene. It is that there are so few of them.

It has long been said that wealth begets wealth. In the 1890s, John D. Rockefeller hired Rev. Frederick T. Gates to guide his philanthropy. After assessing his employer's assets, Gates warned the oil tycoon, "Mr. Rockefeller, your fortune is rolling up like an avalanche! You must distribute it faster than it grows! If you do not, it will crush you and your children and your children's children!"[38]

The "problem" of burgeoning fortunes has largely been limited to whites because wealth is fundamentally intertwined with power. With influence. With access to others who have power, who build power and portfolios together. As is becoming increasingly evident—although there are certainly those who would argue otherwise—the United States has systematically worked to prevent nonwhite Americans from accessing power and, hence, from accumulating fortunes in the manner of the families enjoying the fruits of multigenerational wealth. That has enduring implications: A study by researchers at the U.S. Federal Reserve found that financial inheritance is a more important predictor of a child's future earnings than the child's IQ, personality, and education combined.[39]

There are always exceptions to so-called heartless capitalism. There are even socialist-minded millennial heirs trying to live their values by getting rid of their money.[40]

And then there is MacKenzie Scott, who was Mrs. Bezos until 2019.[41] She left the marriage with 4 percent of the outstanding stock in Amazon, or 19.7 million shares. The value: $38.3 billion.

A year later, thanks largely to a spike in online shopping during the pandemic, that stock was worth about $62 billion. If her holdings are less now, it is because, by December 2020, she had given away $4.2 billion.[42]

In making donations, she solicits no applications. Instead, working with a team of advisors, she identifies potentially worthy organizations, conducts due diligence, and gives, in most cases, to very surprised recipients. Many of her donations have gone to organizations focused on basic needs, such as food banks (her $9 million gift to Vermont Foodbank is the largest in its history[43]) and Meals on Wheels. Morgan State University, a historically Black university in Baltimore, received $40 million, the largest private gift in its history.[44] Howard University received a "transformative" gift.[45] Perhaps even more stunning, Scott was responsible for 20 percent of all COVID-19-related charitable funds donated globally in 2020, according to tracking organization Candid.[46]

Chuck Collins, director of the Charity Reform Initiative at the Institute for Policy Studies, said that by moving quickly rather than creating private foundations through which her descendants eventually distribute funds, Scott is "disrupting the norms around billionaire philanthropy."[47]

MacKenzie Scott is disrupting philanthropy by ignoring the bureaucracy of charitable giving—removing an institutional veil that often reinforces the power dynamic of wealth. Unlike philanthropists of old who doled out funds to support the arts, feed the poor, and see their names adorn buildings—often with a tangle of strings attached—Scott is using the wealth her ex-husband amassed to empower others, both individuals and organizations. Her gifts are unrestricted, giving recipients the flexibility to use the funds as they see fit. It is a more activist form of philanthropy, intended to redress wrongs and support those laboring on the front lines of the war against poverty and inequity.

The divide between rich and poor can be an abstraction, but it was harder to ignore during the lockdowns when one portion of the population struggled while another was marveling at the rise in their 401(k)s. A study published in the *Nature Food* journal found that more than one in three people globally faces malnutrition due to COVID-19.[48] The full cost of the pandemic borne by those at the lower echelons of society may not be felt for years. Children in impoverished circumstances already start at a disadvantage educationally, and not just because of substandard schools. A landmark 1995 study in the United States found that, on average, a child of parents in professional occupations is exposed to 2,153 words an hour—nearly twice the number of words heard by the average working-class child (1,251). The average child on welfare? Only 616 words an hour. That matters because vocabulary development during the preschool years is correlated with later success in reading and academics generally.[49]

This deficit will be accelerated by COVID-19 and its related shutdowns and the move to remote learning. What will the impact be on the workforce—and on society—in 2038 because of the millions of adults who lost one, even two critical years of learning a decade and a half earlier? Already, according to a report by insurance company Horace Mann, a majority of public school teachers say the pandemic has resulted in a "significant" learning loss for students. This impact is being felt both academically and in terms of social and emotional progress, especially among the most vulnerable.[50] In mathematics, for instance, analysis by McKinsey in December 2020 estimated that students of color would lose six to twelve months of learning, compared with four to eight months for white students.[51] "While all students are suffering," the report's authors conclude, "those who came into the pandemic with the fewest academic opportunities are on track to exit with the greatest learning loss."[52]

An earlier McKinsey study, released in June 2020, found that even if all U.S. students were back in the classroom by January 2021 (they were not), the drop in earnings over forty years as a result of classroom time lost would be $87,440 for Blacks and $72,360 for Hispanics, compared with $53,920 for whites.[53] The gap widens still further.

Living in disparate places has given me a new perspective on the wealth gap in America—one that I was largely oblivious to growing up in the comfortable middle-class bubble of River Edge. I live and work mostly in Canton Vaud, Switzerland, but, until recently, my family and I also moved between two hometowns: Tucson, Arizona, near the Mexico border, and New Canaan, Connecticut. These places could not be more different.

Despite similar numbers of residents born outside the United States—15 percent in Tucson and 13 percent in New Canaan—Tucson feels like an extension of Mexico and is very much a Hispanic city; New Canaan looks, feels, and functions like a stage set for a J.Crew catalog. Data from the Census Bureau for 2015–19 shows that the median household income in Tucson was $43,425 (in 2019 dollars), with 22.5 percent of its population living in poverty. In stark contrast, the median household income in New Canaan was $190,277, and just 3.2 percent of residents lived below the poverty line.[54]

The real differences between these two places are found not in the demographic breakdowns but in residents' expectations and dreams—what they hope for, and at what cost those dreams might be realized.

A short story—a classic by Ursula K. Le Guin, a much-admired novelist, often of science fiction—dramatizes the issue. It is called "The Ones Who Walk Away from Omelas."[55] The town featured in the story is a remarkably happy place, but its happiness depends on the misery of one person, a child kept confined in a dank, dark, dirty room the size of a broom closet. The child, of indeterminate sex, "looks about six," writes Le Guin, "but actually is nearly ten. It is feeble-minded. Perhaps it was born defective or perhaps it has become imbecile through fear, malnutrition, and neglect."

The townspeople enter to bring the child food. They do not speak. Nor do they react when the tiny prisoner says, "Please let me out. I will be good!"

Why does this cruelty persist? Because everyone understands that "their happiness, the beauty of their city, the tenderness of their friendships, the health of their children, the wisdom of their scholars, the skill of their makers, even the abundance of their harvest and the kindly weathers of their skies, depend wholly on this child's abominable misery."

Do the townspeople feel bad about this? Oh, yes. But not in a way that would threaten their comfort. They understand that if they were to bring the child into the sunlight and care for it properly, "all the prosperity and beauty and delight of Omelas would wither and be destroyed." And so the child stays put.

This, in hyperdramatic terms, is the dilemma of modern economic systems. Wealth, traditionally regarded as a cushion and a comfort, has created an enormous divide in this century—and it hinges on the wealthy and middle class alike turning a blind eye to the plight of the less fortunate. As the British have discovered post-Brexit, the system starts to fall apart when underpaid immigrants and guest workers are no longer there to drive the lorries and harvest the crops. And yet how many made an effort to keep them there?

Across the developed world, we have grown accustomed to purchasing garments and other goods sold at ultralow prices made possible by subsistence-level workers laboring in often unsafe conditions. In 2019, a six-year-old in the U.K. was writing Christmas cards to send to her classmates, using a pack of cards her parents had purchased from a major grocery store chain for £1.50. One card had already been filled in. It said, in English, "We are foreign prisoners in Shanghai Qingpu prison China. Forced to work against our will. Please help us and notify human rights organisation."[56] The retailer announced it would delist the card supplier if it was found to use prison labor, but we all know by this point that—held as prisoners or not—many workers in emerging markets are being called on to sacrifice their quality of life to boost ours.

Distance contributes to the problem. Physical distance, because we can no longer just pop down the street to see how our goods are being made. And emotional distance, because of the enormous chasm between the lives of the haves and have-nots.

In 2011, with a presidential election looming, *The New York Times* asked people who were not involved in politics or punditry to describe how they would lead if they were president. Michael

Sandel, a professor of political philosophy at Harvard, had a proposal that speaks directly to the increasing isolation of the rich from what the rest of us think of as life:

> *I would lead a campaign against the skyboxification of American life. Not long ago, the ballpark was a place where CEOs and mailroom clerks sat side by side, and everyone got wet when it rained. Today, most stadiums have corporate skyboxes, which cosset the privileged in air-conditioned suites, far removed from the crowd below. Something similar has happened throughout our society. The affluent retreat from public schools, the military, and other public institutions, leaving fewer and fewer class-mixing places. Rich and poor increasingly live separate lives.*[57]

No politician, to my knowledge, has stepped up to this challenge. If anything, some of those who have endorsed the Omelas solution to ensure their "happiness" have added willful cruelty to their indifference. During the 2020 pandemic, Goop enjoyed record sales of infrared sauna blankets ($500) and gemstone heat-therapy mats ($1,050).[58] In Miami, the rich bought waterfront homes just for a place to park their yachts.[59] And yet there was still dissatisfaction. A San Diego woman complained, "It's almost impossible to get a tee-off time at Del Mar."[60]

More and more, the wealthy live in a bubble. When that happens, Sandel has suggested, money is no longer a currency. It is a culture.

As a rule, I shy away from unbridled optimism, but I will admit that the aftermath of the "Great Pause" of 2020 has given me cause for hope. With even the world's busiest places stopped in their tracks, many of us had an opportunity to slow down and reflect in a way our frantic lifestyles rarely, if ever, permitted in earlier times. For many, that reflection included thinking more deeply about thorny issues such as systemic racism, privilege, and inequity.

Disparities have become even harder to ignore during the pandemic. As the lockdowns went into effect, it became apparent to those of us afforded the luxury of staying at home that many of the workers deemed essential—and compelled to report to their workplaces—were people of color and minimum-wage workers. Many began to pay attention to these workers in a way they never had, becoming more aware of their struggles and needs. We began to consider more closely how grocery store clerks and delivery drivers, warehouse workers and hospital custodians are compensated, and we noted with interest which employers were increasing salaries for in-store workers as the virus spread. Suddenly more tuned in—and grateful—we began tipping food-delivery persons and others far more generously than we would have just a few weeks prior. As related in *The Atlantic,* data from Square, a digital payments company, shows that, as of August 2021, the average tip remains well above the pre-pandemic norm.[61] We also were more apt during the lockdowns to donate to crowdfunding efforts to help those in need. In a six-month period in 2020, users of GoFundMe raised more than $625 million for frontline workers and others impacted by the pandemic.[62]

For some of us, it has been especially hard to overlook reports about inequities in healthcare, access to medical facilities, and even transmission and death rates. Put simply, in the United States, being a member of a racial or ethnic minority group puts a person at higher risk of contracting and dying from COVID-19.[63] And disparities have been stark on the global stage. A UN report indicated there would be enough vaccines produced in 2021 to cover 70 percent of the world's population.[64] Instead, as of mid-November 2021, we see 68.8 percent of Australians, 68.4 percent of British, and 58.6 percent of Americans fully vaccinated compared with just 25.8 percent in India, 8.9 percent in Iraq, 1.5 percent in Nigeria, and 0.49 percent in Chad.[65]

In the United States and beyond, the great racial reckoning brought about by the murder of George Floyd and the Black Lives Matter movement (and, more recently, the outcome of the Kyle Rittenhouse trial in Wisconsin) further cemented our sense that current inequities are untenable and must immediately be addressed. Many are no longer willing to look away from racial and economic injustices but instead look for opportunities to confront and maybe even fix them.

How will these new feelings and priorities play out between now and 2038? For one thing, the notion of a universal basic income (UBI) will become less and less radical. When entrepreneur Andrew Yang tossed his hat into the ring for U.S. president in 2017, he used the 2020 primary process to introduce many Americans to the concept of UBI. His platform stood out thanks to what he termed a "freedom dividend"—a guaranteed monthly payment of $1,000 to every American aged eighteen and older. Not long after Yang dropped out of the race, leaders of twenty-five U.S. cities, including Atlanta, Los Angeles, Shreveport, and St. Paul, put together the Mayors for a Guaranteed Income coalition aimed at addressing the twin pandemics of COVID-19 and structural racism. UBI pilot programs are being set up in other cities as well, including Hartford, Connecticut; Long Beach, California; Denver, Colorado; and Gainesville, Florida. In an extraordinarily short time, a universal basic income has gone from a fringe, far-left fantasy to what many consider a commonsense solution to income inequity.

Another lasting effect of our newfound economic awareness will be, with plenty of exceptions, a toning down of blatant excess. I read with interest an article about the reboot of *Sex and the City* on HBO Max. The writer pointed out that lead character Carrie Bradshaw's bags were making headlines once again—only this time the bag in question was neither an Hermès nor a Fendi but a tote bag from National Public Radio affiliate WNYC.[66] Rather than reflecting conspicuous consumption circa 1998, her choice of bag in 2021 signaled a prioritization of information and knowledge—and a willingness to financially support public radio.

I am not naïve enough to think that infrared sauna blankets, gemstone heat-therapy mats, and billionaire space races are behind us. Still, what might be the result if we were no longer to accept the price of a child suffering in the dark so that we might live in the light?

What happens next—what we collectively choose to do, to prioritize, to permit—will set the foundation for our future. How society navigates the pressing challenge of inequity globally and locally will act as a bellwether for who we will become. And who we become will be very much influenced by shifts gathering speed in the areas of gender roles and gender identity.

PART THREE

WHO WE ARE

✳

In late 2000, I released my annual trends report, outlining the ten trends to watch for in the year to come. Number six on the list, "Everyway People." I wrote:

> *The query "Who are you?" will be more difficult to answer. Defining ourselves will no longer be a matter of checking one box or another: Sometimes we'll be single, sometimes we'll be partnered; we'll be corporate executives one day and contract workers the next. We'll identify with multiple ethnicities, interest groups, and philosophies. Marketers seeking to segment consumers will try in vain to set their sights on a moving target.*[1]

Twenty years on, the Everyway People trend infuses several of the megatrends outlined in this book and is gaining force in multiple directions, with people increasingly reluctant to squeeze themselves into societal boxes prescribed by others. This is the case concerning everything from work titles to household composition—but is of special relevance regarding gender.

In part three of this book, we will explore the recent evolution of gender, gender roles, and self-perception, beginning with a look at the uneven progress experienced by women over the past two decades.

Chapter 12

Is the Future Really Female?

In the mid-1990s, I was an avid reader of Candace Bushnell's Sex and the City column in *The New York Observer*. She personified the ambition and angst of the women of my generation: as anxious to win at work and love as she was obsessed with her wardrobe. And so, when her column was turned into a television series, I rarely missed an episode.

Carrie, Samantha, Charlotte, and Miranda, all white and all privileged, did not conform to any feminist ideal. They were walking advertisements for guilty pleasures: alcohol, Manolo Blahnik heels, and of course, sex. And yet the foursome also embodied the values of empowered women at the turn of the century: advancing in one's career, supporting one's friends, landing a trophy husband. Granted, many of their aspirations were shallow, but they felt credible, even familiar. These were women who, like so many of us in that age group, were working to level the playing field in a man's world.

Artists, including the creators of television shows, are the antennae of the human race. They hear the rumblings of distant trains. They see around corners. And they share these glimpses and faint impressions with their audiences. It was through pop culture that many in my generation were introduced to big ideas and alternative realities—alternative *aspirations*—including feminism and women's equality. From Marlo Thomas's singleton lead character on *That Girl* to Mary and Rhoda on *The Mary Tyler Moore Show,* Diahann Carroll's Julia, and Bea Arthur's Maude, the images projected onto my television screen introduced me to a world filled with far more possibility than I witnessed outside my living room window while growing up in New Jersey.

The year *Sex and the City* debuted, my life in the advertising world of Manhattan was more frantic, fraught, and fulfilling than anything I might have imagined when I was a girl. I had just moved back to New York City from the Netherlands and finally had a taste of a leadership position, which left me struggling to figure out what women in business, let alone women on Madison Avenue, were supposed to do to exude confidence and power. Times were changing, but the rules were unspoken, selectively applied, and forever in flux. I got myself in hot water that spring when I informed the largely male audience at a senior leadership meeting that their days were numbered because I was envisioning a world where if you couldn't type, you couldn't compute, and if you couldn't compute, you couldn't compete. The observation went down like a lead balloon. No one wanted to imagine a world in which everyone would be attached to keyboards.

Technological change was in the air in the late 1990s—and so was change for women. I felt the latter shift as far back as primary school, when girls gained the right to wear pants to school on cold days. In 1971, Alice Munro, the short story writer who won a late-life Nobel Prize, summed up the spirit of the times thusly:

> *There is a change coming I think in the lives of girls and women. Yes. But it is up to us to make it come. All women have had up till now has been their connection with men.*[1]

By 2000, signs of progress were everywhere. Consider this as a metaphor: 2000 was the year Gloria Steinem married. The preliminary goals of feminism? Seemingly achieved. The next goals: eliminating gender stereotypes and expanding outreach to women of color.

But any celebration was premature. In the new millennium, the progress of women, though considerable, stalled. The numbers tell the story.[2]

On the plus side in the United States, women had been awarded more college degrees than men since way back in 1978. On the minus side, women with high school degrees still earned $8,000 less a year than men. Women with college degrees earned $12,000 less. Women with professional degrees earned $35,000 less. And 72 percent of women employed outside the home worked in clerical jobs, as administrative and managerial support, or as service workers. This explains why an apparent gain—57 percent of women used computers at work, 13 percent more than men—is deceptive; these women were not executives. They were performing administrative duties for higher-paid males.

Nevertheless, Alice Munro was right. Change was afoot, even if it was far-from-evenly distributed globally. And it wasn't just about education and careers. Women were making different life choices.

In the United States, nearly one in five women aged forty to forty-four was childless in 2000, up from one in ten in 1976. Similar increases in childlessness among women in this age range between 1990 and 2010 were seen in other countries, including Australia, Austria, Finland, Italy, and the United Kingdom.[3] And fewer women were getting married. In 2000, 22 percent of thirty- to thirty-four-year-old U.S. women had never married, up from just 6 percent in 1970. (If you are betting on that trend to reverse, consider this: Research conducted in 2019 by Paul Dolan, a professor of behavioral science at the London School of Economics and a noted expert on happiness, reveals that "the healthiest and happiest population subgroup are women who never married or had children.")[4]

In my life, I have seen a remarkable expansion of choices for females, starting in academia. When I applied to colleges in fall 1976, I wasn't rejected by Harvard, but that is likely only because, as a female, I didn't have the opportunity to apply; I applied instead to its sister school, Radcliffe College. Had I made the cut (I didn't), I would have received a diploma from "Harvard-Radcliffe." Now Radcliffe is gone, and 51 percent of undergrads at Harvard are female. I did make the cut at Brown, which had subsumed its sister school, Pembroke College, five years earlier—and I suspect my gender was more an advantage than a hindrance.

Girls my age were right on the cusp of the ascent of coeducation.

I was in junior high when Princeton University considered admitting women to its class of 1973. Other admissions offices, alumni, and current students were appalled. As Nancy Weiss Malkiel related in *Keep the Damned Women Out*, "It disgusts me to be in competition with girls," a male undergraduate told *The Daily Princetonian*. "If I had wanted to go to classes with girls, I would have gone to Stanford."[5]

College administrators were little better:

> *From the director of admission at the all-male Hobart College in upstate New York: "At least your office will be brightened by the sweet young things and their shorty skirts." . . . From the University of North Carolina, where freshman women had only recently been admitted: "I can only offer my condolences to you. We find that females are much harder to deal with than their male counterparts."*[6]

Undergraduates and administrators alike have had to get used to the presence of females on campus over the last fifty years. In the United States in 2020, women outpaced men in college enrollments, graduation rates, and degrees earned.[7]

The story of female students on the rise can be found worldwide, though not everywhere. In China, women make up 51.7 percent of undergraduates.[8] In Italy, women are dramatically more likely to pursue higher education than are their male counterparts.[9] A huge gender gap persists in higher education in Africa, South Asia, and the Middle East, however, due to factors ranging from cultural norms to poverty and violence.[10]

For all the doors that opened to women in advanced economies around the turn of the millennium, one statistic remained relatively unchanged: the percentage of women at the executive level in business.[11] Even as more women entered the workforce in the 1970s, the infamous glass ceiling kept them from reaching the upper echelons of corporations. The new millennium brought a fresh twist: the "glass cliff."

Erin Callan was a prominent victim of that cruel ruse. The daughter of a New York City police detective, she made the leap from a Long Island, New York, public high school to Harvard. She advanced rapidly on Wall Street. She delivered keynote speeches. Women cheered.

Little did Callan realize that she would soon be ensnared in a deceitful ploy. Cynical executives who knew their businesses were imploding devised the stratagem of elevating a pawn, a dupe—in the form of an unsuspecting female—to a leadership position.[12] They did not care whether she had sufficient experience or resources to do the job. All that mattered was her visibility. And when the end came, they would escape blame; she would take the fall.

In 2007, as Lehman Brothers began to promote women, gays, and ethnic minorities, bright minds in its executive offices sensed trouble ahead for Wall Street—and for their firm. That December, Callan was appointed chief financial officer. "They promoted somebody who wasn't remotely qualified, and they made a big 'to do' about it," effectively setting up a woman to take the blame, recalls Vicky Ward, author of a book on Lehman's demise. "She didn't even have a basic accounting degree."[13]

But Callan willingly stepped into the limelight. During an interview with *The Wall Street Journal,* she disclosed that she used a personal shopper at Bergdorf Goodman. She was photographed in her office overdressed by Wall Street standards. In 2008, she was third on the *New York Post*'s list of "The 50 Most Powerful Women in New York City," behind Hillary Clinton and Anna Wintour.[14]

Her moment in the sun did not last long. Callan's efforts to right the ship were "smacked down by the kind of diversionary tactics that men rarely are forced to confront in the workplace," wrote Dominic Elliott for CNBC.[15] She found herself criticized for being "off-putting and challenging" with members of the all-male Lehman executive committee and for dressing in a "provocative" way that "distracted" her colleagues.[16]

Callan left Lehman Brothers in spring 2008. Three months later, the firm declared bankruptcy. Wall Street was gobsmacked. How could the firm have missed the danger signs? A 2,200-page report from the bankruptcy court offered this explanation: The bank had been using accounting tricks to beautify its balance sheet by $50 billion. As CFO, Callan should have recognized these deceits. She was one of four Lehman executives cited for ignoring "ample red flags" over contentious deals.[17]

Michelle Ryan, an associate professor of psychology at the University of Exeter, sees the rise and fall of Erin Callan as "a really classic case of the glass cliff. Women often tend to occupy these dangerous leadership positions in dangerous times, when things are getting hairy. When things are going great, it's usually men who occupy these roles."[18]

In 2008, the year of Callan's public flogging, Catalyst, a nonprofit group that supports businesswomen, reported female executives were three times as likely to lose their jobs during the recession.[19]

Erin Callan cast a long shadow. All these years later, she is still viewed by some as the poster child for the proposition that women should not be elevated to positions of ultimate authority. In 2016, after years of "falling off the earth" (her words), Callan published a memoir, *Full Circle: Leaning In Too Far and the Journey Back,* in which she describes her career crumbling because it had no foundation. This is an incredible admission from a person once considered the woman to watch on Wall Street. It is also speaks to the complicated relationship many women have with Sheryl Sandberg's notion of "leaning in." While some see it as encouragement to assert themselves with courage and confidence, others regard it as faulty feminist advice that relies on a rose-colored view of a meritocratic world that doesn't exist. Even Sandberg backtracked on her jaunty advice in the wake of her husband's death at age forty-seven. In a Mother's Day post on Facebook in 2016, she acknowledged that when she'd written *Lean In,* she "did not quite get it."[20] She hadn't understood, she said, "how hard it is to succeed at work when you are overwhelmed at home" and the true extent of the financial burden so many single mothers and widows face. Three years after the publication of *Lean In,* she called for a rethinking of public and workplace policies to offer more support to single parents and struggling households.

One way to judge a culture is to measure what it considers important. Historically, the sexual harassment of women has been dismissed, ignored, or used as fodder for jokes around the world.

Two U.S. lawsuits reveal how much this has changed in the last two decades.

In 2000, two hundred female technicians at WCCO-TV in Minneapolis and five other network stations sued CBS for discrimination on the basis of sex.[21] They claimed the network denied them promotions, gave better-paying jobs to men, and allowed the creators of hostile work environments to go unpunished. In the settlement, CBS agreed to make significant changes. Cost to the network: $8 million, or $40,000 for each woman.

Sixteen years later, Gretchen Carlson, who had been a highly regarded broadcaster at Fox News, filed a sexual harassment lawsuit against Roger Ailes, who was Fox News chairman and CEO at the time.[22] Fox settled quickly, paying Carlson a reported $20 million and issuing a public apology. Carlson's suit and its stunning outcome helped launch the #MeToo movement (a term originally devised by American activist Tarana Burke); in the aftermath of Carlson's legal settlement, women shared accusations that toppled media executives like bowling pins.

This case demonstrated the increased status and power wielded by media—and women. If settlement dollars are any indication, Carlson's cachet on Fox and the audience she could reach if she were to make the details of her story public were deemed extremely dangerous.

The #MeToo movement soon ricocheted around the world, generating hashtags in multiple languages. Consider the Netherlands: *Dutch Review* reported on more than twenty cases of inappropriate sexual behavior on the part of director and producer Job Gosschalk, one of the most influential people in the Dutch film industry, who had allegedly forced actors to "satisfy him" sexually.[23] Another twenty men and women have accused Julian Andeweg, a relatively successful Dutch visual artist, of rape and sexual harassment, with allegations stretching back over fourteen years.[24] Several of the country's leading art institutions stand accused of covering up his bad behavior.[25] In other countries, however, the movement fizzled out. In Italy, the #MeToo-equivalent hashtag #quellavoltache (#thattimewhen) failed to gain momentum—not because harassment doesn't exist in the culture but because, according to *The New York Times,* "Italian women feared the repercussions of speaking up."[26] If the United States and the Netherlands are any indication, Italian women's time, too, will come.

The Carlson settlement and the humiliation of powerful men who had humiliated women occurred in a decade of increasing polarization. In that climate, politics extended far beyond government.

In 2016, Hillary Rodham Clinton won the Democratic presidential nomination, becoming the first woman to lead the ticket of a major party. Few predicted Donald Trump's victory over her. How did it happen? Conventional wisdom has it that Clinton lost key midwestern states because she failed to campaign aggressively there and because she wasn't "likable."

Let's consider another possible factor in Clinton's defeat. In the first debate between the two, Trump left his podium while Clinton was speaking at center stage and moved behind her. At six foot three and with no small heft, he was a lurking alpha male, his invasion of her space intended to establish his dominance. Clinton responded the way many women of her generation had been socialized to do: She ignored the bad behavior. What might have happened if she instead had turned to Trump and ordered him back to his podium—and, if he refused, calmly asked the moderator to order him back? In that scenario, Clinton might have been seen as the dominant candidate and established Trump as a bully. And she might have won more of the white women's vote, which was 47 percent for Trump compared with 45 percent for Clinton.[27] And yet, how could she have done that successfully while at the same time showing the world that she was "likable"—an expectation that male candidates are free from?

The deferential approach toward bullies—meeting belligerence with politeness, professionalism, and poise—likely will prevent you from being suspended from middle school or called onto the carpet by human resources. In this century, it won't necessarily win elections or give you the latitude to do your job to the best of your ability.

With Trump's victory, the patriarchy in the United States flexed its muscles. But already we are seeing a change in how women respond to that kind of aggression. Consider the steely-eyed, prosecutorial resolve of Kamala Harris, a Gen Xer, when Mike Pence cut her off during the 2020 vice presidential debate: "Mr. Vice President, I'm speaking."

The story of Amy Acton's brief tenure as director of Ohio's Department of Health serves as a reminder that female right all too frequently falls victim to male might. When Governor Mike DeWine appointed Acton to the state's top healthcare post in February 2019, she was a licensed physician with a master's degree in public health and more than thirty years' experience in medicine, healthcare policy and advocacy, community service, data analysis, and more.[28]

The first COVID-19 death in Ohio was reported early in March 2020. A week later, the governor ordered bars and restaurants closed. Dr. Acton reached out to the people of her state, holding frequent and exceptionally candid press conferences that were instantly popular, especially among girls and women. A documentarian turned clips from her press conferences into a six-minute film, asserting that other leaders should pay attention to Acton's effective use of vulnerability, empowerment, and "brutal honesty."[29] Soon, there was a tribute video on YouTube,[30] a bobblehead available for purchase, and 130,000 fans on Facebook.

The state's lockdown was unpopular, however, and the protests were relentless: people chanting outside Acton's press conferences; anti-Semitic slurs; men with guns, MAGA caps, and Trump flags gathering outside her home. Republican lawmakers proposed to strip her of her powers. The governor would have vetoed that bill, but Dr. Acton did not stick around while that played out. In June 2020, she resigned. A month later, the governor appointed a new state health director, Joan Duwve. She quit hours after agreeing to the position; the job, she said, would pose a risk to her family.[31]

Amy Acton is hardly a featherweight. A mother of six, she endured her parents' divorce, poverty, homelessness, and sexual abuse—all when she was only a child. And what she took away from those and other experiences is that anger and opposition are not how to solve problems. After stepping down from her government position, she took on the directorship of Kind Columbus, a nonprofit "dedicated to spreading the words and actions of kindness as a defining value" of the region.[32]

One state over, in Michigan, Governor Gretchen Whitmer was being bullied even more severely than Acton because of her social-distancing and mask mandates. In May 2020, a large group of protestors—some armed with rifles—stormed the state capitol (with seemingly no objection from police), where they proceeded to pound on a door they believed to be Whitmer's office and demand an end to the lockdowns. No one was harmed, but several months later, thirteen members of the Wolverine Watchmen extremist group were arrested and charged with orchestrating a domestic terror plot to kidnap Whitmer and overthrow the state government.[33]

Upon learning of the plot, Whitmer responded, "I knew this job would be hard. But I'll be honest, I never could have imagined anything like this."[34]

Writer and editor Kathleen Walsh terms the events "a window into American misogyny." Writing in *The Week,* she described a Republican candidate for the Michigan House hanging an unclothed effigy of the governor by a noose, and posts inciting violence against the governor in the form of beating, lynching, and even beheading. Tellingly, these threats were saturated with misogyny. Walsh noted, "She's been likened to a menopausal teacher, an overbearing mother, and a 'tyrant b*tch.'"[35]

Writing in *Vox,* Anna North agreed that the governor's gender was central to the backlash against her pandemic restrictions. Historically, she said, "female leaders and candidates around the world have often been portrayed as treacherous, two-faced, corrupt, or power hungry."[36] She notes that the use of the term *bitch* was popularized after the passage of the Nineteenth Amendment in the United States, which gave women the right to vote. "When women like Whitmer try to restrict people's ability to spread a deadly virus," says North, "they're infringing on men's freedom to be men."[37]

As of January 2021, only twenty-two of the nearly two hundred countries recognized by the United Nations have had a female head of state or government. Still, the trend is toward an equal gender balance in governance, even if the UN estimates it will take another 130 years for gender parity in politics and business to come to fruition.[38]

As we await that day, evidence is beginning to emerge of what that more equitable power structure might look like. In the early stages of the COVID-19 pandemic, the potential of a more "female"—i.e., a more collaborative, people-centered—approach to governance was on display. Media channels were full of reports of female heads of state shining during this period, including Germany's Angela Merkel, Taiwan's Tsai Ing-wen, and Denmark's Mette Frederiksen. An analysis in *U.S. News & World Report* described how they were "proactive in responding to the threat of the virus, implementing social distancing restrictions early, seeking expert advice to inform health strategies and unifying the country around a comprehensive response with transparent and compassionate communication."[39]

In October 2020, a study published by the website medRxiv confirmed this pattern, showing that countries headed by women leaders experienced sixfold fewer deaths per capita from COVID-19 in the first six months of the pandemic than those led by men.[40]

Especially impressive, in my view, was New Zealand's Jacinda Ardern. At around the same time antimask and antilockdown mobs were gathering outside Dr. Acton's home in Ohio, Ardern was practicing Acton's philosophy of humanity—and her country was celebrating its rapid exit from the pandemic. When Ardern became prime minister in 2017, she was thirty-seven and the world's youngest head of state. A year later, she became the first world leader to bring a baby—three-month-old Neve Te Aroha—to the United Nations General Assembly in New York. New Zealand now allows government ministers with young children to travel with a nanny or other caregiver at government expense.[41] Imagine that: parenthood normalized.

I took note of Ardern's parenting decision at the time, but what really struck me in terms of the potential for a shift in power dynamics was her response to a terrorist atrocity. In 2019, a white supremacist invaded two mosques in Christchurch, killing fifty-one congregants and injuring another forty. Ardern mourned alongside the Muslim community, even donning a headscarf. Then she went to work. Less than a month after the attack, the New Zealand Parliament banned most semiautomatic weapons and assault rifles and restricted machine guns, semiautomatic rifles, and shotguns capable of holding more than five rounds.[42]

Ardern's political strategy has been centered on a trait not often found in government: inclusiveness. After the Christchurch massacre, she expressed this eloquently in discussing the Muslim victims: "'They' are 'us.' The person who has perpetuated this violence against us is not."[43]

When New Zealand experienced its first COVID cases in March 2020, the prime minister prioritized people and health over short-term economics, immediately announcing that the government would require anyone entering the country to self-quarantine for fourteen days. That was just the beginning for what she termed "the widest ranging and toughest border restrictions of any country in the world." A few days later, she closed New Zealand's borders to noncitizens and nonpermanent residents. Then came a national lockdown.[44]

Once again, Ardern preached inclusiveness. She gave dozens of candid interviews and posted regularly on social media, often referring to New Zealand's residents as "our team of five million." In a Facebook Live video that captured as many viewers as there are New Zealanders, she wore a faded green sweatshirt and asked everyone to be kind. "Stay at home, break the chain, and you'll save lives," she said.[45]

The outcome was spectacular. Over the first six months of the pandemic, New Zealand experienced fewer than 1,900 confirmed cases of COVID-19 and just 25 deaths. According to NBC News, that equates to around 320 cases per million, compared with some

25,000 per million in the United States.[46] When Ardern ended the lockdown, she said, "We can let ourselves once again feel pride that we managed to get to that position together," and she capped off the announcement with a little celebratory dance in her living room.[47]

Here is something to ponder: Do women lead differently because of innate characteristics related to their gender? Or do women lead differently as a workaround to avoid male censure and opposition?

We know for certain that women in business have an extremely fine needle to thread. Writing in *Fast Company,* Martin Abel, an assistant professor of economics at Middlebury College, reported on a study that demonstrated the extra burden female managers face. The research revealed that both men and women responded more negatively to criticism when it came from a woman.[48]

Researchers at three universities—Washington State and Northwestern in the United States and Bocconi in Italy—conducted a series of experiments in which they uncovered that many men in subordinate positions feel threatened by female superiors and behave more assertively toward them than they would a male manager.[49] As reported in *Vice,* subordinates were especially hostile toward female managers regarded as ambitious.[50]

The researchers concluded that because women are aware of the negative stereotypes surrounding powerful women and the consequences of violating gender norms, they tend to adopt a leadership approach that is more collaborative—ensuring that the team is kept apprised of the bigger picture and working to keep everyone connected and on board.

It is a double-edged sword: Women know they will be denied job promotions if they're perceived as weak, but they also recognize the downside of being branded as power hungry or aggressive. "As it stands," the researchers concluded, "in order to reach the dizzying heights of business success, women have to be far smoother operators than men vying for—or working in—the same positions."[51]

This delicate dance adopted by women to help them succeed in a society in which men make all the rules is proving to be a better approach to business. Research conducted by *Harvard Business*

Review in 2012 and again in 2019 found that, judged by objective measures rather than personal perspectives, women in leadership positions were every bit as effective as men. "In fact," said the study's authors, "while the differences were not huge, women scored at a statistically significantly higher level than men on the vast majority of leadership competencies we measured."[52]

I grow more convinced every year that injecting women's voices into conversations and decision-making will lead to better outcomes for businesses and society. Yet progress is slow, including in pay equity. The World Economic Forum's Global Gender Gap Report 2020 estimates it will take 99.5 years to achieve gender parity in wages at the current rate of progress.[53] And the circumstances have only grown bleaker during the pandemic.

Throughout 2020 and into 2021, women worldwide with children at home paid a steep price, taking on the brunt of homeschooling, household management, and childcare responsibilities during the pandemic. In a MetLife survey, 58 percent of American women said the crisis had negatively impacted their careers because of the disproportionate burden placed on them at home.[54] And the 2020 Women in the Workplace study from McKinsey and Lean In, Sheryl Sandberg's nonprofit, found that at least one in four women was considering downshifting her career or leaving the labor market entirely because of COVID-19.[55] In the United States alone, 5.1 million women quit their jobs during the pandemic; a year later (as of May 2021), 1.3 million were still not employed.[56] The study's authors call this an "emergency for corporate America," concluding, "Companies risk losing women in leadership—and future women leaders—and unwinding years of painstaking progress toward gender diversity."[57]

McKinsey reported that the three groups of women most likely to have departed full-time employment during the pandemic were working moms, Black women, and women in the most senior roles in the corporate world.[58]

This is hardly a phenomenon unique to the United States. Research conducted in the U.K. and Switzerland during spring 2021 found that women in those countries handled more childcare and homeschooling compared with their male partners, regardless of wage bracket.[59] Societal perceptions contribute to the problem: "Men who are out of work are still presumed to be workers, but women aren't, because we frame work for women as a choice," said Sarah Damaske, a sociologist at Penn State. "So when they unexpectedly lose a job in a society in which their working was in question all the time, it really throws how they're thinking about who they are into question."[60]

In stark contrast with their husbands, most married women never considered that they had a choice in taking on the additional household labor. *The New York Times* surveyed a large sample of U.S. women who had left their jobs and discovered that only two in ten had even spoken with their partner about which of them would quit to take on childcare responsibilities when the children could no longer go to school. "Eighty percent had no discussion," the paper reported. "There would have been no point."[61]

It might be easy to dismiss this inequity within households as an aberration brought on by the pandemic, but we all know it extends well beyond this crisis. For all the gains women have made in the workplace since the 1970s, they are still considered the default parents, the default housekeepers, the default runners of the home.

Addressing why women face barriers to career advancement, Mekala Krishnan, a partner at the McKinsey Global Institute, reported that the uneven division of unpaid care work (globally, women do three times as much as men) affords women less time to reskill or search for employment. "At first glance," Krishnan concludes, "it looks like men and women are running the same race into the age of automation, but while the distance may be similar, women are running with a weight around each ankle."[62]

Will generations of women to come cast off those ankle weights? Is equality in the workplace—and at home—even an aspiration for younger generations?

A frequently cited (and sometimes derided as methodologically faulty) Netmums survey conducted in the United Kingdom in 2012 found that only one in seven women identifies as a feminist, with younger women the least likely to do so.[63] This has been held up as evidence by some that feminism is waning, but I do not think that is accurate. In my experience, many young women reject the label but, when pressed, reveal that they embrace the principles behind the movement. Moreover, feminism is morphing and expanding to be more diverse and to incorporate other movements, from environmentalism to racial and economic justice. They are all intertwined.

"Feminism has to be able to work for all women, not just white women or upper-class women or middle-class women," Celisa Calacal, a student at Ithaca College who identifies on Twitter as an "intersectional feminist and foodie," told *USA Today.* "It has to work for poorer women, for transgender women, for black women, for Indian women, for Latina women."[64] In her popular TED Talk on intersectionality, Kimberlé Williams Crenshaw, a civil rights advocate and professor of law at Columbia University and UCLA, spoke about a legal case involving Emma DeGraffenreid, a Black woman denied employment at an automotive manufacturing plant. The judge who dismissed the case argued that the employer had a history of hiring (white) women—primarily for secretarial or front-office positions—and Black men—usually for industrial or maintenance jobs. He didn't appear to recognize that by being both Black and female, DeGraffenreid faced a double discrimination.[65]

And it's not just DeGraffenreid. Awareness is growing that anyone who has more than one strike against them—whether because of gender, race, religion, ethnicity, or any other part of their identity—suffers an extra serving of discrimination and bias. The dominant form of feminism moving forward will not limit itself to jobs, maternity leave, reproductive rights, and other traditional concerns of women's equality. The movement will be broader, more holistic—confronting inequities and challenges across society.

In most parts of the world, the accomplishments of last-century feminists are apparent. Women are catching up to (and even surpassing) men in education. They have increased access to jobs. They are slowly gaining a foothold in the corridors of government. What many girls and women still lack, however, is an essential component of equity: autonomy, or the freedom to make independent decisions and act accordingly.

And that, as we look ahead to 2038, is at the crux of the change for which many are fighting. Put simply, a major hindrance to women's equality—to a better future for women and for society—is men's desire to control them: how they behave, how they look, even how they think.

Reproductive rights is an obvious place to start this discussion. Without question, many antiabortion activists and their supporters are motivated by a genuine desire to protect the unborn. There is plenty of anecdotal and statistical evidence, though, that others are motivated more by a desire to control the women whose bodies house those fetuses. A 2019 survey by Supermajority/PerryUndem Research of likely voters in the 2020 general election in the United States divided respondents into two camps: those who want abortion to be legal in all or most cases (whom I will refer to as "pro-choicers") and those who want abortion to be illegal in all or most cases ("pro-lifers"). The researchers then posed a series of questions pertaining to gender equality to see how the opinions of those two groups differed. The contrasts were stark.

Looking at women's political power:

- A majority of pro-lifers (54 percent) agreed that men generally make better political leaders than women, and only 47 percent wanted to see equal numbers of men and women in positions of power in society. Among pro-choicers, those figures were 24 percent and 80 percent, respectively.
- Similarly, 82 percent of pro-choicers agreed the United States would be better off if more women were in political office, compared with 34 percent of pro-lifers who said the same.
- Among pro-choicers, 70 percent thought the lack of women in political office affects women's equality; less than a quarter (23 percent) of pro-lifers agreed.[66]

A divide was also apparent in how respondents viewed broader issues related to women's equality and experiences.

- Nearly 77 percent of pro-lifers said women are "too easily offended," and 71 percent agreed that "most women interpret innocent remarks or acts as being sexist." Among pro-choicers, just 38 percent agreed with each of those statements.
- Similarly, 71 percent of pro-choicers had a favorable opinion of the #MeToo movement, compared with just 23 percent of pro-lifers.
- And while 67 percent of pro-choicers believed systems in society have been "set up to give men more opportunities than women," only 19 percent of pro-lifers agreed.[67]

Reproductive rights are about more than abortion. They are part of a broader culture war being waged to determine who in society wields power and influence.

The desire to "put women in their place" continues to be prevalent among many men (and even some women). We can see that in the misogynistic catchphrase "Make me a sandwich" regularly posted in response to "uppity" women on Twitter and shouted at female politicians on the campaign trail. We can see it, too, in the "Women: Get back in the kitchen!" T-shirt sold on Zazzle.com[68] and the "Nice new girlfriend / What breed is she?" tee sold at Topman in the United Kingdom before protests led the retailer to pull it off the shelves.[69]

Denigrating girls and women, restricting their options, positioning them as lesser than men, and regulating their dress and appearance—all of it forms a pattern of control. For years, there have been efforts to offset the power of women by alternately hypersexualizing them and imposing gendered modesty mandates. In *Everyday Sexism,* Laura Bates writes about female high school students "being hauled out of class, publicly humiliated, sent home, and even threatened with expulsion for such transgressions as wearing tops with 'spaghetti straps,' wearing leggings, or (brace yourself) revealing their shoulders."[70] The insidious message girls receive is twofold: They must alter their appearance to avoid infringing on boys' learning environment, and they—not boys—are responsible for controlling male behavior.

At the same time that schoolgirls are being sent home to cover up, female athletes are under pressure to don skimpy or sexualized outfits, presumably to attract male audiences—but also to counteract the strength and physical power these females are displaying. Why else would the men who run the International Boxing Association have tried to mandate that female boxers wear skirts during their bouts at the London 2012 Olympic Games?[71]

In 2021, the Norwegian women's beach handball team brought the debate to global attention when they accepted a monetary fine rather than wear the tiny bikini bottoms mandated during the European championship tournament. The International Handball Federation requires women to wear bottoms "with a close fit and cut on an upward angle toward the top of the leg" and sides that are no more than four inches. Meanwhile, the male athletes can wear shorts as long as four inches above their knees as long as they are "not too baggy."[72] "We are forced to play [in] panties," the Norwegian team captain told the media. "It is so embarrassing."[73]

The Norwegian team's refusal to don teeny bikinis was not the only harbinger of change in the sports world in 2021. Also momentous were the decisions by tennis champion Naomi Osaka and superstar gymnast Simone Biles to stand up for their mental and physical well-being by opting out of some competitions and, in Osaka's case, media appearances. They broke with tradition by putting themselves above any obligation they felt to their sport, sponsors, or fans. In an op-ed in *Time,* former college gymnast Katelyn Ohashi spelled out the import of these choices: "We start so young, and we have no autonomy over our bodies. . . . And what we're seeing now is a manifestation of athletes taking back their autonomy and redefining what winning is."[74]

Another recent sign that women's autonomy is being supported: the #FreeBritney campaign, which has brought the issue of conservatorships into public view. Just a few months shy of her fortieth birthday in 2021, pop star Britney Spears had been under a conservatorship for thirteen years. Initially in response to diagnosed mental health issues, in 2008 her father had been handed control over most aspects of her life: her finances, her business contracts, even her healthcare choices. She was not permitted to own a smartphone or have unfettered access to the internet. Nor, as she petitioned the courts to have her father removed from his oversight position, was she free to choose her legal counsel.

Speaking of the years-long oppression of Spears, Ashlie D. Stevens wrote in *Salon* about the "incredibly aggressive misogyny" of which Spears was a victim—a misogyny that went largely unchecked for two decades.[75] Stevens questions what impact "incessant tabloid portrayals" of Spears as promiscuous and a bad mother played in her losing custody of her sons. The question on the minds of many: What are the odds that a male star in similar circumstances would be stripped of his rights, his dignity, his agency? Most of us would agree, those odds would be slim indeed.

In a Los Angeles courtroom in November 2021, Judge Brenda Penny finally brought the Spears conservatorship to an end.[76]

In the United States, a multimillionaire pop star fights for and eventually regains control over her life. In Norway, female athletes resist efforts to sexualize and diminish them. In New Zealand, a female head of state is lauded for keeping a lethal virus at bay.

Is the future female, as placards at demonstrations so often claim? What does that even mean in a world where we have Alexandria Ocasio-Cortez and Lauren Boebert in the same legislative body, where Rachel Maddow shares airwaves with Laura Ingraham, where Marine Le Pen and Anne Hidalgo are both seen as threats to Emmanuel Macron's continued reign, where Polly Toynbee and Melanie Phillips offer diametrically opposed political commentary, where Sheryl Sandberg tells members of her sex to lean into their careers while Laura Doyle urges them to surrender to their husbands? And what does it mean at a time when gender is fluid and increasingly deemed a social construct?

Will the future be female? No. For the first time, though, I think we can say with confidence that neither will it be male.

Chapter 13

GUY PROBLEMS

Imagine a pickup truck so long you cannot easily park it—a truck that extends farther than a 1959 Cadillac Eldorado. A generous public parking space is eighteen feet long. This truck is nineteen feet.

The Ram—until 2010, it was called a Dodge Ram—is a legend. It has won *Motor Trend*'s Truck of the Year award eight times. In 2021, it became the first truck in history to win in three consecutive years.

Described by its maker as the "apex predator of the truck world," the 2021 Ram 1500 TRX is superpowerful. Its 6.2-liter, 702-horsepower Hemi V-8 engine can tow 8,100 pounds.[1] It accelerates from zero to sixty miles per hour in 4.5 seconds. Its 900-watt premium Harman Kardon audio system is good enough for a restaurant.[2] The seats in the back have business-class legroom. And the ride? *Car and Driver* equates it to gliding along in a Mercedes-Benz GLS.[3] The truck costs upward of $72,000. The (premium) Launch Edition will set you back more than $90,000.

The nickname for the vehicle is "Cowboy Cadillac." While this is slang for any high-end pickup truck, the Ram is not a truck. It's an identity.

Who wants to identify in that way? A great many people. About fifty-five thousand Americans buy a Ram each month.[4] To no one's surprise, more than eight in ten of those buyers are male.[5]

Much of the news we receive about male behavior these days is negative. When a man scales a building to save a toddler dangling from a balcony, we marvel at the bravery of the individual involved rather than applauding the heroics of men in general. In contrast, when a man makes headlines for some misbehavior—an abuse of power, sexual violence, or the like—the perpetrator's gender becomes part of a more sweeping discussion: What's going on with men, and how can we fix it? The same broad-brush tendency plagues women, of course. Erin Callan's "failures" as CFO of Lehman Brothers have been used to tarnish other women in finance. The difference of late is that so much more attention directed at men—especially older straight, white men—seems to be critical and framed within broader questions about males' perceived negative societal impact.

Many of today's world leaders sit at the extreme of what has come to be known as "toxic masculinity." There is a reason we call autocrats strongmen. (The word *strongwoman*, in contrast, refers to a carnival oddity, not anyone to be feared or even respected.) In this era, the number of strongmen in positions of power is growing. *Time* magazine reported in 2018:

> *In every region of the world, changing times have boosted public demand for more muscular, assertive leadership. These tough-talking populists promise to protect "us" from "them." Depending on who's talking, "them" can mean the corrupt elite or the grasping poor; foreigners or members of racial, ethnic or religious minorities. Or disloyal politicians, bureaucrats, bankers or judges. Or lying reporters. Out of this divide, a new archetype of leader has emerged. We're now in the strongman era.*[6]

There have been iron-willed women leaders—Margaret Thatcher, Golda Meir, and Indira Gandhi spring to mind—but so far, none of the world's strutting dictators has been female.

Mass murder is another male specialty. As of late November 2021, only 3 of the 124 mass shootings in the United States since 1982 have been carried out by women.[7] And no one is confused about who is behind the sexual abuse that launched the #MeToo movement.

There are some traditional male strongholds, though, in which men's dominance is beginning (however slowly) to be challenged by women. On the domestic front, *head of household* and *man of the house* are antiquated terms, even if the U.S. Internal Revenue Service continues to use the former and even if the division of household duties remains gendered and deeply skewed. As discussed in the last chapter, girls and women are surpassing their male classmates in school.[8] And while Erin Callan's story remains a cautionary tale, female chief financial officers are by and large outperforming men,[9] and there's increasing emphasis on bringing more women into the upper ranks of management.

Not every man is embracing this change. I had a conversation recently with an Italian executive who told me that as a father of girls, he is happy with all the ways companies are pulling women forward. Still, as a business leader competing for his next job, he felt like an underdog. "Who knew my gender could be a liability?" he said to me. Welcome to the club.

Watch this sentiment rise as inequities are slowly diminished. As men's long-standing domination is threatened on every front—in politics, in the classroom, in the workplace, and in their relationships with women—we can expect pushback, especially as more men begin to feel they are being forced to change (or mask) something essential about them. We have entered the "emo years," when a man without a high emotional intelligence quotient, or EQ (the ability to understand, use, and properly manage one's emotions, will find himself disadvantaged in ways previous generations of men did not. Look for gender-blind emotional intelligence training to take hold in more workplaces by the end of this decade.

"A woman's place is in the home." Not anymore. "Boys don't cry." They do now. Strictly delineated male and female identities have faced steady erosion since the 1960s. The thinking that rigid gender roles are innate has been increasingly discredited, if not outright demolished—at least in secular, liberal cultures.

Patrimony is bleeding—and maybe even bleeding out. Oppressors who feel like victims are angry that women are invading their domains. Privileges to which they have always been accustomed are being called into question; the "divine right" of men is rejected at every turn. Thinking back to my family dinner table in the 1970s, I remember well my mother serving my father dinner, my father presiding over after-dinner conversation, and then both of them retreating like clockwork to watch my father's favorite television shows, which included *Hogan's Heroes* and *M*A*S*H*. Dad was king, Mom was his cheerleader and enabler, and we three daughters were accustomed to receiving—and acquiescing to—decrees. "You are not wearing pants to school unless it is snowing." "Act like a lady." "You bet your sweet bippy you will do as I say."

Now, as the rules change—as men are asked to be less macho and maybe even (dare I say it?) slightly more female—males are facing some of the same issues that have plagued their female counterparts for millennia. Case in point: body image. A 2021 survey by U.K.-based suicide prevention nonprofit CALM (Campaign Against Living Miserably) found that nearly half of males aged sixteen to forty struggle with their mental health because of poor body image. (Fifty years earlier, such a statistic would have been unthinkable. Back then, men were unlikely to even consider talking about something so personal and, well, "unmasculine.") The situation will likely worsen: 58 percent of respondents said the pandemic had negatively impacted how they feel about their bodies.[10] Organizations are springing up to combat the trend. The EveryMAN Project, for instance, started by American artist and activist Tarik Carroll, aims to "liberate men worldwide from self-hate" and to "challenge society's standards of what the *real* male aesthetic is" as well as its "obsession with hypermasculinity and perfection."[11]

Too often, males are left behind as notions of gender change. In Western cultures especially, *woman,* for the most part, can now mean whatever a woman thinks it does. Women are being invited to adopt attitudes and behaviors once considered the domain of men. They can be edgy, assertive, commanding—and take on virtually any role (which is not to say there isn't a price to pay, as

Hillary Clinton found out). Or they can opt to adhere to more traditionally female traits—e.g., demureness, nurturance, peacemaking, hospitality—and prioritize family and homemaking above all else. To a large extent (barring financial pressures), the choice is theirs, and while there may be pushback from some quarters, females can anticipate a far larger dose of support for their right to choose and to be whoever they wish.

Meanwhile, the male of the species is admonished to "fix" himself. Behaviors previously dismissed on the grounds that "boys will be boys" are now called out for what they are: actions and attitudes that are frequently predatory, violent, boorish, crass, antisocial, unethical, or illegal. The modern world—at least in some regions and cultures—is slowly evolving toward one standard of human behavior, with males and females being judged against a single code that rejects some of the behaviors previously considered acceptable for men. Watch this space for a new, gender-neutral way forward.

As males come of age with a new set of rules and so much ambiguity, they are inundated with conflicting messaging—the new and the old. They should be sensitive but stoic. Gentle but assertive. Empathetic but confident. Whereas society has mobilized to create equal opportunities for girls and women, fewer resources and less energy have been devoted to helping boys and men navigate a world in which the rules have changed but haven't quite settled.

This lack of attention is beginning to be addressed. As boys and men struggle to find a balance that wins society's approval, support groups are cropping up globally to help them navigate changing societal mores and embrace their "better" (i.e., less macho) selves. Among them: Humen in the United Kingdom, a mental health charity offering group therapy on topics such as inadequacy, shame, fear, and guilt;[12] Evryman, a U.S.-based organization that uses retreats, peer-led group discussions, coaching, and events to "destigmatize men's vulnerability and emotionality" and help them lead more fulfilling lives;[13] and The Man Cave, an organization that works with boys, parents, and teachers across Australia to "allow young men to explore and express their full humanity."[14]

These groups provide a safe space for men grappling with these issues, but the underlying message is clear: Boys and men must adapt to changed expectations and standards. Society needs them to behave and think differently.

When threatened, animals have a common set of reactions. At their peril, they can ignore the threat. They can acknowledge the threat and adapt. They can flee the threat in hopes that it will not follow. Or, cornered and feeling their survival is at stake, they can fight back.

In the United States, that last reaction has enjoyed a high media profile in recent years. Love him or loathe him, looking back over President Trump's years in office, it is hard not to see a caricature of the beleaguered male mounting one last stand against the forces he sees poised to disempower him and those like him.

One reason some men identify with Trump is his views on the male prerogative. If pushed, he would acknowledge that women are legally equal, but—wink, wink—they really aren't, and no way would he ever be emasculated by one. This is not a turnoff for some voters; instead, it is part of Trump's appeal. Reporting for *The New York Times,* Jennifer Medina interviewed dozens of Mexican American men to understand why they identify so closely with a politician who has made no secret of his anti-immigrant sentiments. Her conclusion: "To them, the macho allure of Mr. Trump is undeniable. He is forceful, wealthy and, most important, unapologetic. In a world where at any moment someone might be attacked for saying the wrong thing, he says the wrong thing all the time and does not bother with self-flagellation."[15]

The 2016 election results suggest that this sort of male hubris also holds appeal among many women.

If you tally Trump's remarks about women, it is clear that his world remains sharply delineated between male and female. A sample from a compilation in *The Week:*

- On his 2016 rival: "If Hillary Clinton can't satisfy her husband, what makes her think she can satisfy America?"
- On actress Lindsay Lohan, at the time eighteen years old:

"She's probably deeply troubled, and therefore great in bed. How come the deeply troubled women—deeply, deeply troubled—they're always the best in bed?"

- On the #MeToo movement: "You've got to deny, deny, deny and push back on these women. If you admit to anything and any culpability, then you're dead. . . . You've got to be strong. You've got to be aggressive. You've got to push back hard. You've got to deny anything that's said about you. Never admit."
- On women, generally: "[Women are] really a lot different than portrayed. They are far worse than men, far more aggressive, and boy, can they be smart!"[16]

Women, smart? Who would have thought?

Trump's most entrenched supporters may even cheer his solidly mid-twentieth-century views on fatherhood. In his view, men who change diapers and care for their children are acting "like the wife."[17]

Meanwhile, in the United Kingdom, a ban on harmful gender stereotypes in advertising has been instituted. Supporters of the ban include hands-on fathers fed up with stereotypical depictions of dads as being "useless" around the home.[18] (The ever-present yang to the yin.) An international group of fathers has created *Dope Black Dads,* a podcast and a "digital safe space for fathers who wish to discuss their experiences of being black, a parent and masculinity in the modern world." Their aim: "to celebrate, heal, inspire and educate black fathers for better outcomes for black families."[19] Along with gender norms, diapers will be changed.

And yet old habits die hard. Women may serve in the military, but men are still the ones to decide to go to war. This is increasingly unwise. In our hyperconnected world, countries on both sides of a military conflict are part of the same global supply chain, with any damage inflicted potentially harming economic partners. And we can see with the most recent wars fought by the United States that even when the opponents cannot possibly win on the battlefield, they drain America's resources and political will just by continuing to fight.

Simply put, war—historically the exclusive territory of men—is increasingly obsolete, arguably useful only for those industries that supply the military; in modern conflicts, a few keystrokes and a disinformation campaign on social media can be more effective than a thousand bombers and a hundred thousand soldiers. Why hasn't society evolved to a place where the notion of putting young bodies in harm's way is anathema?

There is something else to consider here on the topic of conflict and aggression: Where can warriors focus those energies when there is no more war? How can we channel these traditional male strengths to serve the greater good? How can we encourage heroism and honor off the battlefield? Both qualities are sorely needed.

Sociologist Philip Slater examines the endurance of outdated institutions in *The Chrysalis Effect: The Metamorphosis of Global Culture*. He identifies the phenomenon of male resistance to any change as "control culture," which he connects to "authoritarianism, militarism, misogyny, proliferating walls, mental constriction, and rigid dualism"—all expressions of male dominance.[20]

With the ascent of women, that world is crumbling. "Modern men have been trained in macho skills over many years and at severe cost," says Slater, "only to discover that those skills are no longer of any use to anyone. Strutting, boasting, fighting, destroying, and killing just don't seem as important to the world as they used to."[21] In other words, not only have women invaded male domains, they have also proved that they are no longer dependent on men—and the men in question are not happy about it.

What matters more than strutting and fighting now? Empathy, compassion, accessible emotion—values associated with women and what some deem "feminized" men.

The men who feel the need to express hypermasculine behaviors to feel authentically male are likely to have increasing difficulty finding female companionship. If current trends continue, macho men looking for a Saturday night date are very likely to be knocking back beers and amusing themselves at the pool table with other men. As a result, the ranks of incels will balloon. Members of this subculture and hate group—which is already responsible for at least one mass killing[22]—blame women for their shortcomings and their unfulfilling lives. As Jennifer Wright put it in *Harper's Bazaar,* "Their existence is not about being lonely. It is about blaming women for their loneliness."[23]

Will such men lash out as they see "feminized" men get all the "good" women in movies, television shows, and real life—or will they learn to adapt? One can hope for the latter. But some facts intrude: Oversized pickup trucks rarely get good gas mileage. They do not fit in some parking spaces. Their resale value is generally not as good as that of more versatile vehicles. And yet men, in large numbers, continue to covet and buy them.

Chapter 14

Unmooring from Gender and Cis-Sameness

Back when men were men and women were helpmates, the terms *sex* and *gender* were used interchangeably (at least outside academia). According to traditional precepts, a man was hunter and protector, the financial provider for his family. Within his household, he dominated. His word was law. A woman, in contrast, was defined solely in relation to others—first as a daughter and then as a wife and mother. Her place was in the home. For no salary and with no agency, she worked all day, cooking, cleaning, chauffeuring the children. At night, she serviced her man. For both men and women, the rules were clear.

Then the planets realigned. In the early 1960s: the Pill, Betty Friedan's *The Feminine Mystique,* a younger generation in the White House. Followed by a "youthquake" of marijuana and LSD, cheap airfares, the "Summer of Love." Then antiwar protests with the enticing claim that "girls say yes to guys who say no," popularized by activist folksinger Joan Baez. And women's lib, which was less about bra-burning and much more about women going to work.

Bella Abzug was elected to Congress in 1971. Her campaign slogan: "This woman's place is in the House—the House of Representatives." She could say that (and live that) because, back in New York, she had a support system. A nanny and housekeeper lived with the family for twenty-three years. Her daughter recalls that her father was "always going food shopping and doing laundry"[1]—far different from what most families experienced in that era.

For women, the 1970s were powered by a new sense of possibility. Freedom to marry or not. Freedom to become a mother or not. Freedom to pursue a career or not. But the sexual choice was still narrow: straight or gay. And only one choice was acceptable. *Transsexual* wasn't coined until 1949, *transgender* not until 1971[2]—but having a word to describe such "transgressive" natures did not make them any more socially acceptable. "Unnatural" sex could bring criminal prosecution. In fact, it was not until 2003 that sexual acts between persons of the same gender were legalized nationwide in the United States.[3]

What forces jump-started public awareness and even some acceptance of expanded gender definitions and loosened gender roles? As is often the case, it was art. David Bowie appeared in long hair and a dress.[4] The Kinks recorded a love song in which "girls will be boys and boys will be girls; it's a mixed up, muddled up, shook up world, except for Lola." On his gender-bending 1972 album, *Transformer,* Lou Reed sang about a walk on the wild side—"Shaved her legs and then he was a she . . ." Androgynous punk-rock band the New York Dolls hit the stage as "tarted-up toughs in boas and heels,"[5] followed a decade later by the überpopular Boy George. On the flip side, model-singer-actress Grace Jones introduced much of the world to a stunningly beautiful woman deeply in touch with her masculine side.

What once was spectacle, limited mainly to the world of the arts, has seeped into the broader society. It was always there, of course—just well hidden. A generation or two after "Lola" hit the scene, rigid notions of gender appear to be on the way out, though opposition to change remains widespread. The debate is settled in the minds of many outspoken celebrities, the mainstream media, and much of the population (especially the young), but local communities across the country are battling it out on issues ranging from how gender is taught in schools to whether it's OK for a lesbian couple to be elected homecoming king and queen.[6] Even as these debates rage, gender is now up for discussion, and sexual orientation is far more complicated than straight versus gay. "Love is love" is the ethos of the day in more progressive pockets of society. A person may identify as transgender* or nonbinary† or gender-fluid‡ or even as "name only" because they have decided they cannot be defined by the chromosomal pattern with which they were born. More than a dozen countries have added a third gender designation to passports (typically, "X") for use by people who don't identify as male or female. The Netherlands is removing gender designations entirely from national identification documents.

More people—including those who identify as cisgender§ —are declaring their preferred personal pronouns on their email signatures, name tags, and social media profiles. Facebook now allows its members to choose from more than fifty gender identifiers.[7]

Others fight the trend, sometimes making it about grammar but more often revealing underlying discomfort with this significant societal shift that has turned a once binary option into a complex calculation that produces any number of gender identities. An affronted former Foreign Service officer sent this email to linguist and author Geoffrey Nunberg after he discussed personal pronouns on NPR:

> *If you give them your pronouns today they will come for the rest of your free speech tomorrow. . . . You may be willing to call a person "they" but that is a slippery grammatical slope towards the bastardization of our language to say nothing of capitulation to the absolute slimmest portion of society that is intent on "wagging the dog" with their "new age nonbinary" tail. Wise up, please. We who love the language will not sit idly by while the Left and liberal professors such as yourself [take] unfair advantage of Americans' confusion on the gender issues facing us.*[8]

* A person whose sense of personal identity and gender does not correspond with their sex at birth

† A person who considers themselves neither exclusively male nor exclusively female or who is in between or beyond both genders

‡ A person whose gender identity is not fixed

§ A person whose gender identity matches the sex assigned to him or her at birth

Comedian Sarah Silverman has a different take: "We learn how to say Galifianakis and Schwarzenegger like nothing. Why can't we figure out pronouns?"[9]

Of course, we can figure out the pronouns. The question is: Do we want to? Some cultures are already embracing the notion that gender is nonbinary; others likely never will.

Symptomatic of the tussles playing out in many countries was an incident on a London train in 2021. A conductor welcomed passengers on board with "Good afternoon, ladies and gentlemen, boys and girls." A passenger who heard the announcement tweeted: "As a non-binary person this announcement doesn't actually apply to me so I won't listen." London North Eastern Railway apologized, and—right on cue—anti-LGBTQ+ voices pitched in to criticize "fake gender ideology."[10]

Traditionalists lost no time in declaring war on gender fluidity, considering it a threat to "normal" life—i.e., the environment in which they were comfortable. Like so many political issues, the words are not the real target. The aim is to limit people's freedom to make choices with which traditionalists disagree. And this especially applies to women.

This is a battle traditionalists have been losing for decades, starting with the push for gay rights. Some say the fight began in earnest on April 30, 1997, when Ellen DeGeneres revealed on her sitcom, *Ellen,* that she is a lesbian.[11] In that "special episode," Oprah Winfrey played her therapist. Laura Dern appeared as a possible love interest. And there were drop-ins by Melissa Etheridge and Demi Moore. The episode attracted more than forty million viewers, a record for the show.

Even though the episode carried a warning label from the network—"due to adult content, parental discretion is advised"[12]—the blowback was swift. A bomb threat was called in to the studio. Televangelist Pat Robertson labeled the comedian "Ellen DeGenerate." Chrysler, JCPenney, Domino's Pizza, and McDonald's pulled advertising. A year later, the sitcom was canceled.

But *Will & Grace* and *Glee* and *Queer Eye* followed. In 2012, JCPenney, the same retailer that had rejected Ellen a decade and a half earlier, hired her as a spokesperson—albeit not without a huge backlash from its board, investors, some customers, and organizations such as the American Family Association's One Million Moms group, which criticized the retailer for "jumping on the pro-gay bandwagon" and promised its support of DeGeneres would cause it to "lose customers with traditional values that have been faithful to them over all these years."[13]

Through all the vitriol and personal attacks, DeGeneres persevered (though at no small cost[14]). A 2015 poll named her the most influential figure in transforming public opinion about gay rights. In 2016, President Obama awarded her the Medal of Freedom. It turned out that gays were harder to hate once you knew them as individuals. While Ellen's reputation has suffered since then amid accusations of a toxic work environment on her talk show, her impact as a gay icon stands.

The public's hearts and minds were not quite so open when the conversation expanded beyond sexual orientation to gender identity. In the early 2020s, these became hot-button questions: Should transgender students be allowed to use the school bathrooms or play on the sports teams of the gender with which they identify? Should transgender adults be permitted to serve in the Armed Forces? Should medical insurance cover reassignment surgeries?

It is not just conservatives and evangelical Christians who are alarmed by the changing definitions of gender. Harry Potter creator J. K. Rowling retweeted an article that referred to "people who menstruate." She added this: "'People who menstruate.' I'm sure there used to be a word for those people. Someone help me out. Wumben? Wimpund? Woomud?"[15]

Rowling is a savvy writer. She knew her tweet would generate discussion, but she couldn't have anticipated the firestorm of criticism it unleashed. Actors in the Harry Potter and Fantastic Beasts franchises—Daniel Radcliffe, Eddie Redmayne, Emma Watson—distanced themselves. On Twitter, there were threats of "cancelling, punching and death."[16] There was no middle ground.

The opposition to gender fluidity and a broader range of sexuality will accelerate, and for a good reason: Shifts in how we define and discern gender are accelerating. Yin, meet yang. Among Gen Zers, one in six adults describes themselves as LGBTQ+.[17] For many of them, coming out was far less fraught than it was for Ellen DeGeneres. As *The Washington Post* noted about this generation, "They were eight years old when same-sex marriage became legal in Maryland, about twelve when they realized they were attracted to girls and fourteen when they came out as nonbinary, using they/them pronouns."[18]

Why are gender-nonconforming youth receiving broader (though far from universal) support these days? Twenty-first-century media is standing on the shoulders of *Ellen, Will & Grace,* and other hit shows, with no courage now required on the part of network executives and corporations. And, thanks to the internet, any tribe is but a click away. Gays and transgender people become YouTube and TikTok stars. Support groups announce meetings on school bulletin boards. And, on occasion, LGBTQ+ youth inspire their closeted parents to come out, or at least to join them along parade routes and express their pride.

The trend has also had a boost from celebrities. Well-known parents who have publicly embraced their transgender or gender-nonconforming children run the gamut from actors (Charlize Theron, Gabrielle Union, Warren Beatty and Annette Bening) and musicians (Cher) to athletes (Dwyane Wade). In 2019, Grammy Award–winning musician Sam Smith came out as gender nonbinary, saying: "I'm not male or female. I think I float somewhere in between."[19] In 1976, my family and I cheered on U.S. decathlon champion Caitlyn Jenner (then known by her birth name, Bruce) at the Montreal Olympics, where Jenner won a gold medal and set a new world record. Some forty years later, Jenner's announcement that she is transgender and her accompanying physical transition became breaking entertainment news, since it came at a moment when much of the world was trying to keep up with the Kardashians—her family by marriage and children. In late 2020, Elliot Page—beloved star of *Juno* and *The Umbrella Academy*—came out as trans and discarded his birth name, Ellen. In 2021, Mj Rodriguez became the first openly transgender performer to be nominated for an Emmy in a lead acting category—a first that sparked conversation and consternation over why awards are gendered at all. A week earlier, a trans woman was crowned Miss Nevada USA, putting her on track to compete in the Miss USA pageant later in the year.[20]

In my view, one of the strongest signs of how much the pendulum has swung is the existence of summer camps for LGBTQ+ kids. New Hampshire's Camp Aranu'tiq, which is specifically for transgender youth,[21] takes its name from a Chugach word used to describe Two-Spirits—people thought to embody both a female and a male spirit. Gender differences that once provoked censure and exclusion are increasingly accepted as part of a spectrum that is far broader and more dynamic than people could have imagined half a century ago.

What started in the last century with unisex fashion and morphed into metrosexuality has become a rainbow of potential identities. It may take some of us going through a handful of gender definitions before we find one that fits us. Or our gender definition may be an endlessly moving target.

How will society adapt to the growing recognition that the human population cannot be shoehorned into traditional binary roles? Without question, unisex bathrooms (typically for a single user) will become the norm. (It has been estimated that North Carolina's controversial "bathroom bill"—which prevented transgender people in the state from using bathrooms aligned with their gender identities and led to boycotts by the likes of Bruce Springsteen, Demi Lovato, and Nick Jonas, and pullouts by businesses that include PayPal, the NBA, Adidas, and Deutsche Bank—cost the state more than $3.76 billion in lost revenues over a dozen years.)[22] Following a 2019 online discussion among human-resources experts on the topic of making workplaces more gender-neutral, one participant commented, "A good 60 percent—at least—of the conversation was about bathrooms."[23] My advice: Urinal manufacturers should be looking to diversify into new product categories.

Unisex clothing and gender-neutral branding have been around for years. Now we can expect more fashion designers to expand their lines to include a broader array of sizes to fit trans women and men. The brand Humankind already offers gender-neutral swim- and loungewear in a wide range of sizes.[24]

More-established brands also are stepping up. Levi's has debuted the Unlabeled collection, which it notes has been "curated by our LGBTQ+ staff—for everyone."[25] The retailer's website explains: "This curated collection resists conformity to celebrate individuality and self-expression. These are clothes inspired by fluidity and the freedom to live, love, and be your authentic self." The brand's Beauty of Becoming campaign features gender nonbinary Jaden Smith, who several years earlier had been the face of a Louis Vuitton women's wear campaign.[26]

Toymaker Mattel also has moved toward inclusivity, unveiling a line of gender-neutral Barbie dolls. In launching the line, the company tweeted, "In our world, dolls are as limitless as the children who play with them. Introducing #CreatableWorld, a doll line designed to keep labels out and invite everyone in. #AllWelcome."[27]

Gender fluidity is hardly a modern phenomenon. Transgender people have been recorded at least as far back as Roman emperor Elagabalus in A.D. 200.[28] And many cultures, going back centuries, have accepted the notion of a third gender. Third-gender people are called *hijra* in India, *mahu* in some Polynesian cultures, and *muxe* by the Zapotec of Oaxaca, Mexico. Speaking of the tradition of Native American Two-Spirits, musician and activist Tony Enos addressed the societal role these nonbinary people have played:

> *Before colonization, we were balance-keepers. We were the only ones that could move between the men's and women's camps. There was a special role for these gender-queer, gender-fluid, gender-non-conforming tribal individuals who had this special medicine, this blessing to be able to see life through male and female eyes.*[29]

The difference today, and the trend we will see strengthen over the next two decades, is the more inclusive nature of our thinking—

not just our actions. With every passing year, we are less inclined to focus on the otherness of nonbinary people and more inclined to consider the human population as existing along a broad and colorful spectrum. Barriers will continue to crumble, even as opponents work feverishly to reinforce them by promoting a return to rigid gender norms that have already been rejected by all but the most patriarchal societies.

Ironically, even as we get better at embracing and expressing our authentic selves, we are losing our sense of connection to others. Welcome to the era of skin hunger and tables for one.

Chapter 15

Me, Myself, and I

The Buddha said, "There is no one in the universe more dear to us than ourselves. The mind may travel in a thousand directions, but it will find no one else more beloved. The moment you see how important it is to love yourself, you will stop making others suffer."

—Thich Nhat Hanh, *Teachings on Love*

We do not always like to admit that we love ourselves, but most of us would like to continue playing our part in the human drama for as many years as possible.

Increasingly, these parts we play are documented and promoted. Much has been said about selfie culture and the tendency of millennials and Gen Zers to chronicle their lives for friends and strangers alike. We have all seen images of young people using disaster sites—burning buildings, rubble from earthquakes—as backdrops for their self-portraits. And we have mused about the narcissism of a practice that *The New York Times* called "an emergent form of folk art for millennials."[1]

Selfie culture extends beyond photos, of course. It encompasses a cultural trend toward self-everything: self-absorption, self-promotion, even self-loathing. As American aphorist Mason Cooley noted, "Self-hatred and self-love are equally self-centered."[2]

It has been said that the baby boomers' "me" culture has given rise to their children's "me, me, me" culture. And not everyone casts that in an entirely negative light: Alicia Eler, the millennial author of *The Selfie Generation,* considers selfie culture a new style of empowerment, a powerful megaphone through which young people make themselves heard rather than an expression of narcissism. While there may be truth to that, evidence is mounting that this predilection for oversharing may not be harmless. A study by researchers at the University of Maine, for instance, found that some young social media adherents have chronicled their lives through screens to such an extent that their ability to decode nonverbal cues in real life has been damaged.[3] And in her testimony before the U.S. Congress, Facebook whistleblower Frances Haugen pointed to evidence the social media giant had compiled on how its Instagram platform negatively affects mental health, especially among girls, contributing to eating disorders and suicidal ideation, among other impacts.[4]

Even beyond heavy social media use, human existence on planet Earth is inexorably growing more self-centric and individualized. We use smartwatches and other devices to monitor our steps, our heart rate, our blood glucose, our sleep patterns, our water intake . . . our everything. It is estimated that the number of Americans using health and fitness apps increased more than 27 percent in 2020.[5] We also carefully curate our personal brands, designing online personas that may bear little relation to reality.

Arguably most impactful: We curate bespoke media and content streams. It is entirely conceivable that no one else on Earth enjoys precisely the same media diet as you. It is yours and yours alone. That points to a great paradox of our time: One might think that with nearly six in ten of the world's peoples connected to social media,[6] humankind would be more in sync than ever before. Instead, we are isolated by both preference and AI smart-data systems that personalize content consumption to such an extent that it has defeated the most obvious promise of the web: our links to one another.

It's no coincidence that we are more likely to work alone—or at least independently—than ever before. There were six million more gig workers in the United States at the start of 2020 than in 2010, according to the ADP Research Institute.[7] How does that compare with our starting point of 2000? There have long been freelance workers, but the term *gig economy* did not even join the lexicon until celebrated magazine editor Tina Brown (*Vanity Fair, The New Yorker*) started talking about it nearly a decade later, in 2009.[8]

Between today and 2038, we can expect more people to jump on the entrepreneurial bandwagon—far more likely as solopreneurs[9] than as proprietors of companies with employees, let alone mega-buck corporations. The hunger is there: An estimated 21 percent of employed adults in the United States were self-employed in 2019, but an academic study conducted in 2000 suggests that 70.8 percent of Americans would like to be self-employed.[10] The percentage is even higher in Poland and Portugal.

We are also more isolated within our neighborhoods. In 2000, political scientist Robert D. Putnam explored Americans' growing social disconnectedness in his landmark book *Bowling Alone*. He detailed that between 1975 and 2000, attendance at club meetings had plummeted 58 percent, while family dinners decreased 43 percent and having people over to one's home dropped by more than a third.[11] This increasing isolation has a cumulative impact on both individuals and society, affecting everything from personal health and satisfaction to involvement in democratic institutions.

With his book, Putnam hoped to revive the sense of community that once united his country—that same sort of community Tocqueville had lauded more than a century earlier. Instead, the disconnection and isolation have intensified. A study conducted just prior to the pandemic found that nearly one in six Americans—rising to more than one in four millennials—did not know their neighbors' names.[12] No wonder sales of home surveillance cameras are booming, forecast to reach nearly $12 billion globally by 2027.[13] The Elks social club saw its membership fall by half between 1980 and 2012.[14] They are not unique: U.S. country club membership declined 20 percent between 1990 and 2014,[15] and the percentage of Americans who belong to a religious institution dipped to 47 percent in 2020, down from 70 percent in 1999, according to Gallup.[16] Honestly, our pre-pandemic selves likely would have asked, Who has the time?

We can see this trend of social isolation globally, too. Clinical psychologist Shabnam Berry-Khan calls loneliness "a worldwide public health matter."[17] Both Japan and the U.K. have appointed ministers of loneliness, with the latter distributing funds to help organizations "connect small groups of people through projects and activities they enjoy."[18] Analysis by the EU's Joint Research Committee of data from the European Social Survey in 2019—so even before social distancing—determined that nearly one in five adults in Europe is socially isolated, a situation particularly pronounced in Hungary and Greece.[19]

Adding immeasurably to the problem is the trend toward living alone, which you have seen referenced in several chapters—a sure sign of a trend with tentacles that extend into myriad aspects of modern life. In his book *Going Solo,* sociologist Eric Klinenberg deemed this trend "a remarkable social experiment" that extends across ages, geographies, and political views.[20] I mentioned earlier that more than 40 percent of Tokyo's population live alone.[21] By 2040, according to Japan's National Institute of Population and Social Security Research, nearly 40 percent of *all* households in the country will be solo-occupant.[22] That pales in comparison with Sweden, where a majority of households are already single-occupant.[23] In the United States, the proportion of people living alone has nearly doubled in the past fifty years, to 14.6 percent in 2019.[24] In some cities, including Cincinnati, Pittsburgh, and St. Louis, more than one in four adults live alone.[25]

Academic researchers in Spain concluded that the rise in people living alone "has come to be emblematic in many ways of modern Western societies because it represents the importance conceded to the individual and to individual goals at the expense, basically, of the family."[26] Researchers at Our World in Data have found another correlation besides Western values: People are more likely to live alone in wealthier nations.[27] The new nuclear household: me, myself, and I.

There is a fine line between self-empowering independence and isolation. Earlier generations would have marveled at the notion that their grandchildren would have an endless store of movies, TV shows, books, articles, music, and other content available twenty-four hours a day. I am old enough to remember when the television channels (we only had four) closed the day's broadcasting around midnight by playing our national anthem and then dissolving into static. That's all, folks. Go to bed.

My mind would have boggled at the idea that a person could shoot, edit, and distribute a movie on their own, let alone on a personal phone. Or work from home and have video meetings with colleagues thousands of miles away—sharing screens and files instantaneously. Or renovate and decorate a home without ever once stepping foot in a store. Let's face it: Our digital capabilities are amazing. But what price have we paid?

At a primal level, humans are social animals. We need to be connected to one another—emotionally and physically. Long before the social distancing of the COVID-19 era, I was writing and speaking about the disturbing twenty-first-century trend of touch deprivation. The psychological term for it: *skin hunger.*

Being deprived of touch is detrimental to all animals, including humans. Infants who are not held and cuddled fail to thrive.[28] Adults respond in other ways, including through antisocial behaviors, depression, anxiety, and stress. A lack of touch can even weaken one's immune system.[29]

So hungry are we for physical contact that a consumer market has emerged. In the past two decades, we have seen the emergence of cuddle parties, in which strangers get together—sometimes clad in pajamas—to snuggle and caress one another in nonsexual ways.[30] Cow cuddling saw a spike in popularity during the pandemic. According to the owner of a farm in upstate New York, "You cannot hug your friends, or hug your grandkids," but for seventy-five dollars an hour, "you can hug [Angus cows] Bella and Bonnie."[31]

People are also gravitating toward inanimate objects that mimic the sensation of human contact. Weighted blankets have been around since the late 1990s, but sales have only taken off in the last several years. In 2020, the global market for these blankets was valued at just under $530 million; the market is expected to grow more than 14 percent annually through 2026, to more than $1.1 billion.[32] The manufacturers of these blankets, which typically retail for between $100 and $300, claim that the even pressure they exert on the body reduces the stress-related hormone cortisol while promoting the release of the well-being chemical serotonin and the sleep hormone melatonin. A less sciency explanation is that the blankets make users feel comforted and cuddled.

Also increasingly popular: compression wear—tight-fitting garments worn not to enhance athletic performance but to reduce anxiety. An Australian company selling compression clothing likens it to a "constant soft 'hug' for the wearer's body"—a feeling that can reduce anxiety and even avert a panic attack.[33]

Living in a single-person household does not necessarily mean being alone. One of the few positive media stories early on in the pandemic was the news that animal shelters were running out of pets. Shelter Animals Count, an organization that tracks rescue facilities across the United States, recorded twenty-six thousand more pet adoptions in the first ten months of 2020 compared with the same period in 2019, an increase of around 15 percent.[34] A similar response was seen in other countries. For instance, researchers in Hong Kong and Pakistan conducted a Google trends search using keywords associated with the adoption of dogs and cats between 2015 and the end of 2020. They found that searches peaked between April and May 2020, shortly after the World Health Organization declared the pandemic.[35]

There are indications that some people made the choice to adopt because they finally were spending enough time at home to properly train and care for a pet. I think it is safe to say, though, that many of these furry friends were brought home simply because they offered companionship, solace, and comfort in an especially stressful time.

L. F. Carver, an assistant professor at Queen's University in Canada, conducted a study of pet owners during the pandemic. She wrote:

> *One participant said, "I don't know what I would do without the company of my dog, she has kept me going." Another said, "It is the only thing that is keeping me sane." And others*

said the presence of a pet was salvation (a life saver) and brought joy. There were also those who said they talk with their pet and that it helped stave off loneliness.[36]

People and pets go back thousands of years, but there has been a change in the relationship since the start of this century: With global spikes in stress and anxiety, dogs, cats, and other four-legged adoptees have morphed into "support animals"—providers of nonverbal therapy. In the United States, the National Service Animal Registry—which sells official-looking animal vests and "support pet" certificates—had 2,400 service dogs, psychiatric service dogs, and emotional-support animals in its registry in 2011. By mid-2021, that number exceeded 220,000.[37]

Support-documented or not, pets fill a gap in modern life—providing the comfort, unconditional love, and physical affection that used to be integral to human society when we lived more communally. Part of that comes back to touch. Petting an animal has been found to lower heart rate and blood pressure—hence, the trend of "comfort dogs" being brought to universities during exams and "crisis-response dogs" being deployed to provide comfort in the aftermath of natural disasters.[38] For some people, petting or cuddling their cat, dog, or hamster is the only sustained contact with a living being they experience most days. It may be just what the doctor ordered.

Allergic to cats? No time to walk a dog? Enter the robots. We may be connecting less often with our fellow humans, but many of us are filling our homes with digital interactors—from AI-powered speakers to robotic vacuums.

Estimated at just under $12 billion in 2019, the global market for smart speakers—Amazon Echoes, Google Homes, and the like—is forecast to exceed $35.5 billion by 2025.[39] With so many of these devices now in our homes, it stands to reason that some people interact more with their smart appliances on a given day than with friends or family. Anyone who has one in their home may even develop feelings toward it, good or bad. (If you have never apologized to Alexa for getting snippy with "her," I would venture to guess you don't own an Amazon Echo.) As our devices get smarter and more responsive, we will increasingly turn to them for companionship, therapy, and even romance, as dramatized in Spike Jonze's 2013 film *Her*.

In 2017, my former communications agency conducted a global study that found that one in four millennials believed humans will develop deep friendships and even romantic relationships with robots. In some markets, that figure was even higher—reaching 54 percent in China and 45 percent in India.[40] That time is drawing nearer. Technologist Scott Dewing confirms that "sexbots are a rapidly emerging technology that will have a profound impact upon the future of human sexual relations."[41] Already on the market from manufacturer RealDoll: a selection of customizable, life-size dolls. If you are willing to shell out several thousand dollars for an artificially intelligent sex partner, you can dictate her body type, skin tone, eye color, hair and makeup style, and more. (The company does not currently offer male "companions.")

Dewing considers a potential impact of such AI devices growing increasingly humanlike:

> *Maybe the human race doesn't go extinct due to a sudden and fantastic catastrophe like nuclear war or an errant asteroid slamming into Earth. Maybe we'll just self-select our extinction by no longer procreating because we've stopped having sex with other humans and instead are having sex with advanced AI robots that have climbed their way out of the uncanny valley* and into our beds.*[42]

Getting under the sheets with us is about as intimate as technology can get. And it speaks to people's dissatisfaction with the current reality. As former Google CEO Eric Schmidt put it: "All of the people who talk about metaverses are talking about worlds that are more

* *Uncanny valley* is a term used by roboticists to describe the unsettling feeling people can get when they encounter an android that closely resembles a human but is not convincingly realistic.

satisfying than the current world—you're richer, more handsome, more beautiful, more powerful, faster. So, in some years, people will choose to spend more time with their goggles on in the metaverse."[43] Despite his position as one of the gods of Silicon Valley, Schmidt laments, "The world will become more digital than physical. And that's not necessarily the best thing for human society."[44]

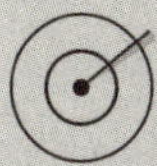

On the radar:

By 2038, we will see further development of "thought technologies"—apps and devices controlled by our minds. Already, in 2021, the U.S. Food and Drug Administration has authorized such a device that enables stroke patients to regain significant control over their hand-and-arm movements.[45] A scientist at MIT has even devised a headset that turns thoughts into speech.[46] Imagine traveling abroad and having your thoughts translated automatically into spoken words in another language. Cue privacy concerns: What happens when devices allow us to intercept the thoughts of others?

Verbal spats with our smart speakers. Kinky encounters with sexbots. Fantasies lived out in a virtual universe. Welcome to our new AI-mediated reality.

Imagine if there had been a pandemic back in 1989. How would we have handled weeks on end of sheltering in place before the internet? Reading books. Plenty of TV, supplemented with taped shows and movies. Phoning around. Maybe some writing, maybe some board games. But would there have been a safe way to keep businesses running, let alone schools?

What a difference thirty years has made. Imagine what the next thirty will bring.

Even before the COVID-19 crisis, hundreds of millions of people were choosing to live a lot of their lives remotely through screens. Yet, across cultures, many retained a sneaking feeling that screen-based living was a poor substitute, a lazy, morally inferior version of the "real life" that "should" take place face-to-face with physical objects in physical space.

The pandemic has fundamentally reframed that view, although there will always be some who lament the crossover. Place-independent living through screens became an essential workaround for the physical limitations of lockdowns. It became the only way that homebound people could carry on working, socializing, and learning. What might once have been a lesser option became the only option.

In April 2020, my partner celebrated Passover with his family—scattered from Tucson and Brooklyn to Melbourne, Australia—via Zoom. (I got a recipe for matzoh, which was hard to buy online at the last minute, from a British friend who shared it with me via WhatsApp.) The family had the option of sitting instead at a virtual Seder table with a whole host of celebrities—Jason Alexander, Ben Platt, Sarah Silverman, Harvey Fierstein, Tan France, Idina Menzel, Finn Wolfhard, and Josh Groban, among many others—as they celebrated Passover via storytelling, music, and comedy. The Saturday Night Seder did more than entertain and bring people together; it raised some $2 million for the CDC Foundation's Coronavirus Emergency Response Fund.[47] That same month, Pope Francis presided over Easter Sunday Mass online, and millions of users—not all Catholic—registered to watch that and other Holy Week broadcasts from the Vatican.[48]

The COVID crisis has shown all but the most committed Luddites just how useful screens can be for providing the necessities of life, including convenient and safe forms of social connection. We had the technology to enter into business and personal and educational relationships through screens well before the pandemic, but we rarely took advantage of it. Now, enough mindsets have shifted to make screens not just possible but potentially even preferable for many—and challenging for others. In other words, the COVID crisis has raised flashing-light question marks over many assumptions that were already in doubt.

What is the point of businesses running expensive offices when many employees can work just as well or better from home without wasting time and energy on commuting? (Counterpoint: Are the savings sufficient to offset the loss of community that comes from bringing workers together?) Why would organizations continue to incur the hefty financial and environmental costs of far-flung meetings when essential work can be achieved with videoconferencing? (Counterpoint: Can enduring client relationships be cultivated from a distance?) What is stopping secondary schools and universities from moving on from centuries-old teaching models and making better use of online methods that are less expensive and more effective? (Counterpoint: What happens when students in precarious situations are denied the support services typically offered in schools?) Why wouldn't more healthcare systems use video consultations and telemedicine technology to work more effectively and improve health outcomes? (Counterpoint: Will doctors miss physical indicators of ill health or fail to establish the levels of trust needed in times of crisis? Will mental health professionals be as adept at reading body language via screens?) With each digital advance, we have much to gain but also much to lose. How can we progress without inadvertently eliminating essential elements of the human experience?

It seems to me that the real question is not which aspects of life can move online but which cannot. Opportunity abounds for trusted brands to create portals to certified professionals across industries—medical, financial, legal, and more. Would you be more apt to hire a financial consultant certified by Google? A web designer verified by Apple? I would. In the absence of in-person interaction, the imprimatur of a trusted source instills confidence. A Switzerland-based friend was recently looking for a reliable dogsitter in the Netherlands; I sent her to the website I use in Connecticut to find someone competent to dogsit our goldens, Ben and Harley, when we are away for a weekend. A Lebanese friend asked me for advice on apartment-hunting in New York City; I sent him to the website through which I had found the one-bedroom apartment we gave up when I moved to Europe in 2018.

Recommendations from friends are vital, but so are reviews by strangers on sites such as TripAdvisor and Edmunds. A 2020 survey by BrightLocal found that 94 percent of respondents were more likely to use a business that has positive online reviews, while 92 percent were less likely to use one with negative reviews. Moreover, 79 percent of those surveyed said they trust online reviews as much as they do personal recommendations from family and friends.[49] It's a far cry from my parents' world, where recommendations came from the neighbor across the street or from familial experience that may have accumulated over decades. It also reinforces the heightened role of media affirmation of brands in building personal trust. Can I welcome you into my world? It's a question we will find ourselves asking with increasing frequency.

Conducting more of our lives via screens rather than face-to-face kept many of us physically safe during the pandemic. The flip side is that it made us digitally more vulnerable.

The digital environment has long been a breeding ground for human pathogens: fraudsters, scammers, phishers, spoofers, hackers, identity thieves, and disinformation agents. Until now, people's cybersecurity has been largely left to the private market, with companies providing protection and internet users buying it—or not. All too many users have woefully inadequate cybersecurity awareness and practices—the digital equivalent of not masking up or washing their hands.

As people and organizations move more of their lives online, we are at ever greater risk of a digital pandemic.

As people and organizations move more of their lives online, we are at ever greater risk of social alienation and the loss of human connection.

What feels like progress now may soon seem more like an erosion of individual development, life satisfaction, and societal wellbeing. The trick will be to proceed mindfully—but how good are we at that?

While our collective prospects feel less bright than most of us would like, getting a stronger grip on the forces arrayed against us and the trends taking shape on the not-so-distant horizon will better position us to make smart choices straightaway to create a future we can live with. And so we move now to the sightings that will inform those decisions.

PART FOUR

What's Next?

✳

Whatever was . . . is over. That TV series that everyone marathoned just a few weeks ago—do you even remember its name? That song that blanketed the airwaves and stubbornly adhered to your auditory cortex last winter—can you even hum it now? The celebrity news that rocked your world last year—does it even seem worth knowing anymore?

Hits and fads are ephemeral. Here today, gone tonight. True trends are different. Like a rocket, it takes enormous power for a trend to lift off and gather speed. Once aloft, it tends to stay aloft—at least for a while. And if it is powerful enough, it does not burn out but instead morphs into one or multiple new trends, changing our culture in the process.

One cannot fully understand trends without grasping the context in which they arise and grow. So I began this book by stepping back and looking at two crisis periods, two decades apart.

I started in 1999, focusing on technology—specifically, the global threat of Y2K. It never burgeoned into a true global crisis because nations and businesses took the problem seriously and spared no expense in solving it. They collaborated. Teams of programmers not only fixed the immediate problem but also looked ahead and improved computer functionality. Crisis averted. Future crises prevented. Relief palpable.

In the years since, the internet has developed from a narrow, rickety rope bridge to a multilane superhighway with feelers into virtually every nook and cranny of our lives. The golden age of communication is upon us: one world, connected; and yet we have come to discover that this interconnectivity is more fraught with peril than many would have imagined.

Two decades after Y2K, we faced another global crisis—only this one was not averted. COVID-19 was a medical mystery that forced citizens to shelter in their homes, businesses to lock their doors, and governments to close their borders. Science stepped up in a huge way, producing effective vaccines at record speed. And yet, even with masks mandated in most places, we saw the number of confirmed COVID deaths skyrocket from fewer than 4,000 on March 9, 2020, to more than 2.6 million as of that same date in 2021.[1]

The virus found a perfect vector in ignorance, suspicion, and disinformation. Conspiracy theories ran rampant, making it all the more difficult for scientific reason and restraint to break through. Depending on whom you believed, the virus was a natural phenomenon or one intentionally unleashed by China, Bill Gates, Jews, the European Union, or Big Pharma. Or else it was all a hoax—no worse than the seasonal flu. The vaccines? Obviously, according to some conspiracists, a false front by which microchips would be implanted into unsuspecting bodies, ensuring total control over the populace by the government—or by the much-maligned Bill Gates.[2] A post on the blog of the Foreign Affairs Intelligence Council (sounds legit, doesn't it?) warned that the mRNA COVID-19 vaccines authorized in the United States were designed to transform recipients into bioweapons factories containing "super-strain" variants that will be unleashed to kill the unvaccinated.[3] The pandemic is, the authors claim, part of a massive, nefarious plot. The shared goal of Dr. Anthony Fauci, the National Institutes of Health, and the Chinese Communist Party, according to these conspiracy spreaders: genocide.[4]

You might think outlandish theories of this nature would have a hard time gaining traction. You would be wrong. The reality is that fiction and fantasy spread fast, far, and deep thanks to social media.

It was not meant to be like this. The most popular social media platforms began with idealism at their core—at least if we are to believe their marketing. Facebook's 2009 mission statement was to "make the world more open and connected."[5] Fast-forward a dozen years, and founder and chairman Mark Zuckerberg is in the hot seat, his company accused of "pushing users toward extremism to increase their engagement with the site."[6] The platform is blamed for all manner of bad behaviors, from helping to incite violence in Ethiopia[7] to facilitating human trafficking[8] and fomenting the storming of the U.S. Capitol in early 2021.[9]

What went wrong?

People, mainly. Or, rather, techno-idealists' naïve notions about human nature.

By the time the COVID-19 virus escaped Wuhan in 2020, politicians, activists, rabble-rousers, con artists, and the paranoid, ignorant, and biased were already using social media to divide us and set us against one another. People died as a result.[10]

Americans are seeing unprecedented societal division—the greatest since the U.S. Civil War, it is said[11]—as we step further into the 2020s. The European Union, once regarded as a unifying regional force, is deemed "broken" by majorities in Austria, France, Germany, Italy, and Spain.[12] And around six in ten respondents surveyed by Pew Research in seventeen advanced economies across Asia-Pacific, Europe, and North America say their societies are more divided now than before the pandemic.[13]

And twenty years from now? Where will we find ourselves then?

Our target year of 2038 is not quite two decades from 2020, but it is close enough for our purposes.

In that year, experts have warned, we could see a variation on Y2K. Specifically, we will witness the end of Unix time—a way of tracking time in seconds that has been around since 1970. On January 19, 2038, any 32-bit computers still around would run out of numbers with which to store time. Those running on Unix time would reset to December 13, 1901, which 32-bit computers would not like at all. In my view, Y2038 is a potent metaphor for running out of time and space.

Some would argue that this is a trivial problem that will mostly affect devices not connected to the internet, unlike Y2K. More important, it appears to have been fixed—or at least put off until the year 2486—by a smart guy at Oracle named Darrick J. Wong.[14] Still, it is worth noting that some issues are cyclical in technology. And built into the operating system. And scheduled.[15] We would be naïve not to expect an abundance of conspiracy theories to arise in tandem with this potential technological time bomb. After all, we live in an era in which Neddy Games' Conspiracy Theory Trivia Board Game ("Tinfoil hat not included"[16]) has been released in three editions and multiple expansion packs since its creation in 2017. The game tests players' knowledge of internet conspiracies and includes QR codes to "uncover the truth." (I potentially could muster more concern over conspiracy theorist Bruce Cyr's *After the Warning to 2038,* prophesying civilization "running out of time," were it not preceded by his book *After the Warning 2016.* Then again, there are many who did consider 2016 an especially wretched year.)

There is another item on the calendar that will only cause limited problems, but it speaks to a broader issue. Brood X cicadas appear every thirteen or seventeen years. They appeared in 2021. They will be back in 2038. We tend to confuse cicadas with locusts. Beyond their sheer numbers and the noise they make—males trying to attract females—they have nothing in common. For starters, unlike locusts, cicadas can be eaten; in Chinese cuisine, chefs deep-fry the nymphs.

Why care about cicadas in 2038? Again, technology. Until recently, it has been difficult to predict their emergence with accuracy. In 2019, scientists devised Cicada Safari, an app that has been downloaded more than 150,000 times. By geotagging and uploading photos of the insects, observers in far-flung locations help scientists track "periodical" cicadas that have spent years underground.[17]

Thanks to technology, we can see that some of those highly evolved cycles of thirteen or seventeen years are shorter than they used to be. Because of climate change, they may shrink even further. The cicada is the new canary in the coal mine.

Writes Ian Frazier in *The New Yorker*:

> *The insects emerge when soil temperatures reach sixty-four degrees. What happens when that temperature starts being reached every January? Or when the soil never goes below sixty-four degrees? Our part of the planet may be too hot for today's cicadas' fourth-great-grandchildren, who will be coming a hundred and two years from now, in 2123.*[18]

Clearly, it is not only cicadas at threat. The World Wildlife Fund reports that species are being lost at a rate of between one thousand and ten thousand times higher than the natural extinction rate (the rate at which species would go extinct if humans did not exist).[19] The group estimates that between ten thousand and a hundred thousand species are dying out *each year.*[20]

Don't find that especially concerning? Perhaps you will if you take the time to consider this assessment by celebrated biologist Paul R. Ehrlich: "In pushing other species to extinction, humanity is busy sawing off the limb on which it perches." That warning adorns the walls of the American Museum of Natural History's Hall of Biodiversity in New York City. As we saw with the starlings released into New York City's Central Park, humans, plants, and all other life-forms compose an ecosystem, with each variable affecting all of the others. We can think of our near-term future in the same light. An action taken in 2025 will have repercussions in 2038, and there is no way to calculate precisely what those repercussions will be. The best we can do is remain mindful of that interconnectedness as we seek to prevent our world from spiraling out of control.

Throughout this book, I have touched on two significant factors that will shape our world in the next two decades: technology, a boon and a danger; and climate change, an issue so fraught that terror and activism are equally appropriate responses. Add a third megafactor: the long-term effects of the COVID-19 pandemic—not so much the health impacts as the shifts in how we work, learn, and live. And how we prioritize our lives.

Technology, climate, and pandemic: the three threads that will weave new patterns from the present to 2038 and beyond. Now that I have armed you with the content and context of the forces that have shaped society since 2000, I will introduce the ten megatrends that promise to determine our trajectory for at least the next two decades, along with dozens of feeder trends that will reinvent our personal and professional worlds.

Chapter 16

Our World in 2038

Even from my vantage point as an early adopter and trends diviner (I hate that term, by the way), I find it astonishing how thoroughly digitalization has transformed our world in just twenty years. In the late 1990s, if you wanted to stream a movie, you had to have your television set connected to a phone line, call to order a certain title, and then wait for it to connect.

According to a piece in *The Guardian,* Pamela Paul, editor of *The New York Times Book Review,* still rents movies from Netflix via DVDs sent in the mail.[1] I wasn't aware the option even existed anymore. She makes it a point to severely limit her (and her children's) digital use, still listening to music on CDs, sending checks via snail mail, and eschewing tablets. Like many of us, she laments all we have lost with our move away from the analog world, from the ability to navigate without a GPS to childhood boredom. "Boredom serves a function," she says. "When you have no input coming in, you generate output. That's how you become resourceful."[2] She hits on an issue of real concern to me: How can we raise new generations of creative, resilient kids when they are so connected to devices that they rarely have an opportunity to think deeply and create worlds of their own imaginations? Do children even have imaginary friends anymore, or have those been replaced by cartoon or video game characters and other figures streamed to them via their devices?

When I look ahead to 2038 and beyond, it is clear that the world today's youth will inherit is far more complex than I ever could have envisioned during my childhood days. Imagine the world into which *their* children will be born.

Growing up, my bookworm self was a big fan of *Treasure Island* and *Kidnapped,* and I think on occasion of a quote from their author, Robert Louis Stevenson: "Don't judge each day by the harvest you reap but by the seeds that you plant."

With this trends book, I seek to plant seeds that others will sow. So far, I have shared personal and professional insights into the sociopolitical, cultural, environmental, and technological trends that have shaped our lives over the past two decades and that will influence our tomorrow. I have come back again and again to several themes, and I present them here once more, as a collection of ten megatrends:

1. **Mother Nature is striking back, and she is angry as hell**—and has every right to be. The world is on fire, and the age-old conflict between humankind and nature is turning out to be a battle to preserve our planet and future.
2. **The chaos of now and next is turbocharged,** posing a constant challenge to our mental health and well-being. With multiple parts moving at hyperspeed, few reliable rules of engagement, and forces of chaos so persistent and powerful that we cannot adapt quickly enough to tame them, there is no such thing as certainty—or peace of mind.
3. **The world has two superpowers, and neither is equipped to deliver the future we need.** Both the United States and China are fumbling as they move fast to retain or gain ground in a battle for economic and political supremacy. The historic dominance of nation-states is increasingly unsustainable at a time when the immense challenges the world faces require global cooperation and sacrifice.
4. **Desperate times require plans born of desperation,** including a bunker mentality and a batten-down-the-

hatches *modus vivendi* (peaceful coexistence) mindset that includes exit strategies. Each of us is forced to ponder with whom and to where we will escape, how, and for what purpose.

5. **The pressure is on to establish clear swim lanes in a world increasingly blurred and blended.** Many boundaries are newly fortified even as other borders break down and absolutes become muddled and harder to enforce.
6. **Small becomes the new big** as we seek to savor the simplest pleasures and to master minutiae. A sense of manageable scale is an antidote to the stress of chaos and the speed of change.
7. **The new luxury is the simplest of all: breathing space.** Time to find oneself and to restore order in a world overloaded by the clutter of materiality, uncertainty, and emotional burdens has become a premium. We all crave a secure space—physical and mental—in which to absorb the trials and tribulations of modern life.
8. **Equity is the new battle cry.** Society is egregiously unbalanced in most respects, none more so than wealth and access to critical resources. A select few have an abundance, while the rest have an excess only of anger and resentment at the inequities of their lot.
9. **Identity is mutable.** Rigid gender roles and procrustean definitions of femininity and masculinity are giving way to a mix-and-match flexibility that simultaneously heals wounds and opens up battle fronts. Identities are cast in sand, not in concrete.
10. **Self is at the center.** With social and cultural institutions in flux, our focus has turned inward, emphasizing personal experiences, growth, and branding. People will endeavor to create or join new institutions and systems in which individuals "like them" are front and center—both to safeguard their interests and devise and implement what they consider the best solutions.

To varying degrees, these megatrends intersect and overlap, but each speaks to a radically changed environment in which humans are fighting to exert control, safeguard the future, and find authenticity and meaning.

The ten megatrends I have laid out will have an outsize impact on how we live, work, and think in 2038, both as a collective and as individuals. There will be other component trends, shifts, and developments that will challenge and shape us as well. I share here the ones I believe will be especially impactful.

Early-Warning Systems and Cybersurveillance

Jarred by the massive death toll, economic devastation, and social disruption of the pandemic, tech companies and health authorities worldwide will have collaborated to create contagion advanced warning systems (CAWS). Much as people used wearable fitness trackers in the 2020s, in 2038 they will use noninvasive individual CAWS technology that detects changes in bioindicators (e.g., oxygen saturation, inflammation markers) and aggregates the data to flag potential emerging infections. This will require a lot of guarantees (or compromises) related to confidentiality and civil liberties. And it will create big temptations for corporate interests, authorities, and criminals to abuse these systems.

To date, concerns about surveillance and abuse have not done much to slow the adoption of sensor-embedded bracelets and watches—used in some countries as health devices, and considered for use in others as mandatory ID bracelets that pick up on the wearer's pulse, temperature, and perspiration to permit more effective contact tracing. China, as noted earlier, appears to be working on perfecting the art of deep control, to the point of tracking facial muscle movements, vocal tone, body movements, and more to infer a person's feelings.[3] You had best be enthusiastic when viewing that portrait of Xi Jinping.

By 2038, more countries—and corporations—will be using technology to monitor responses to both political and commercial messages. Such technology already exists in Silicon Valley. It is not yet used for political control, but in seventeen years, it could be tapped in response to perceived threats.

Big Brother's street cameras and satellites can see you now—and probably hear you, too, if you use any form of connected device. Again, the technology is already in place, and societal permission to use it is growing. In 2038, surveillance will be much more pervasive. Because security.

The Robo-Revolution

The pandemic accelerated emerging shifts in the way people work and heralded new changes—all enabled by technology. Rapid advances in AI and robotics will revolutionize work and economies further. Many functions previously carried out by human workers, from manual labor to highly specialized tasks, will be accomplished faster and at far lower cost by machines. This will create extraordinary wealth for the relatively few people who create and control the machines, huge displacement for tens of millions of workers, and ingredients for explosive social and political conflict. After a lot of pain and experimentation, societies will create a New AI Deal. Among other measures, this deal will facilitate meaningful activities for those people—including displaced warehouse workers and delivery drivers—who no longer have conventional work. You do not have to be religious to believe that the devil makes work for idle hands. To feel genuinely connected to society, people require self-worth and a sense of how they are contributing.

Work: Beating the Clock

"Who first invented work and bound the free . . . to plough, loom, anvil, spade—and oh! most sad, to that dry drudgery at the desk's dead wood?" English essayist and poet Charles Lamb wrote those words in 1819.[4] Two centuries on, society is taking steps to forge a more sensible way forward.

In 2038, hybrid approaches, including various mixes of onsite and remote work, will be a ubiquitous component of life—as commonplace as a morning cup of coffee, the school run, food deliveries. "You're on mute" will remain part of the soundtrack of our everyday lives. For many, going to work will involve a commute only occasionally, if ever.

This reimagining of work practices means rethinking time. Across industries, the Monday–Friday industrial clock—working and schooling on a schedule created for industrial workers—will be replaced by asynchronous living. The luckiest among us will log on, work, and study when it suits our biological clocks, lifestyles, and household rhythms. We will recognize that "always on" only applies to e-commerce. Work will be continuous, but we will dip in and out of it, with coworkers contributing on a schedule that best suits them.

Conventional offices will still exist, but many will serve as community centers for collaborating, hosting events, and meeting clients and partners rather than as primary workspaces. The most productive organizations will equip their people with tools that allow them to drop in at will via digital technologies, so they can contribute their best from anywhere. Hours logged will still matter, but people will be judged primarily on their output—as used to be standard for white-collar workers before lawyers realized in the mid-twentieth century that they could make more money by charging by the hour.[5]

One hundred years after U.S. president Franklin Roosevelt signed the Fair Labor Standards Act of 1938, establishing a five-day, forty-hour workweek for many employees, a drop to a four-day workweek will be standard in many industries and countries. It has already been implemented with success in Iceland. And do not be surprised if those days are shorter. Already, an experiment conducted in Sweden has shown us that six-hour workdays can boost productivity, energy, and happiness.[6] Automation and job displacement, both of which are coming and fast, will mean that what remains of work culture, besides robots as colleagues, will be much less rigid.

There will come a day when parents have to explain to their children what a traditional office was like, or that a Monday-to-Friday nine-to-five, each day bracketed by a lengthy commute, was standard.

School Days

As with work, so with education. The forced global experiment of school closures and homeschooling during the 2020–21 lockdowns allowed us to recognize the positives and negatives of the approach and learn from our mistakes. In the future, younger (primary school) children may be the only age group that sits in a physical classroom four to five days a week—and that will be mostly to benefit their working parents and give youngsters the benefits of socialization. Older students will learn in online classes (provided the technology and bandwidth gaps are resolved), going into school at semiregular intervals to participate in extracurriculars. Academics will be more skills-focused, modular, and customized, with students accumulating certifications and work experience as they go.

We will still talk about "going to school," just as oldsters talk about "checking the answering machine" and "playing the tape." But in 2038, going to school may involve just going to the in-home or neighborhood study space where the interactive equipment is located. It will be a dramatically different experience from the internet education we now know. Thanks to extraordinary developments in haptic technologies—tech that stimulates the senses of touch and motion so you feel you are interacting directly with physical objects—remote learning will feel "real," paving the way for apprenticeships and virtual on-the-job training.

The key is—yes, that again—technology. With computers and connectivity nearing universal levels by 2038 (as of 2021, more than six in ten people worldwide are online[7]), digital learning will expand access to education to an extent unthinkable just a couple of decades earlier. This will be a game changer for those who in the past could not afford to leave home for college or were stuck within a substandard school district. *Upskilling*—the new buzzword—will see people buying education in affordable chunks. For some, the motivation will be credentials that lead to promotions, better jobs, and more money. For others, the impetus will be knowledge for its own sake, just because it feels good to build a new body of wisdom and understanding.

Fintech

As in many domains of life, technology will upend money. Most transactions, big and small, are already electronic—shifting 1s and 0s between digital ledgers. Still, those bytes represent traditional currencies—dollars, euros, yen, yuan, pounds, and more—issued and controlled by national governments. By 2038, cryptocurrencies will be increasingly the norm.[8] Some form of cryptocurrency may even replace the dollar as a global reserve currency.[9] Digital currencies' key point of appeal (and concern) is that they are neither issued nor regulated by national treasuries—which means they will be outside government control.[10]

With our lives going digital in pretty much every realm, it makes sense that cryptocurrency will be our go-to payment method. (Eric Adams, mayor of New York City as of January 1, 2022, asked to receive his first three paychecks in the form of bitcoin.) It also makes sense that it may fail spectacularly, and we will come to talk about it as the latest incarnation of failed currencies—à la Dutch tulip mania. A lot will depend on whether governments can prevent cryptocurrencies from undermining their ability to raise revenue and enforce laws.[11]

Tech Titans and Trillionaires

One of the many surprises to come from the pandemic was the massive increase in the wealth of a few—especially tech moguls. Several of the world's wealthiest made their billions building companies that were barely more than startups (if they existed at all) when Y2K was the big news. Now the world is looking to various branches of technology—medtech, edtech, cleantech, and biotech, to name a few—to address its most pressing challenges. Some of today's teens and early-twenty-somethings will become wizards in these fields and will join the ultrawealthy elite of 2038.

As the rich grow exponentially richer, the standards for who is considered truly wealthy will rise, too. Billionaires, not millionaires, will be the new benchmark of serious wealth, and there are even some who suggest that trillionaires will become a reality—starting with Tesla CEO Elon Musk.[12]

Addressing Inequity

If justice and common sense prevail, the poor—and those whose jobs were lost to automation or the elimination of entire industries—will be doing a bit better. A universal basic income[13] will have been implemented, funded primarily—though not voluntarily—by ultra-successful corporations, including those that gained wealth disproportionately during the pandemic. More people will embrace the notion that Robin Hood had it right all along—in his intentions, if not his methods. Taking from the rich to give to the poor is, as it has always been, the most direct way of helping the impoverished and balancing the scales of economic justice—in the process, shoring up social stability and cohesion. MacKenzie Scott's style of philanthropy will inspire other high-net-worth individuals to use targeted donations to drive social progress.

It's a Digifab Life

Until around 2025, people will shop for physical goods through the internet—goods that have to be warehoused, packaged, dispatched, and delivered. But as 3D printing becomes more sophisticated and affordable, an increasing number of physical products will be delivered directly via digital fabricators:[14] digifabs, or computer-controlled manufacturing machines. In 2038, many homes and offices will have them. We will come to curse our digifab machines just as previous generations cursed their ink-jet printers. And where would we be without the technicians who service and repair our digifabs and the companies that supply the raw materials? Thanks to this new print-as-you-need-it technology, the world will produce far less wasteful packaging. There will be many fewer cargo ships filled with plastic knickknacks moving across the world's oceans (or caught up in traffic jams at ports). Some of those vacant storefronts on Main Street—more on those later—

will prove the ideal place for digifabs to set up and serve the local community.

The Environment: Saved or Savaged?

Over the last two decades, scenes of plastics-choked waterways, disappearing glaciers, and distressed wild animals have created an abiding sense of emergency. The enforced slowdown and reduced travel of the pandemic gave us a glimpse of a world that had seemed impossible to re-create. As frantic human activity eased off in 2020, some highly polluted parts of the world saw blue skies.[15] Wildlife came out of hiding.[16]

By 2038, we may be treading more lightly on the earth as a result of the lessons learned during our great "anthropause." In two decades' time, the generation coming of age when climate activist Greta Thunberg burst onto the world stage will be well into adulthood—and increasingly in control of business, government, and culture. They will devise better paths forward. The phasing out of internal combustion engines and the temporary collapse of widespread air travel in the pandemic era, combined with the rapid development of renewable energy technologies, have created a new low-impact normal. More citizens than ever before will have ethical aspirations and seek to live in alignment with them. Smart technologies to measure individual carbon footprints will give citizens the means to see day by day what impact their actions are having on the spaces and species that matter to them. By 2038, scientists will have developed super-enzymes[17] from strains of plastic-eating bacteria,[18] finally getting a seemingly intractable plastics pollution problem under control.

As usual, some countries will be more attentive to the environment than others. Germany has already developed a plan to phase out fossil fuels entirely; by 2038, it will be at the end of its coal-burning days.[19] Finland will stop using coal as of 2029.[20] The United States has set a goal to reach 100 percent carbon-pollution-free electricity by 2035.[21]

What about employees of fossil fuel companies? If all goes according to plan, countries with a vestigial economic dependency on coal will have worked through the objections of the coal industry and upskilled their employees for jobs in new industries.[22] Some displaced workers will find careers in clean energy. Many will be put to work improving infrastructure that will have fallen into disrepair. Some members of the younger generation will be working in fields that did not exist in 2021. The artifacts of the now extinct coal industry will be relegated to museums around the world, with some mining regions getting a new lease on life as family vacation destinations.

Next-Gen Energy Sources

Technology will come to the aid of the planet with the widespread adoption of distributed generation and microgrids—local and even hyperlocal power generation. Most of the fundamental technologies have been around for a while: solar, wind, hydro, geothermal, biomass, biogas, and microkinetic devices. As with computers in the 1970s–1990s, the challenge has been to make these technologies smaller, more powerful, and more affordable, and then to network them. It is a challenge that will have been met by 2038.

The United Kingdom is one of the leaders in moving households over to sustainable sources of power. Already, through the government's Renewable Heat Incentive, homeowners receive quarterly cash payments over seven years for installing renewable heating technologies such as solar hot-water or biomass systems.[23] The Smart Export Guarantee program pays households to generate small amounts of renewable energy, which they export to the grid.[24] It's adding up: In 2020, just 1.8 percent of electricity in the U.K. was generated from coal, down from 40 percent a decade earlier, and the country is on track to reach net-zero carbon emissions by 2050.[25]

A Thirsty Planet

One of the most urgent ecological problems to be solved is drought. Potable water will be even scarcer and more valuable[26] in 2038; countries will go to war over it and even wield it as a weapon.[27]

Improved desalination technology will help developed countries meet the needs of their citizens, but those in less developed regions will be under severe water stress. Expect crops to fail, rivers and lakes to dry up, death in the desert, and mass migrations—even more of humanity will be on the move, and not by choice.

Who Wood Have Guessed It?

Not all climate-supporting technology is digital. Who would have thought that after the Stone Age, the Iron Age, the Bronze Age, and the Plastic Age, modern humans would usher in the Wood Age? With high-tech engineered timber, we will be able to live in a variation on the traditional wood-frame houses of past times—and in more complex modern wooden buildings, including high-rises.[28] Thanks to out-of-the-box ingenuity—as exemplified by a Japanese wooden satellite announced in 2020[29]—there are now few areas of life where wood has not gone some way toward replacing environmentally harmful concrete, plastic, and steel. As we have discovered, wood has multiple advantages over those materials. It is a renewable resource, it fixes carbon, it can be recycled—and it looks good. It is almost as if nature knew what it was doing.

Move Over, Meat

Biotech is also technology. Proponents of veganism used to say that if there were foods available that were cheaper than meat, tastier than meat, healthier than meat, and less environmentally harmful than meat, then nobody would want or need to eat meat. They will be proved right. Technologies for creating delicious, nutritious, lab-grown protein products are already reducing the need for commercial livestock in the most developed parts of the world. Some will insist that only animal meat is "the real thing," but their numbers will shrink every year. I can already foresee a time when restaurant-goers will need to request the special "meat menu" to satisfy their carnivore hankerings, much as people are able to request a vegan or gluten-free menu in some restaurants today. Mushrooms—a popular meat substitute—earned a spot as *The New York Times'* Ingredient of the Year for 2022, with a rise in urban mushroom farming forecasted.[30]

Meanwhile, the decline of the global livestock industry will have a significant beneficial effect on the environment. One difficulty: deciding on suitable names for these protein products. In the 2020s, protein technology companies boast that their "meat-free meat" has the taste and texture of this or that cut of this or that animal. By 2038, animals will no longer be the point of reference, as more consumers react to the association with revulsion.

Tree Chic

For as long as there have been cities, they have competed to garner prestige and residents. Which city has the tallest buildings? The richest arts scene? The best restaurants and schools? The most efficient mass transit? In the next two decades, we will see a different type of competition ramp up: Which is the greenest, healthiest, most sustainable city?

In a concrete jungle, trees bring bragging rights. They help to offset the heat-trap effects of concrete and tarmac. They filter air pollution. They boost happiness, reduce stress, and encourage city dwellers to get out and about. They reduce wind speed and absorb storm-water runoff.

Even prior to the COVID-19 pandemic and the attendant reevaluation of living spaces, Paris made plans to plant an urban forest around four historic sites. Seoul planted more than two thousand groves and gardens.

As the option of remote work beckons many city dwellers to greener locales, metropolitan leaders will inject more verdure into urban spaces to satisfy people's enthusiasm for nature and maintain the tax base. Atlanta, Georgia, prides itself on its reputation as the "city in a forest," but there is stiff competition for which city can claim the most extensive canopy. To help resolve some of the competing claims, Treepedia is building up a store of interactive city maps based on aerial images and street-view data. Leading in the rankings so far is Tampa, Florida (36.1 percent of its surface is covered by trees), but several other cities also boast canopies in excess of 25 percent; among them: Breda (Netherlands), Montreal, Oslo, Singapore, Sydney, and Vancouver.[31] Melbourne also is vying to make that list. It has announced plans to nearly double its canopy cover to 40 percent by 2040.[32] That is the point at which the maximum cooling benefits of trees start to kick in.[33]

Country Living

If you don't have to work in an office in the city, why live in the city? For that matter, why live in the suburbs? Why not step into your dream life at the end of a country road, a cottage on the beach, a houseboat in the Caribbean? With powerful communication technology and new ways of working, it is all suddenly possible.

We can already see this trend taking shape. Pre-pandemic, everyone wanted to be near places of work and entertainment, so competition for housing and services drove up prices and made cities the most expensive places to live. Now the countryside, with its smaller and less dense populations, its greenness, its fresh air, and, not least, its mythology, has become more desirable. We are more astute about security issues—both pandemic security and physical safety—and the countryside appeals on both counts. We are more attuned to the physical health benefits of clean air and the mental health benefits of natural vistas, "forest bathing,"[34] and walking barefoot on dirt, grass, or sand. Plus, the countryside has long appealed to survivalists and other preppers, who are growing in number.

Small-town Main Streets around the planet will have a renaissance. The stores that used to draw people to public spaces are mostly long gone, driven away by low turnover, unaffordable costs, and crushing competition from online retailers and mega-box stores just outside town. Now small cities and large towns are experimenting with new uses for their centers. In small towns, as in big cities, people can only endure so much virtual life; they want opportunities and places to hang out, to do things together.

How will city economies adjust to losing a chunk of their most affluent tax base? Will they find clever ways to lure young college graduates who previously could not afford life in the most expensive urban areas? Can rural areas absorb the urban migrants? Do they want to? And what measures will be put in place to discourage home building on plots that encroach on the wilderness or in areas especially susceptible to extreme weather events? Every migration—no matter in which direction—brings with it the potential for new challenges.

Staying Battle Ready

As I've mentioned, doomsday preppers and others seeking to live apart from the masses will be part of the population decamping to remote areas. I have talked about the rise of a bunker mentality for several years now—a trend that is in part a reaction to chaos as the new normal. At the extreme end of this trend are the doomsday preppers, many of whom have been stockpiling goods (and, in the United States, guns) for years.

COVID-19 promises to swell the ranks of preppers by both adding more hardcore adherents and incorporating regular folks who simply want to be ready for the next crisis. We can expect individuals to get a lot more serious about stockpiling (bottled water, canned food, fuel) and for businesses to step in to fulfill these new desires (while stoking our fears). Already, you can buy long-term emergency supply rations from Walmart. By 2038, it will be normal for upscale apartment complexes and housing developments to boast not just of their state-of-the-art gyms and fancy clubhouses but of their emergency preparedness. In the United States, we have seen small-town police forces outfitted with military vehicles, personal protective equipment, and other items more commonly spotted on the battlefield than during traffic stops. How long before upscale communities equip commando squads to patrol their perimeters?

Healthcare

For those who can afford it, advances in healthcare will offer cutting-edge cures and enhancements. With hundreds of millions of people desperate to counteract the effects of aging, geriatric research will top the agenda for medical and tech professionals.

Today's bioelectric implants—pacemakers to regulate heart rhythms and cochlear implants to improve hearing—are just a preview of what lies ahead. The brain—the seat of our operating system, if you will—may be the organ that offers the greatest potential to improve lives.[35] Computer-chip implants that can restore memory and repair damage due to injury, stroke, or Alzheimer's will be readily available.[36] Cellular transplant and regeneration offer the prospect of restoring function to people with spinal cord injuries.[37]

The fast-tracked COVID-19 vaccines introduced the masses to the wonders of mRNA technology.[38] In the coming decades, researchers will more fully tap the potential of mRNA drugs to tackle viral diseases. And with rapid advances in CRISPR techniques,[39] it is not outside the realm of possibility that noninfectious diseases such as cystic fibrosis, multiple sclerosis, and many types of cancers will be eradicated.

But the biggest prize will be reserved for treating the most widespread, costly, and deadly health conditions of the twenty-first century: type 2 diabetes, stroke, and cardiovascular disease, which cause 80 percent of the world's deaths from noncommunicable diseases.[40] There is little hope that affected populations will improve their lifestyles fast enough to make a difference; in fact, the trend is in the opposite direction. So it will be up to scientists to save the day.

Diseases of Despair

Not so long ago, mental health issues were widely considered shameful—an affliction to be hidden from employers, neighbors, and even family at all costs. Mental health was a taboo subject, broached only when discussing troubled geniuses such as actor and comedian Robin Williams or artist Vincent van Gogh. Now it is increasingly difficult not to talk about mental health, especially in light of the pandemic. More than four in ten people surveyed by the U.S. Census Bureau in December 2020 reported symptoms of anxiety or depression, an 11 percent increase over the previous year.[41] Similarly, the Office for National Statistics in the U.K. found 19 percent of respondents surveyed in December 2020 reporting symptoms of depression, nearly double the rate in that country just prior to the pandemic.[42]

Although COVID-19 exacerbated the problem, rising rates of anxiety, depression, substance abuse, alcohol dependency, and suicidal thoughts and behaviors regularly made headlines years beforehand (including in relation to social media use), with health authorities having dubbed the issue "diseases of despair."[43] A report from the UN noted that mental health disorders carry enormous social and economic costs, and that suicide is now the second leading cause of death among people aged fifteen to twenty-nine. Many of these people have no expert to whom to turn: Worldwide, there is less than one mental health professional for every ten thousand people. It is estimated that the global economy loses more than $1 trillion annually as a result of workers suffering from depression or anxiety.[44]

Between now and 2038, the world will get wiser about declines in mental health and will put more money behind finding solutions. We'll see fine-tuned apps that work with wearable neurofeedback devices such as Mendi and Muse. Therapy—whether online or in-person—will be seen as a standard implement in people's wellness toolboxes, not as something to conceal. And companies of all sizes will become more serious about putting support systems in place, including employee resource groups that foster diverse and inclusive workplaces and create a closer feeling of community.

Democracy in the Age of Disinformation

Maintaining control is no small matter for governments. The rise of cryptocurrencies, the concentration of massive wealth in the hands of a relatively small number of people, and the impacts of climate change represent severe threats to the stability and even viability of nation-states. While some countries may start or continue on the path to becoming totalitarian giants, others may succumb to fragmentation—breaking into smaller units to maintain ethnic or religious purity and stave off sectarian conflict.

Around the world during the first two decades of this century, we have seen a lessening of faith in democracy's ability to solve our most urgent challenges.[45] Two decades hence, democracy will no longer be assumed to be the best (or least bad) way to run the affairs of a country. Here, too, the impact of technology is evident.

As the COVID-19 pandemic illustrated, our consensus on reality is fragmenting. Twenty years ago, you and I may not have agreed on an issue, but we would at least have agreed on what constituted reality—aka the basic facts. Twenty years ago, there were people out there holding wacky beliefs about space aliens and cabals and conspiracies, but they were mostly isolated individuals or members of small groups. Now and in the future, those individuals and groups can easily find one another online and coalesce into groups of many millions. In a world where so much of reality is already virtual—mediated by screens—there is plenty of scope for people to hunker down in their separate realities with their unique sets of "alternative facts," as presented by their selected information gatekeepers.

The rapid development of deepfake technology will help to drive the evolution of these alternate realities.[46] Video and audio will be used to create invented scenes indistinguishable from the truth. Even the biggest lies can be spread with the imprimatur of "documented" visual proof.

For all the positive change driven by our newest generations of youth, the rise of deepfakes will make it even harder for governments and international bodies to muster enough popular support to tackle big issues such as climate change and species extinction. And the widespread adoption of nonstate cryptocurrencies will reduce government revenues. Democracy dies not just in darkness but also in discontent and disconnection.

The Mother Continent

With all eyes on a rising China, we sometimes overlook a landmass to its southwest that is larger than China, India, most of Europe, and the contiguous United States combined: the continent of Africa.[47] Africa is benefiting from the transformational technologies of the Fourth Industrial Revolution, a shift "characterized by a fusion of technologies that is blurring the lines between the physical, digital, and biological spheres," according to the World Economic Forum.[48] Research from the Brookings Institution in 2020 suggests that economic growth across Africa will continue to outperform that of other regions. At present, the continent is home to seven of the world's ten fastest-growing economies.[49]

While Africa has long maintained trading ties with Europe, China now accounts for nearly a fifth of its trade, and connections also are being developed across other parts of Asia, South America, and the Middle East.[50]

Between 2020 and 2050, the population of Africa will double. In 2050, the continent will be home to some 2.5 billion people,[51] half of whom will be under age twenty-five. Looking further ahead, to the next millennium: Africans will make up one-third of the world's citizens. And at the turn of the next century, nearly half of all the young people on the planet will live in sub-Saharan Africa.[52]

As city dwellers on other continents begin to heed the siren call of the countryside, Africa will move in the opposite direction, embracing urbanization. There are already as many cities in Africa with populations over a million as there are in Europe, and the continent is just as urban as China.[53] By 2030, half its population will live in cities,[54] boosting productivity and shifting the workforce from agricultural to industrial, high-tech, service, and manufacturing jobs. The film industry in Nigeria, known as Nollywood, produces some 2,500 films a year. Its output is already larger than Hollywood's and second only to that of Mumbai's Bollywood.[55] And the M-Pesa mobile payments company, which began in Kenya in 2007, is now seen as a world leader in mobile finance.

Africa is a land of great promise, but, as in India, its transition to a more modern economy will be slowed by a high infant mortality rate; low life expectancy (sixty-six years for females born in 2021 and sixty-three for males, compared with a global average of seventy-five and seventy-one years, respectively);[56] sluggish jobs creation; poor governance in some countries; and an acute vulnerability to climate change.

The Other Half of the Americas

No country's or region's future is cast in concrete. Destinies are dictated by how these entities make use of their advantages (e.g., natural resources, access to trade routes) and respond to externalities beyond their control. Who would have foreseen that South Korea, devastated by war throughout the 1940s and '50s, would become a wealthy, educated, and technologically advanced powerhouse? Who would have expected in the late 1970s that in barely two generations, China would go from political turmoil and poverty to being the world's second-largest economy with a growing middle class? What chance was there that Iceland, a poor, bleak, barely populated island in the North Atlantic, would develop into one of the world's most advanced information societies, replacing South Korea at the top of the ICT Development Index (measuring information and communication indicators)?[57] Similar "who would have expected" observations could be made about other countries, not least Japan, Ireland, Germany, Finland, and Singapore. One way or another, each of them overcame difficult conditions and defied expectations.

In South America, the trend—at least for now—is moving in the opposite direction. Venezuela was a wealthy country for several decades of the twentieth century until oil prices plummeted in the late 1980s. Economic problems led to political turmoil and the election of Hugo Chavez as president in 1998.[58] By the time he died in 2013, the economy had declined further, not least due to the impact of U.S. sanctions. Plagued by shortages and hyperinflation, around 4.6 million Venezuelans—approximately 16 percent of the population—have fled the country as economic refugees.[59] Like Venezuela, Argentina was one of the wealthiest countries in the world a century ago, but its position has declined ever since[60] through cycles of political instability, debt defaults, and hyperinflation extending into the twenty-first century. Despite the setbacks, it is still one of the largest economies in Latin America, with a GDP of approximately $450 billion and vast natural resources in energy and agriculture.[61]

So what is to come between now and 2038? The nations of Latin America range from the massive (Brazil, Argentina, Mexico) to the relatively minuscule (El Salvador, Costa Rica, Panama). Despite their many differences, all the countries are facing the future with more or less pronounced versions of the same impairments:

- **Political:** Weak institutions, unreliable governance, lack of political participation, and lurking violence and corruption
- **Economic:** Overreliance on raw materials, modest productivity growth, and low rates of savings and investment
- **Human:** Poor quality of education and low innovation capacity

Recent events in the United States have shown that democracy isn't invulnerable even in countries with a long history of civic engagement and political stability, let alone in less stable countries. For decades, many of the countries of Latin America have found it difficult to sustain stable political systems that enjoy widespread popular legitimacy and balance out competing interests. Instead, many have at some point fallen under the sway of strongman military dictators, either through coups or "democratic" takeovers that turned into dictatorships. Among them: Bordaberry in Uruguay, Stroessner in Paraguay, Castelo Branco in Brazil, Pinochet in Chile, Videla and Galtieri in Argentina, Noriega in Panama, and Ríos Montt in Guatemala. The region's people also have a track record of pinning their hopes on populists able to exploit disparities and resentment, notably Juan Perón in Argentina, Chavez and now Maduro in Venezuela, and Bolsonaro in Brazil.

By and large, these strongmen and dictators kept a lid on social unrest, although primarily through intimidation and human rights abuses. However, the outcomes indicate that the strongman formula is a dead end. It doesn't foster the sort of developments countries need to deal with current issues, let alone prepare for the future. We have seen evidence of this in Latin America's response to the COVID-19 pandemic; its infection and mortality rates are among the worst in the world.

As we consider the direction in which this region is moving, we see that support for democracy is declining among the populace, especially among the youngest group of voters and soon-to-be voters: those aged sixteen to twenty-four.[62] Describing democracy in Latin America as "on the ropes," the National Endowment for Democracy noted that the downward trend is exacerbated by "low trust in sources of information, including traditional news media and scientists."[63]

And yet, even with ongoing corruption scandals, resurgent violence, and the weak rule of law plaguing this region, I, like others, see reason for hope. Internet access in the region has given youth new pathways to success, and entrepreneurship is on the rise in all countries.[64] Optimism is also apparent among business leaders: The Mazars C-suite barometer found that 91 percent of C-suite leaders surveyed in Latin America expected their business revenues to increase in 2020, compared with a global average of 71 percent.[65] Reasons for a positive outlook include technological advances and the adoption of business models once the preserve of more advanced economies, including remote work.

The "Multi" Mandate

Multilateral. Multinational. Multilingual. Multiracial. Multiplatform. Multigenerational. The world is far too complex for individuals and organizations to tackle alone. It brings me back to a Woodrow Wilson quote I have shamelessly appropriated time and again over the years: "I not only use all the brains that I have but all that I can borrow." It's an approach I highly recommend.

In business especially, we will see a stronger emphasis on collaboration and cooperation. Cases in point: the nonprofit Accumulus Synergy, a data-sharing platform that has brought together ten biopharmaceutical companies (Amgen, Astellas, Bristol Myers Squibb, GSK, Janssen, Lilly, Pfizer, Roche, Sanofi, and Takeda) "to transform how drug innovators and health regulators interact to bring safe and effective medicines to patients faster and more efficiently"[66] and the Climate Collaborative, an independent organization made up of more than seven hundred companies working "[to leverage] the power of the natural-products industry to reverse climate change."[67]

I have every expectation that we will see an expansion of private-public partnerships such as we witnessed in the last century when General Electric teamed with NASA on Apollo 11.

Seen as a whole, the trends that will take shape and strengthen between now and 2038 speak to a world keenly attuned to threats to its long-term survival and to a broad awareness that the way things are now—the ways in which people work and live—are not how we want them to be in the future.

In some ways, this is promising. The first step to solving any problem is accepting that there *is* a problem, and there are very few people today who would claim the road ahead looks smooth. The numbers are terrifying, people are scared, and change is in the air. Now the hard work begins.

Conclusion

What's in It for Me?

Now that you have digested my analysis and predictions, it is time to consider how to apply these foresights to your unique circumstances and goals. The first step is to keep soaking in sightings and patterns. If you have learned anything from my travels through place and time, I hope it is to keep your ears and eyes open to the trends I haven't mentioned here or that have yet to burst forth on the cultural or sociopolitical scene. Be nosy, ask hard questions, don't accept the obvious, learn to discern between fleeting fads and enduring trends. Consider all the negative revelations but never forget to ask what's happening that is better, that you can embrace and enjoy. Inject optimism into your contemplation of the future, near and far. And determine what you can do today to create a life that offers more satisfaction for all.

In *The Global Village: Transformations in World Life and Media in the 21st Century,* Marshall McLuhan wrote, "The greatest discovery of the 21st century will be the discovery that man was not meant to live at the speed of light."[1] In 2020–21, much of the world stopped cold. As ever, that unleashed a yin-and-yang response. We hated that the world slowed down, and we loved that it gave us time to think, to fashion a new home life, to decide what mattered. Those of us able to work from home appreciated the change in environment even as we chafed against it. We were reintroduced to our families, deepened bonds with close friends, and let acquaintances we once considered friends drift away. We discovered new interests. We breathed deeply. We looked to the sky and wondered, perhaps for the first time, what our lives meant. And then, as more people became vaccinated and more workplaces reopened, some of us returned to a variation of life "before," and some adjusted to a hybrid "after."

Here is one last prediction: The dream scenario for many of us by 2038 may be the slow life—a life we sampled for several months in 2020 and 2021. We saw this trend start to emerge long before COVID-19 broke into the headlines. The slow movement, originally known as the slow *food* movement, began in 1986 on the Piazza di Spagna, at the foot of the Spanish Steps in Rome, with a protest over the opening of a McDonald's restaurant. It was an appropriate setting given that Italians are a people who embrace the expression *dolce far niente*—"the sweetness of doing nothing." A few years later, in Chianti, in Tuscany, Italy, Città Slow[2] was born to help cities and towns embrace a better quality of life by literally slowing down. Cities worldwide are now members of its global offshoot, the Cittaslow movement;[3] each commits to slower, more purposeful living and opposition to mass-produced culture.

"Slow" will become a rallying cry around the globe as more and more people who have achieved middle-class status reject the immense pressure of competitive lifestyles. (For the hundreds of millions of the world's most impoverished people, stuck in survival mode, these pressures would very much be considered a "first-world problem.") The lucky members of the consumer classes will organize themselves, along with their families and friends, around a philosophy the Nordics describe as "enough is as good as a feast" or "perfect-simple" or the trendy Danish concept of hygge. This "cozy togetherness," this safe space for social flow, has become what many of us seek as an antidote to our ever-increasing anxiety: a lifeboat from which we can more easily navigate the uncertainty of the future. This slower, quieter life is likely to be just the thing for the many parts of the world where older people will constitute a much larger proportion of the population—notably Europe, East Asia, and Latin America.[4] Chinese youth have begun to embrace a philosophy called *tang ping*—meaning "lying flat"—a response to the relentless pressure to work and excel.[5] Savoring time for oneself will be a version of luxury the many can afford.

I experienced a version of "lying flat" when I lived in Amsterdam in the 1990s. For this hyperkinetic American, it was eye-opening to experience sociable, unhurried evenings full of meaningful conversation and real connections. No networking, no scrambling to fit things in, no long lines; just time enjoyed with other perfectly imperfect humans. The kind of evenings where anxieties melt away. Twenty-five years later, I still crave the Dutch emphasis on authenticity, peace, sociability, and stability—and have tried with varying degrees of success to recapture it as I navigate a world that hurtles forward at breakneck speed.

No matter who you are, no matter what you believe, it is all but certain that you go to sleep wanting a safe place in which to wake up, a safe place for children and for people you care about. And people who care about you.

I was still living in Holland when my coauthor and I wrote *Next,* forecasting life and work in the new millennium. With the benefit of working at the cutting edge of the new connectivity (we were helping to create momentum for pioneering internet service provider AOL, which had gone global), we accurately foresaw the importance of the digital economy, the end of American hegemony, and the deterioration of so many of the invisible divides—home versus office, education versus entertainment, nutrition versus medicine—that had once delineated the various sectors of life. It was all beginning to blur. But what we missed completely was the rise of the self, or, more accurately, the rise of laser-focused selfishness that put the "Me decade" of the 1970s to shame.

By 2013, you could not miss the culture of self-absorption (*selfie* was *Oxford Dictionary*'s Word of the Year[6]). In a speech I gave in 2015, I predicted that *self* would be the word of the age—not on its own, but in combination: *self-portrait, self-parody, self-referential, self-obsessed. Self* runs like a red thread through the words that are written or spoken by everyone from pop culture icons and bloggers to the guardians of high culture.

Self-everything, I said at the time, is making itself felt everywhere. Fashioning a positive self-image is now recognized as a vital task for everyone, boosted by healthy measures of self-confidence, self-esteem, self-discipline, self-respect, and self-regard. In other words, self-promotion has become an essential tool for self-preservation. The trend becomes even more striking when we add *personal,* the slightly less self-referential sibling of *self*. Personal trainers, personal computers, personal development, and personal branding are all focused on the individual.

There is another side to the *self* coin: selflessness. Doing good has emerged as a critical component of feeling good and doing well. We embrace activism, allyship, and altruism because they offer satisfaction and connection and propel us forward in business and in the community.

The two competing strands here—selfishness and selflessness—pervade everything. This will continue. And it will accelerate, because as much as we want things to slow down, constant connectivity means we are always keeping score. At every moment, we are pushed to ask ourselves: Am I doing well? Am I doing good? For whom? Everyone on the planet? My community? Or just myself?

Our unending stress may drive us toward a more streamlined approach to what we want, to how much we can manage, to what we can take on—and to a greater willingness to let technology go where it has thus far gone only in science fiction. In 2005, inventor and futurist Ray Kurzweil envisioned the late 2030s as a future in which "mind uploading" is mainstream and "nanomachines" are installed in the brain to receive signals.[7] As for the remainder of the 2020s, Kurzweil foresaw that computers would be capable of "autonomously learning and creating new knowledge"[8] and that supercomputing would be accessible to most: "A $1,000 U.S. personal computer will be a thousand times more powerful than the human brain."[9]

Expect this counterbalance, this duality: slow and cozy, humane, selfless, and warm on one side and turbocharged, self-obsessed, and mechanical on the other.

Frank R. Stockton's "The Lady, or the Tiger?," published in 1882, is a story that has been read to generations of children. It is set in a land ruled by a king who is sometimes cruel, sometimes humane. He devises a unique way to dispense justice: A man accused of a crime is brought to an arena. There are two closed doors, both soundproof. Behind one is a woman considered a suitable match; if he chooses that door, he gets to marry her. Behind the other door is a ravenous tiger; if he opens it, he is lunch. Slaughter? A wedding? Which will chance drive the man to choose?

His situation is like ours, but only to a point. We have history, and we know how we got to this moment. We do not have to choose blindly and hope we get lucky. We can take actions that will see us safely out of the arena. Among the most critical: reassessing our definitions of success and our material ambitions; addressing the mental health challenges that result from the chaos of modern life; forging a new, more sustainable relationship with planet Earth; reducing inequities of gender, race, and wealth; creating stability and certainty by setting smart boundaries; prioritizing collaboration over competition; and balancing our sense of self with a sense of community. There is much to do and two radically different futures before us, one a vision of progress and the other of doom.

By 2038, we will know which door we have chosen.

Acknowledgments

I am forever indebted to Jesse Kornbluth, writer and thinker and Renaissance man, who coached, coaxed, and helped me craft this book over more than one year, working with me remotely except for one long lunch at a Connecticut diner in the spring of 2021, right after we had both been vaccinated. Without Jesse—an intellectual and storyteller who took the time to immerse himself in the art and science of trendspotting—this book would be far less filled with color, charm, and charisma.

Special thanks to those who inspired me and whose brilliant input can be found within these pages. They include global colleagues, family, and friends: Iro Antoniadou (Switzerland), Angie Argabrite (United States), Matteo Bendotti (France), Jackie Bruno Finley (United States), Arthur and Melissa Ceria (United States), Aaron, Isabelle, and Reuben Diamond (United States), Victor Friedberg (United States), Loren and Stuart Harris (England), Emily Irgang (United States), Lutfy Mufarrij (Lebanon), Fernanda Romano (Brazil), Aaron Sherinian (United States), Jody Sunna (Switzerland), and Claire Woodruff (United States). While all the mistakes and dud predictions are mine alone, I am so lucky to be surrounded by smart observers of life, now and next. Seth Goldenberg of Epic Decade in Rhode Island has been an incredible ally and friend through every step of the creation of *The New Megatrends*. His generosity in introducing me to David Drake (and Paul Whitlatch and Katie Berry) launched my epic journey backward and forward. Crown's Paul and Katie have been masterful editors, pushing me hard to sharpen my observations and to fine-tune the prose.

In the middle of writing this book, I got the news that a third brain tumor would need to come out. Surgery at Boston's Brigham and Women's Hospital was scheduled for December 2020 and then postponed due to COVID-19 to March 2021. Thanks to the talents of Drs. Ossama Al-Mefty and Walid Ibn Essayed, among others, I was back at the computer reading, researching, and writing seventy-two hours after they removed my latest meningioma.

André and Margaret Calantzopoulos, Jacek and Iwona Olczak, Suzanne Rich Folsom, Charles Bendotti, Deepak Mishra, Gregoire Verdeaux, Nevena Crljenko, Silke Muenster, Jennifer Motles Svigilsky, Steve Rissman, and other colleagues and their families worldwide have been a source of comfort and inspiration over these last three and a half years. During the pandemic, they have shown me that the inevitable blurring of life and work can be joyful and productive, even when so much of it occurs via a computer screen.

My executive assistant, Fleur Dusée, ensures that both my work and life work; without her, I would be lost. Special thanks, too, to Friso and Toni Westenberg and their family for their friendship and support over the last year and a half. Having Dutchies in Lausanne is a joy. I am also deeply grateful to my colleagues from my past jobs at Havas and Omnicom and WPP, who continue to be a huge support system and great sounding boards, none more so than Donna Murphy, Shazzia Khan, Bob Jeffrey, Colette Chestnut, and Bob Kuperman.

This publication has its roots in earlier books I coauthored on trends. Ira Matathia and Ann O'Reilly made me a much better trendspotter and strategic thinker. Ann's genius is felt in all my work and has been for almost thirty years. (Where has the time gone?) This book also draws from my annual trend reports, which have been made so much better in recent years by Dr. Moira Gilchrist, Tommaso Di Giovanni, Jason Mills, Bessie Kokalis Pescio, Bryson Thornton, Julia Shpeter, Adam Vincenzini, David Fraser, Corey Henry, and their global teams, who have ensured my relevance from Albania and Bulgaria to Korea and Vietnam. Jody Sunna and then the team at CNN Digital set me on the path to 2038 with a timely interview in the early days of COVID. (Who knew an off-the-cuff answer would lead me to the hypothesis that we were feeling the impact of Y2K twenty years late?) My graduate studies in government at the Johns Hopkins University refined my thinking style and research skills considerably—and took me to that special place I had been happily decades ago, during my undergraduate years at Brown University.

Finally, I am deeply grateful for a supportive family that has endured years of my life on the road. Thank you to all the Diamonds, but especially to Jim; to Patsy Jones, who has moved with us one too many times; to my sister Jane Zemba and her family; and to Dr. Steve and Tracy Curtin and their children, who have become our Tucson family. You are my link to American life, to real-world issues such as hurricane and wildfire warnings and pandemic grocery shortages, and to the demands of the present, which would often escape me because I am lost in a "to-do" list that never seems to grow shorter and in the endless newsfeeds in which I am frequently submerged.

—Marian Salzman, Switzerland, Connecticut, and the cloud

Notes

Introduction

1. Clay Risen, "John Naisbitt, Business Guru and Author of *Megatrends,* Dies at 92," *The New York Times,* April 14, 2021.

2. Ibid.

3. Thomas Ling, "Starling Murmurations: Why Do They Form and How Can I See One?," *Science Focus,* March 19, 2021, sciencefocus.com/nature/starling-murmurations/.

4. Simone Ross, "Whatever Happened to the Internet's Promise?," *Techonomy,* March 1, 2017, techonomy.com/2017/03/whatever-happened-to-the-internets-promise/.

5. Miguel Niño-Zarazúa, Laurence Roope, and Finn Tarp, "Global Inequality: Relatively Lower, Absolutely Higher," *Income and Wealth* 63, no. 4 (2017): 661–84, onlinelibrary.wiley.com/doi/full/10.1111/roiw.12240.

6. Doris and John Naisbitt, *Mastering Megatrends: Understanding & Leveraging the Evolving New World* (Singapore: World Scientific, 2018), 35.

7. Zachary Laub, "Hate Speech on Social Media: Global Comparisons," Council on Foreign Relations, June 7, 2019, cfr.org/backgrounder/hate-speech-social-media-global-comparisons.

8. Martin Luther King, Jr., "Letter from Birmingham Jail" (excerpt), World History Archives, hartford-hwp.com/archives/45a/060.html.

9. Paul Bischoff, "Surveillance Camera Statistics: Which Cities Have the Most CCTV Cameras?," *Comparitech,* May 17, 2021, comparitech.com/vpn-privacy/the-worlds-most-surveilled-cities/.

10. Robin McKie, "The Vaccine Miracle: How Scientists Waged the Battle Against Covid-19," *The Guardian,* December 6, 2020.

11. "Will an mRNA Vaccine Alter My DNA?," Gavi, December 15, 2020, gavi.org/vaccineswork/will-mrna-vaccine-alter-my-dna.

12. Sarah Marsh, "Essays Reveal Stephen Hawking Predicted Race of 'Superhumans,'" *The Guardian,* October 14, 2018.
13. "Urban Population to Become the New Majority Worldwide," Population Reference Bureau, July 18, 2007, prb.org/resources/urban-population-to-become-the-new-majority-worldwide/.
14. Jeff Desjardins, "This Is What the Cities of the Future Could Look Like," World Economic Forum, January 9, 2019, weforum.org/agenda/2019/01/the-anatomy-of-a-smart-city.
15. Samantha Schmidt, "1 in 6 Gen Z Adults Are LGBT. And This Number Could Continue to Grow," *The Washington Post,* February 24, 2021.
16. Pudgy Penguins, pudgypenguins.io/.
17. MacKenzie Sigalos, "China's War on Bitcoin Just Hit a New Level with Its Latest Crypto Crackdown," CNBC, July 7, 2021.
18. Midnight Trains, midnight-trains.com/en/home.

PART ONE

1. "Word of the Year 2016," Oxford Languages, languages.oup.com/word-of-the-year/2016/.
2. Kendrick McDonald, "Unreliable News Sites More Than Doubled Their Share of Social Media Engagement in 2020," NewsGuard, newsguardtech.com/special-report-2020-engagement-analysis/.
3. Mark Jurkowitz and Amy Mitchell, "Early in Outbreak, Americans Cited Claims About Risk Level and Details of Coronavirus as Made-Up News," Pew Research Center, April 15, 2020, pewresearch.org/journalism/2020/04/15/early-in-outbreak-americans-cited-claims-about-risk-level-and-details-of-coronavirus-as-made-up-news.
4. Arundhati Roy, "The Pandemic Is a Portal," *Financial Times,* April 3, 2020.
5. Katie Weston et al., "Shelves Empty Across UK," *Daily Mail,* October 9, 2021.
6. Lauren Lewis, Chris Jewers, and Amie Gordon, "Energy Crisis Grips the World," *Daily Mail,* October 9, 2021.

Chapter 1

1. "Timeline of Computer History," Computer History Museum, computerhistory.org/timeline/memory-storage/.

2. Barnaby J. Feder, "The Town Crier for the Year 2000," *The New York Times,* October 11, 1998.
3. Ibid.
4. "Y2K Bug," *Encyclopaedia Britannica,* britannica.com/technology/Y2K-bug.
5. Jack Schofield, "The Millennium Bug: Special Report," *The Guardian,* January 4, 2000.
6. "Y2K Bug," *National Geographic,* Resource Library, Encyclopedia, nationalgeographic.org/encyclopedia/Y2K-bug/.
7. Luke Jones, "How the UK Coped with the Millennium Bug 15 Years Ago," BBC News, December 31, 2014.
8. "What Will Happen When the Clock Strikes Midnight," Greenspun Family Server, greenspun.com/bboard/q-and-a-fetch-msg.tcl?msg_id=00241S.
9. Kelsey Campbell-Dollaghan, "20 Years Ago, the World as We Know It Was Born," *Fast Company,* December 9, 2019.
10. *Will Y2K Snarl Global Transportation? Field Hearing Before the Special Committee on the Year 2000 Technology Problem,* 106th Cong. Rec. S344 (September 30, 1999), govinfo.gov/content/pkg/CHRG-106shrg62346/html/CHRG-106shrg62346.htm.
11. Lee Davidson, "Bennett to Lead 'Millennium Bug' Battle," *Deseret News,* April 29, 1998, deseret.com/1998/4/29/19377250/bennett-to-lead-millennium-bug-battle.
12. Daniel Patrick Moynihan, "Countdown to a Meltdown," Congressional Record Volume 142, Number 129, September 18, 1996, govinfo.gov/content/pkg/CREC-1996-09-18/html/CREC-1996-09-18-pt1-PgS10871-2.htm.
13. Betsy Hart, Scripps Howard News Service, "Christian Y2K Alarmists Irresponsible," *Deseret News,* February 12, 1999.
14. Ibid.
15. "Computer Doomsday Scenarios: Much Ado About Nothing?," Retro Report, July 22, 2018, retroreport.org/transcript/computer-doomsday-scenarios-much-ado-about-nothing/.
16. Jones, "How the UK Coped."
17. Marty Langley, "Cashing In on the New Millennium: How the Firearms Industry Exploits Y2K Fears to Sell More Guns," Violence Policy Center, December 1999, ojp.gov/ncjrs/virtual-library/abstracts/cashing-new-millennium-how-firearms-industry-exploits-y2k-fears.
18. Kate Snow, "FEMA Makes Y2K Recommendations," CNN, March 22, 1999.

19. Edward Yourdon and Robert A. Roskind, *The Complete Y2K Home Preparation Guide* (Hoboken, N.J.: Prentice Hall, 1999).
20. Mark Harris, *Mike Nichols: A Life* (New York: Penguin Press, 2021), 305.
21. Francine Uenuma, "20 Years Later, the Y2K Bug Seems Like a Joke—Because Those Behind the Scenes Took It Seriously," *Time*, December 30, 2019.
22. Matt Gilligan, "People Share Their Most Memorable Stories from Y2K," Did You Know?, didyouknowfacts.com/people-share-their-most-memorable-stories-from-y2k/.
23. George Takei staff, "People Recall Their Craziest Y2K Experiences," January 9, 2020, georgetakei.com/people-recall-their-craziest-y2k-experiences-2644350926/dang.
24. Gilligan, "People Share Their Most Memorable Stories from Y2K."
25. National Commission on Terrorist Attacks upon the United States, "Foresight—and Hindsight," *The 9/11 Commission Report* (U.S. Government Printing Office, 2004), 339–60, fas.org/irp/offdocs/911comm-sec11.pdf.
26. Adam Shell, "13 Years After 9/11, Markets Face New Threat," *USA Today*, September 10, 2014.
27. Farhad Manjoo, "How Y2K Offers a Lesson for Fighting Climate Change," *The New York Times*, July 19, 2017.
28. "Bill Gates TED Talk Transcript from 2015: Warns of Pandemics, Epidemics," Rev, rev.com/blog/transcripts/bill-gates-ted-talk-transcript-from-2015-warns-of-pandemics-epidemics.
29. George W. Bush, "George W. Bush Warned of Not Preparing for Pandemic in 2005," ABC News, April 20, 2020, YouTube, youtube.com/watch?v=spcj6KUr4aA.
30. "Hear What Barack Obama Said in 2014 About Pandemics," *Don Lemon Tonight*, CNN video, April 10, 2010, cnn.com/videos/politics/2020/04/10/barack-obama-2014-pandemic-comments-sot-ctn-vpx.cnn.
31. Victoria Knight, "Obama Team Left Pandemic Playbook for Trump Administration, Officials Confirm," *PBS NewsHour*, May 15, 2020.
32. Nick Bryant, "The Time When America Stopped Being Great," BBC News, November 3, 2017.
33. "Jair Bolsonaro, Brazil's President, Is a Master of Social Media: But to What End?," *The Economist*, March 16, 2019.
34. Bobby Azarian, "An Analysis of Trump Supporters Has Identified 5 Key Traits," *Psychology Today*, December 31, 2017.

35. Stephan Lewandowsky, Michael Jetter, and Ullrich K. H. Ecker, "Using the President's Tweets to Understand Political Diversion in the Age of Social Media," *Nature Communications* 11 (2020), nature.com/articles/s41467-020-19644-6.
36. David Klepper, "Viral Thoughts: Why COVID-19 Conspiracy Theories Persist," AP News, April 6, 2021.
37. David M. Cutler and Lawrence H. Summers, "The COVID-19 Pandemic and the $16 Trillion Virus," *JAMA* 324, no. 15 (2020): 1495–96, jamanetwork.com/journals/jama/fullarticle/2771764.
38. James K. Jackson et al., "Global Economic Effects of COVID-19," Congressional Research Service, updated November 10, 2021, sgp.fas.org/crs/row/R46270.pdf.
39. S. O'Dea, "Forecast Number of Mobile Devices Worldwide from 2020 to 2025," Statista, September 24, 2021, statista.com/statistics/245501/multiple-mobile-device-ownership-worldwide/.
40. Susan Wojcicki, "YouTube at 15: My Personal Journey and the Road Ahead," *YouTube Official Blog,* February 14, 2020, blog.youtube/news-and-events/youtube-at-15-my-personal-journey/.

Chapter 2

1. Kris Epley, "Residents Stockpile Supplies in Fear of Y2K Chaos," *The Grand Island Independent,* August 29, 1999, theindependent.com/news/residents-stockpile-supplies-in-fear-of-y-k-chaos/article_1789cb1b-2e95-5a80-a36a-92fd93cf993e.html.
2. Duncan Green, "Of the World's Top 100 Economic Revenue Collectors, 29 Are States, 71 Are Corporates," From Poverty to Power, August 3, 2018, oxfamblogs.org/fp2p/of-the-worlds-top-100-economic-entities-29-are-states-71-are-corporates/.
3. "Facts: Global Inequality," Inequality.org, inequality.org/facts/global-inequality.
4. Noah S. Diffenbaugh, "Verification of Extreme Event Attribution: Using Out-of-Sample Observations to Assess Changes in Probabilities of Unprecedented Events," *Science Advances* 6, no. 12 (2020), advances.sciencemag.org/content/6/12/eaay2368.
5. "Obesity and Overweight," World Health Organization, June 9, 2021, who.int/news-room/fact-sheets/detail/obesity-and-overweight.
6. Eleanor Bird, "Latest Evidence on Obesity and COVID-19," *Medical News Today,* May 6, 2020, medicalnewstoday.com/articles/latest-evidence-on-obesity-and-covid-19.
7. Nicole Lyn Pesce, "This Is the Most Anti-vaxxer Country in the World," MarketWatch, June 19, 2019.

8. Leah Selim, "Measles Explained: What's Behind the Recent Outbreaks?," UNICEF, December 5, 2019, unicef.org/stories/measles-explained-whats-behind-recent-outbreaks.
9. "New Measles Surveillance Data for 2019," World Health Organization, May 15, 2019, who.int/immunization/newsroom/measles-data-2019/en/.
10. Robert Barnes, "Supreme Court Says Gay, Transgender Workers Protected by Federal Law Forbidding Discrimination," *The Washington Post,* June 15, 2020.
11. A. Tarantola, "Social Media Bots Are Damaging Our Democracy," Engadget, August 15, 2019, engadget.com/2019-08-15-social-media-bots-are-damaging-our-democracy.html.
12. "Internet/Broadband Fact Sheet," Pew Research Center, April 7, 2021, pewresearch.org/internet/fact-sheet/internet-broadband/.
13. Ibid.
14. Emily Sullivan, "Why Aren't Millennials Spending? They're Poorer Than Previous Generations, Fed Says," NPR, November 30, 2018.
15. Brian Pascus and Benjamin Zhang, "Here Are 11 of the Worst Commutes in the World Where Drivers Can Spend More Than 100 Hours a Year Stuck in Traffic," *Insider,* February 1, 2019.
16. "World Bank and WHO: Half the World Lacks Access to Essential Health Services," World Health Organization, December 13, 2017, who.int/news-room/detail/13-12-2017-world-bank-and-who-half-the-world-lacks-access-to-essential-health-services-100-million-still-pushed-into-extreme-poverty-because-of-health-expenses.

Chapter 3

1. S. M. Enzler, "History of the Greenhouse Effect and Global Warming," Lenntech, lenntech.com/greenhouse-effect/global-warming-history.htm.
2. "Declaration of the World Climate Conference," World Meteorological Organization, February 1979, dgvn.de/fileadmin/user_upload/DOKUMENTE/WCC-3/Declaration_WCC1.pdf.
3. Hearing Before the Committee on Energy and Natural Resources U.S. Senate First Session on the Greenhouse Effect and Global Climate Change, 100th Cong. (1988) (statement of Dr. James Hansen, Director, NASA Goddard Institute for Space Studies), pulitzercenter.org/sites/default/files/june_23_1988_senate_hearing_1.pdf.

4. Philip Shabecoff, "Global Warming Has Begun, Expert Tells Senate," *The New York Times,* June 24, 1988.
5. Hamish MacPherson, "Angus Smith, a Glaswegian Pioneer of Environmental Chemistry Should Be Recognised," *The National,* February 14, 2021, thenational.scot/news/19089019.angus-smith-glaswegian-pioneer-environmental-chemistry-recognised/.
6. "Heat and Health," *The Lancet* 398, no. 10301 (August 19, 2021), thelancet.com/series/heat-and-health.
7. Xinran Wang, Anthony Leiserowitz, and Jennifer Marlon, "Explore Climate Change in the American Mind," Yale Program on Climate Change Communication, March 31, 2021, climatecommunication.yale.edu/visualizations-data/americans-climate-views/.
8. "The Peoples' Climate Vote," United Nations Development Programme, January 26, 2021, undp.org/publications/peoples-climate-vote.
9. "Confusion Is the Main Reason Europeans and Americans Underestimate Climate Crisis, Open Society Report Finds," Open Society European Policy Institute, November 20, 2020, opensocietyfoundations.org/newsroom/confusion-is-the-main-reason-europeans-and-americans-underestimate-climate-crisis-open-society-report-finds.
10. "Peoples' Climate Vote."
11. Lizzie Widdicombe, "The Moms Who Are Battling Climate Change," *The New Yorker,* April 12, 2021.
12. Ibid.
13. Ibid.
14. Marta Rodriguez Martinez and Lillo Montalto Monella, "Extreme Weather Exiles: How Climate Change Is Turning Europeans into Migrants," Euronews, June 17, 2020, euronews.com/2020/02/26/extreme-weather-exiles-how-climate-change-is-turning-europeans-into-migrants.
15. Ibid.
16. Ibid.
17. Annie Ropeik, "Americans Are Moving to Escape Climate Impacts. Towns Expect More to Come," NPR, January 22, 2021.
18. Christiana Figueres and Tom Rivett-Carnac, "What the World Will Look Like in 2050 If We Don't Cut Carbon Emissions in Half," *Time,* April 22, 2020.
19. Philip Alston, "World Faces 'Climate Apartheid' Risk, 120 More Million in Poverty," UN News, June 25, 2019, news.un.org/en/story/2019/06/1041261.

20. Marina Romanello et al., "The 2021 Report of the *Lancet* Countdown on Health and Climate Change: Code Red for a Healthy Future," *The Lancet* 398 (2021): 1619–62, thelancet.com/action/showPdf?pii=S0140-6736%2821%2901787-6.
21. "Climate Change in Bangladesh: Impact on Infectious Diseases and Mental Health," The World Bank, October 7, 2021, worldbank.org/en/news/feature/2021/10/07/climate-change-in-bangladesh-impact-on-infectious-diseases-and-mental-health.
22. Tik Root, "Earth Is Now Trapping an 'Unprecedented' Amount of Heat, NASA Says," *The Washington Post,* June 16, 2021.
23. Fiona Harvey, "'The Next Pandemic': Drought Is a Hidden Global Crisis, UN Says," *The Guardian,* June 17, 2021.
24. Ibid.
25. Ibid.
26. "Drought—September 2021," National Centers for Environmental Information, October 13, 2021, ncdc.noaa.gov/sotc/drought/202109.
27. Sarah Kaplan and Cassidy Araiza, "How America's Hottest City Will Survive Climate Change," *The Washington Post,* July 8, 2020.
28. Kirk Siegler, "Colorado River, Lifeline of the West, Sees Historic Water Shortage Declaration," *All Things Considered,* NPR, August 22, 2021.
29. "Facts + Statistics: Wildfires," Insurance Information Institute, iii.org/fact-statistic/facts-statistics-wildfires.
30. "Wildfires," California Air Resources Board, ww2.arb.ca.gov/our-work/programs/wildfires.
31. Lisa Richards, Nigel Brew, and Lizzie Smith, "2019–20 Australian Brushfires—Frequently Asked Questions: A Quick Guide," Parliament of Australia, March 12, 2020, aph.gov.au/About_Parliament/Parliamentary_Departments/Parliamentary_Library/pubs/rp/rp1920/Quick_Guides/AustralianBushfires.
32. "Australia Marks Quietest Fire Season in a Decade," CNN, March 31, 2021.
33. Christianna Silva, "Food Insecurity in the U.S. by the Numbers," NPR, September 27, 2020.
34. "The State of Food Security and Nutrition in the World 2021: The World Is at a Critical Juncture," Food and Agriculture Organization of the United Nations, fao.org/state-of-food-security-nutrition.
35. "FACT SHEET: President Biden Sets 2030 Greenhouse Gas Pollution Reduction Target Aimed at Creating Good-Paying Union

Jobs and Securing U.S. Leadership on Clean Energy Technologies," White House Briefing Room, April 22, 2021, whitehouse.gov/briefing-room/statements-releases/2021/04/22/fact-sheet-president-biden-sets-2030-greenhouse-gas-pollution-reduction-target-aimed-at-creating-good-paying-union-jobs-and-securing-u-s-leadership-on-clean-energy-technologies/.

36. Fiona Harvey, "UK Vows to Outdo Other Economies with 68% Emissions Cuts by 2030," *The Guardian*, December 4, 2020.

37. Julian Wettengel, "Spelling Out the Coal Exit—Germany's Phase-Out Plan," *Clean Energy Wire*, July 3, 2020, cleanenergywire.org/factsheets/spelling-out-coal-phase-out-germanys-exit-law-draft.

38. Eloise Gibson and Olivia Wannan, "'The Government Will Not Hold Back': Jacinda Ardern on How NZ Could Go Zero Carbon," *Stuff* (NZ), January 31, 2021.

39. World Business Council for Sustainable Development, *Vision 2050: Time to Transform*, March 2021, wbcsd.org/contentwbc/download/11765/177145/1.

40. Ibid.

41. Timothy Puko, "Oil Company Leaders Support Carbon Pricing Plan," *The Wall Street Journal*, March 22, 2021.

42. "Our Meatless Future: How the $2.7T Global Meat Market Gets Disrupted," CB Insights, August 9, 2021, cbinsights.com/research/future-of-meat-industrial-farming/.

43. Ibid.

44. Anna Starostinetskaya, "Plant-Based Food Sales Surge by 27 Percent to $7 Billion in 2020," *VegNews*, April 7, 2021, vegnews.com/2021/4/plant-based-food-sales-7-billion-in-2020.

45. "Europe's Plant-Based Food Industry Shows Record-Level Growth," Community Research and Development Information Service, last updated March 30, 2021, cordis.europa.eu/article/id/429495-europe-s-plant-based-food-industry-shows-record-level-growth.

46. Mark Clements, "Strong Outlook for Plant-Based Meat Alternatives in Asia," Wattpoultry.com, July 29, 2021, wattagnet.com/articles/43107-strong-outlook-for-asian-plant-based-meat-alternatives.

47. "Our Meatless Future."

48. Lisa Friedman, Kendra Pierre-Louis, and Somini Sengupta, "The Meat Question, by the Numbers," *The New York Times*, January 25, 2018.

49. "The Global Consumer: Changed for Good: June 2021 Global Consumer Insights Pulse Survey," PwC, pwc.com/gx/en/industries/

consumer-markets/consumer-insights-survey/archive/consumer-insights-survey-2021.html.

50. "New Research Shows Climate and Sustainability Still Top Concern Despite COVID-19 Pandemic," Getty Images, October 7, 2020, press.gettyimages.com/new-research-shows-climate-and-sustainability-still-top-concern-despite-covid-19-pandemic/.

51. "The Eco-Wakening," World Wide Fund for Nature, explore.panda.org/eco-wakening.

52. "Insights on the Ethical Fashion Global Market to 2030—Identify Growth Segments for Investment," PR Newswire, May 25, 2021, prnewswire.com/news-releases/insights-on-the-ethical-fashion-global-market-to-2030---identify-growth-segments-for-investment-301298786.html.

53. Kevin Adler, "Global Electric Vehicle Sales Grew 41% in 2020, More Growth Coming Through Decade: IEA," IHS Markit, May 3, 2021, ihsmarkit.com/research-analysis/global-electric-vehicle-sales-grew-41-in-2020-more-growth-comi.html.

54. "Vision: Net-Zero Carbon by 2040," Amazon TV commerical, iSpot.tv, ispot.tv/ad/Owyn/amazon-we-do-big-renewable-energy.

55. Richard Luscombe, "Amazon's Jeff Bezos Pledges $10bn to Save Earth's Environment," *The Guardian,* February 17, 2020.

56. Gary Brodeur, "Report Ranks San Bernardino County No. 1 in Ozone Pollution," Heritage Victor Valley Medical Group, hvvmg.com/report-ranks-san-bernardino-county-no-1-in-ozone-pollution/.

57. Sam Levin, "Amazon's Warehouse Boom Linked to Health Hazards in America's Most Polluted Region," *The Guardian,* April 15, 2021.

Chapter 4

1. "Mexico's 1968 Massacre: What Really Happened?," *All Things Considered,* NPR, December 1, 2008.

2. S. I. Rosenbaum, "The Age of Trauma," *Harvard Public Health,* Fall 2021, hsph.harvard.edu/magazine/magazine_article/the-age-of-trauma/.

3. "Census Bureau Releases New Estimates on America's Families and Living Arrangements," U.S. Census Bureau press release, December 2, 2020, census.gov/newsroom/press-releases/2020/estimates-families-living-arrangements.html.

4. Ibid.

5. Stephanie Kramer, "U.S. Has World's Highest Rate of Children

Living in Single-Parent Households," Pew Research Center, December 12, 2019.

6. Rachael Kennedy, "Which EU Countries Have the Most Marriages?," Euronews, February 14, 2019, euronews.com/2019/02/14/which-eu-countries-have-the-most-marriages.
7. "Mechanisms Supporting Single Parents Across the European Union," European Commission, July 31, 2019, ec.europa.eu/social/main.jsp?catId=738&langId=en&pubId=8234&furtherPubs=yes.
8. Shannon Schumacher and J. J. Moncus, "Economic Attitudes Improve in Many Nations Even as Pandemic Endures," Pew Research Center, July 21, 2021.
9. Matt Novak, "The Boston Globe of 1900 Imagines the Year 2000," *Smithsonian Magazine,* October 4, 2011.
10. Ibid.
11. Grace Hauck, "20 Predictions for 2020: Here's What People Said Would Happen by This Year," *USA Today,* December 22, 2019.
12. GoZen!, gozen.com/tysupport/.
13. "Try the 'Road to Resilience: Raising Healthy Kids' Program," Mayo Clinic, January 13, 2020, mayoclinichealthsystem.org/hometown-health/featured-topic/try-the-road-to-resilience-program.
14. Janet Borland, *Earthquake Children: Building Resilience from the Ruins of Tokyo* (Cambridge, MA: Harvard University Asia Center, 2020).
15. "Global: Amnesty Analysis Reveals over 7,000 Health Workers Have Died from COVID-19," Amnesty International, September 3, 2020, amnesty.org/en/latest/press-release/2020/09/amnesty-analysis-7000-health-workers-have-died-from-covid19/.
16. Yea-Hung Chen et al., "Excess Mortality Associated with the COVID-19 Pandemic Among Californians 18–65 Years of Age, by Occupational Sector and Occupation: March Through October 2020," medRxiv, January 22, 2021, medrxiv.org/content/10.1101/2021.01.21.21250266v1.
17. "Asian Americans and Pacific Islander Americans on the Frontlines," New American Economy Research Fund, May 21, 2020, research.newamericaneconomy.org/report/aapi-americans-on-the-frontlines/.
18. "Farm Labor," U.S. Department of Agriculture, ers.usda.gov/topics/farm-economy/farm-labor/.
19. "Family, Domestic and Sexual Violence," Australian Institute of

Health and Welfare, September 16, 2021, aihw.gov.au/reports/australias-welfare/family-domestic-and-sexual-violence.

20. "The Effect of COVID-19 on Alcohol Consumption, and Policy Responses to Prevent Harmful Alcohol Consumption," Organisation for Economic Co-operation and Development, May 19, 2021, oecd.org/coronavirus/policy-responses/the-effect-of-covid-19-on-alcohol-consumption-and-policy-responses-to-prevent-harmful-alcohol-consumption-53890024/.
21. Giulia McDonnell Nieto del Rio, Simon Romero, and Mike Baker, "Hospitals Are Reeling Under a 46 Percent Spike in Covid-19 Patients," *The New York Times,* October 27, 2020.
22. Matt Phillips, "Stocks Post Worst Day in 4 Months as Infections Rise Around the Globe," *The New York Times,* October 28, 2020.
23. Tom McTague, "The Minister of Chaos: Boris Johnson Knows Exactly What He's Doing," *The Atlantic,* June 7, 2021.
24. Rob Merrick, "Boris Johnson Welcomed Covid 'Chaos' Because It Made Him More Popular, Cummings Claims," *The Independent* (U.K.), May 26, 2021.
25. Ibid.
26. Paul Bischoff, "Ransomware Attacks on US Healthcare Organizations Cost $20.8bn in 2020," *Comparitech,* March 10, 2021, comparitech.com/blog/information-security/ransomware-attacks-hospitals-data/.
27. "Insurance Giant AXA Victim of Ransomware Attack," *Security,* May 19, 2021, securitymagazine.com/articles/95245-insurance-giant-axa-victim-of-ransomware-attack.
28. "The Global Risks Report 2021," World Economic Forum, January 19, 2021, weforum.org/reports/the-global-risks-report-2021.
29. Ibid.
30. Steve Morgan, "Cybercrime to Cost the World $10.5 Trillion Annually by 2025," Cybercrime Magazine, November 13, 2020, cybersecurityventures.com/hackerpocalypse-cybercrime-report-2016/.
31. "Watch: NYC Subway Station Floods as Downpours Wreak Havoc on Tri-State Roads," NBC 4 New York, July 8, 2021, nbcnewyork.com/news/local/watch-nyc-subway-station-floods-as-sudden-heavy-downpours-wreak-havoc-on-tri-state-roads/3146172/.
32. "China Floods: 12 Dead in Zhengzhou Train and Thousands Evacuated in Henan," BBC News, July 21, 2021.

33. Sam Courtney-Guy, "London Floods Cause Millions in Damage After 'Biblical' Storms Hit City," *Metro* (U.K.), July 13, 2021.
34. Gaia Pianigiani, "3 Arrested in Genoa Bridge Collapse Investigation," *The New York Times,* November 11, 2020.
35. Jeremy Socolovsky, "India Blackout Highlights Power Problems in Developing Countries," Voice of America, August 1, 2012, voanews.com/a/india-blackout-highlights-power-problems-in-developing-countries/1452613.html.
36. Ari Natter and Jennifer A. Dlouhy, "Texas Was Warned a Decade Ago Its Grid Was Unready for Cold," Bloomberg Green, Bloomberg, February 17, 2021.
37. Zach Despart et al., "Analysis Reveals Nearly 200 Died in Texas Cold Storm and Blackouts, Almost Double the Official Count," *Houston Chronicle,* April 1, 2021.
38. U.S. Global Change Research Program, "Infrastructure," *Third National Climate Assessment,* 2014, nca2014.globalchange.gov/highlights/report-findings/infrastructure.
39. Daniel Kurt, "The Financial Effects of a Natural Disaster," Investopedia, October 28, 2021, investopedia.com/financial-edge/0311/the-financial-effects-of-a-natural-disaster.aspx.
40. "German Flood Rebuilding to More Than 6 Bln Euros—Scholz," Reuters, August 3, 2021.
41. "Brianna Keilar Calls Out Fox News Guest's Covid-19 Misinformation," CNN Business, September 17, 2020, cnn.com/videos/business/2020/09/17/brianna-keilar-fox-news-coronavirus.cnnbusiness.
42. Chas Danner and Paola Rosa-Aquino, "What We Know About the Dangerous Delta Variant," *New York,* August 9, 2021.
43. "Coronavirus (COVID-19) Vaccinations," Our World in Data, COVID-19 Data Explorer, ourworldindata.org/covid-vaccinations?country=OWID_WRL.

Chapter 5

1. Dissent of Justice Hugo Black, *Johnson v. Eisentrager,* 339 U.S. 763 (1950), caselaw.findlaw.com/us-supreme-court/339/763.html.
2. Brett Goodin, "Americans Renouncing U.S. Citizenship in Record Numbers," *U.S. News & World Report,* September 9, 2020.
3. Jennifer A. Kingson, "Wealthy People Are Renouncing American Citizenship," Axios, August 5, 2021.
4. Jeffrey M. Jones, "In U.S., Record-Low 47% Extremely Proud to

Be Americans," Gallup, July 2, 2018, gallup.com/poll/236420/record-low-extremely-proud-americans.aspx.

5. "Many Value Democratic Principles, but Few Think Democracy Is Working Well These Days," Associated Press NORC Center for Public Affairs Research, February 8, 2021, apnorc.org/projects/many-value-democratic-principles-but-few-think-democracy-is-working-well-these-days/.
6. Jacob Poushter, "Who's Having a 'Good' or 'Bad' Day Around the World," Pew Research Center, December 30, 2014, pewresearch.org/fact-tank/2014/12/30/having-a-typical-day-in-2014-youre-not-alone/.
7. Charles Handy, "Tocqueville Revisited: The Meaning of American Prosperity," *Harvard Business Review* 79, no. 1 (January 2001): 57–63.
8. Alexis de Tocqueville, *Democracy in America: And Two Essays on America* (London: Penguin, 2003).
9. Leah Platt Boustan, Devin Bunten, and Owen Hearey, "Urbanization in the United States, 1800–2000," National Bureau of Economic Research, May 2013, scholar.princeton.edu/sites/default/files/lboustan/files/research21_urban_handbook.pdf.
10. "2020 Census Statistics Highlight Local Population Changes and Nation's Racial and Ethnic Diversity," U.S. Census Bureau press release, August 12, 2021, census.gov/newsroom/press-releases/2021/population-changes-nations-diversity.html.
11. Ibid.
12. "Read Hillary Clinton's 'Basket of Deplorables' Remarks About Donald Trump Supporters," *Time,* September 10, 2016.
13. Aaron Blake, "Trump Promised His Supporters 'Everything.' He Didn't Deliver on Much of It," *The Washington Post,* January 20, 2021.
14. "2020 Census Statistics."
15. Noah Millman, "America Needs to Break Up Its Biggest States," *The New York Times,* July 7, 2021.
16. Mark Mather, "Three States Account for Nearly Half of U.S. Population Growth," Population Reference Bureau, December 22, 2015, prb.org/resources/three-states-account-for-nearly-half-of-u-s-population-growth/.
17. Millman, "America Needs to Break Up."
18. Ibid.
19. Kaitlyn Tiffany, "How 'Karen' Became a Coronavirus Villain," *The Atlantic,* May 6, 2020.

20. Isaac Chotiner, "The Collapse of American Identity," *The New Yorker,* June 29, 2021.
21. Juliana Menasce Horowitz, Ruth Igielnik, and Rakesh Kochhar, "Trends in Income and Wealth Inequality," Pew Research Center, January 9, 2020, pewresearch.org/social-trends/2020/01/09/trends-in-income-and-wealth-inequality/.
22. Ibid.
23. Ibid.
24. Ibid.
25. Callie Holtermann, "Are C.E.O.s Paid Too Much?," *The New York Times,* May 11, 2021.
26. "2020 Census Statistics."
27. William H. Frey, "The Nation Is Diversifying Even Faster Than Predicted, According to New Census Data," Brookings Institution, July 1, 2020, brookings.edu/research/new-census-data-shows-the-nation-is-diversifying-even-faster-than-predicted/.
28. Jonathan Vespa, Lauren Medina, and David M. Armstrong, "Demographic Turning Points for the United States: Population Projections for 2020 to 2060," U.S. Census Bureau, March 2018, revised February 2020, census.gov/content/dam/Census/library/publications/2020/demo/p25-1144.pdf.
29. Ibid.
30. Ibid.
31. Ibid.
32. Deepa Shivaram and Asma Khalid, "An Indiana Town Is Wooing New Residents with On-Demand Grandparents," *Weekend Edition Sunday,* NPR, October 24, 2021.
33. "How It Works," Umbrella, theumbrella.org/how-it-works.
34. "2021 Index of Economic Freedom: Country Rankings," The Heritage Foundation, heritage.org/index/ranking.
35. Terry Miller and Kim R. Holmes, "Highlights of the 2010 Index of Economic Freedom," The Heritage Foundation, heritage.org/index/pdf/2010/index2010_highlights.pdf.
36. Elliott Davis, "Canada Ranks No. 1 in 2021 U.S. News Best Countries Ranking," *U.S. News & World Report,* April 13, 2021.
37. Sophie Ireland, "Revealed: Countries with the Best Health Care Systems, 2021," *CEOWorld Magazine,* April 27, 2021, ceoworld.biz/2021/04/27/revealed-countries-with-the-best-health-care-systems-2021.
38. "Education at a Glance: OECD Indicators 2012," Organisation

for Economic Co-operation and Development, oecd.org/unitedstates/CN%20-%20United%20States.pdf.

39. "Best Countries for Women," *U.S. News & World Report,* 2021, usnews.com/news/best-countries/best-countries-for-women.
40. "Life Expectancy of the World Population," Worldometer, worldometers.info/demographics/life-expectancy/.
41. "The Things America Leads the World In: Dog and Cat Ownership," Lovemoney, June 24, 2020, lovemoney.com/galleries/70537/the-things-america-leads-the-world-in?page=18.
42. Richard Wike et al., "U.S. Image Suffers as Publics Around World Question Trump's Leadership," Pew Research Center, June 26, 2017, pewresearch.org/global/2017/06/26/u-s-image-suffers-as-publics-around-world-question-trumps-leadership/.
43. Richard Wike et al., "America's International Image Continues to Suffer," Pew Research Center, October 1, 2018, pewresearch.org/global/2018/10/01/americas-international-image-continues-to-suffer/.
44. Julie Bosman, "A Ripple Effect of Loss: U.S. Covid Deaths Approach 500,000," *The New York Times,* February 21, 2021.
45. Ibid.

Chapter 6

1. "Mao's Long March Concludes," History, history.com/this-day-in-history/maos-long-march-concludes.
2. Edgar Snow, *Red Star over China: The Classic Account of the Birth of Chinese Communism* (New York: Grove Press, 1968).
3. Ibid.
4. Ibid.
5. Martin Adams, "Long March to Mythology," *Asia Times,* October 24, 2006, web.archive.org/web/20061106235646/http://www.atimes.com/atimes/China/HJ24Ad01.html.
6. Ibid.
7. Yong Xiong and Pauline Lockwood, "Chinese Communist Party Passes Landmark Resolution Celebrating Leader Xi Jinping," CNN, November 12, 2021.
8. Evan Osnos, "Born Red," *The New Yorker,* March 30, 2015.
9. Ibid.
10. Ibid.
11. Samuel Yang, "China Is Repressing the Feminist Movement but Women's Voices Are Only Getting Louder," ABC News (Australia), June 7, 2021.

12. Osnos, "Born Red."
13. Brenda Goh, "Three Hours a Week: Play Time's over for China's Young Video Gamers," Reuters, August 31, 2021.
14. Gian M. Volpicelli, "China's Sweeping Cryptocurrency Ban Was Inevitable," *Wired,* September 30, 2021.
15. Arjun Kharpal, "Alibaba Shares Dive 7% as Ant Group's Record $34.5 Billion IPO Is Suspended," CNBC, November 3, 2020.
16. Reuters, "China Passes Law to Reduce 'Twin Pressures' of Homework and Tutoring on Children," *The Guardian,* October 23, 2021.
17. Li Yuan, "'Who Are Our Enemies?' China's Bitter Youths Embrace Mao," *The New York Times,* July 8, 2021.
18. Ibid.
19. Ibid.
20. Ibid.
21. Rachael D'Amore, "'Yes, This Drone Is Speaking to You': How China Is Reportedly Enforcing Coronavirus Rules," *Global News,* February 11, 2020, globalnews.ca/news/6535353/china-coronavirus-drones-quarantine/.
22. "China's Response to COVID-19: A Chance for Collaboration," *The Lancet* 397, no. 10282 (2021): 1325, sciencedirect.com/science/article/pii/S0140673621008230.
23. Smriti Mallapaty, "China Is Vaccinating a Staggering 20 Million People a Day," *Nature,* October 14, 2021.
24. Yanzhong Huang, "Vaccine Diplomacy Is Paying Off for China," *Foreign Affairs,* March 11, 2021.
25. Rana Mitter, "Xi Marks the Spot," Air Mail, November 7, 2020, airmail.news/issues/2020-11-7/xi-marks-the-spot.
26. Marie Szaniszlo, "Coronavirus Is Straining Boston Hospitals' Capacity as They Brace for More Patients After the Holidays," *Boston Herald,* December 19, 2020.
27. Peter Egger, Gabriel Loumeau, and Nicole Loumeau, "Unbridled Transport Infrastructure Growth in China," VoxEU & CEPR, November 3, 2020, voxeu.org/article/unbridled-transport-infrastructure-growth-china.
28. Alexandra Ma and Katie Canales, "China's 'Social Credit' System Ranks Citizens and Punishes Them with Throttled Internet Speeds and Flight Bans If the Communist Party Deems Them Untrustworthy," *Insider,* May 9, 2021.
29. Kendra Schaefer, "China's Corporate Social Credit System," Trivium China, November 16, 2020, uscc.gov/sites/default/files/2020-12/Chinas_Corporate_Social_Credit_System.pdf.

30. Alexandra Stevenson and Paul Mozur, "China Scores Businesses, and Low Grades Could Be a Trade-War Weapon," *The New York Times,* September 22, 2019.

31. Ibid.

32. Michael Standaert, "Smile for the Camera: The Dark Side of China's Emotion-Recognition Tech," *The Guardian,* March 3, 2021.

33. Dave Gershgorn, "China's 'Sharp Eyes' Program Aims to Surveil 100% of Public Space," OneZero, March 2, 2021, onezero.medium.com/chinas-sharp-eyes-program-aims-to-surveil-100-of-public-space-ddc22d63e015.

34. Sidney Fussell, "The Next Target for a Facial Recognition Ban? New York," *Wired,* January 28, 2021.

35. Yuan Yang and Nian Liu, "China Survey Shows High Concern over Facial Recognition Abuse," *Financial Times,* December 5, 2019.

36. Allied Market Research, "Emotion Detection and Recognition (EDR) Market to Reach $33.9 Billion at a CAGR of 28.9% by 2023," GlobeNewswire, February 17, 2020, globenewswire.com/news-release/2020/02/17/1985745/0/en/Emotion-Detection-and-Recognition-EDR-Market-to-Reach-33-9-Billion-at-a-CAGR-of-28-9-by-2023-AMR.html.

37. Rachel Cheung, "Hong Kong's Arrested Protesters Now Face Years of Fear and Limbo," *Los Angeles Times,* February 5, 2021.

38. Chan Ho-him, "Hong Kong Officials Ask Schools If They Have Installed CCTV, After Some Lawmakers Called for Cameras to Be Installed in Classrooms," *South China Morning Post,* March 13, 2021.

39. Natalie Lung, Kari Soo Lindberg, and Chloe Lo, "Hong Kong Makes 100th Arrest Using National Security Law," Bloomberg, March 2, 2021.

40. Ibid.

41. Eva Dou, "Who Are the Uyghurs, and What's Happening to Them in China?," *The Washington Post,* February 11, 2021.

42. "Uighur Exploitation in China Slammed as 'Modern Day Slavery,'" Deutsche Welle, December 15, 2020, dw.com/en/uighur-exploitation-in-china-slammed-as-modern-day-slavery/a-55953464.

43. Li Yuan, "What China Expects from Businesses: Total Surrender," *The New York Times,* July 19, 2021.

44. "China Announces Eradication of Extreme Poverty in Last Poor Counties," Reuters, November 24, 2020.

45. Keith Bradsher, "Jobs, Houses and Cows: China's Costly Drive to

Erase Extreme Poverty," *The New York Times,* December 31, 2020.

46. Asit K. Biswas and Cecilia Tortajada, "How China Eradicated Absolute Poverty," *China Daily,* April 12, 2021.
47. "Median Income by Country 2021," World Population Review, worldpopulationreview.com/country-rankings/median-income-by-country.
48. Yuan, "What China Expects."
49. Tracy Qu and Minghe Hu, "Forbes China Names Alibaba Founder Jack Ma Country's Most Generous Entrepreneur in 2020, as Tech Giants Top Charity List," *South China Morning Post,* July 21, 2021.
50. Michael Standaert, "Why Are China's Billionaires Suddenly Feeling So Generous?," Al Jazeera, July 16, 2021.
51. "99 Giving Day," Tencent Foundation, tencent.com/en-us/responsibility/99-giving-day.html.
52. Gabriel Corsetti, "Fifth Tencent 9/9 Charity Day Raises over 2.4 Billion Yuan, Smashing Last Year's Record," China Development Brief, September 11, 2019, chinadevelopmentbrief.cn/reports/fifth-tencent-99-charity-day-raises-over-2-4-billion-yuan-smashing-last-years-record/.
53. "Daryl Morey Backtracks After Hong Kong Tweet Causes Chinese Backlash," BBC News, October 7, 2019.
54. "The NBA Works 'Super Hard' to Reestablish 'Open Dialogue' in China," *The World,* November 9, 2020, theworld.org/stories/2020-11-09/nba-works-super-hard-reestablish-open-dialogue-china.
55. Benjamin Lee, "China Continues to Exert Damaging Influence on Hollywood, Report Finds," *The Guardian,* August 5, 2020.
56. Ibid.
57. Andrew Soergel, "Trading Silence for Access: The Cost of Doing Business in China," *U.S. News & World Report,* October 11, 2019.
58. Natasha Turak, "China's Response to NBA Hong Kong Tweet Was a 'Violation of US Sovereignty,' Condoleezza Rice Says," CNBC, November 11, 2019.
59. Emmanuel Kizito, "Biden's Plan to Rebuild U.S. Supply Chains, COVID-19 Pandemic Accelerates Reshoring," Thomas Insights, September 14, 2021, thomasnet.com/insights/biden-s-plan-to-rebuild-u-s-supply-chains-covid-19-pandemic-accelerates-reshoring/.
60. Hu Yiwei, "'Guochao': China's Younger Generation Embracing

Domestic Brands," CGTN, May 10, 2021, news.cgtn.com/news/2021-05-10/-Guochao-China-s-younger-generation-embracing-domestic-brands-1062GxxNsRi/index.html.

61. Ibid.
62. Shirley Zhao, "Hollywood Struggles for Fans in China's Growing Film Market," Bloomberg, February 15, 2021.
63. Ibid.
64. Peter Hicks, "'Sleeping China' and Napoleon," Napoleon.org, napoleon.org/en/history-of-the-two-empires/articles/ava-gardner-china-and-napoleon/.
65. "Remarks by President Biden in Press Conference," White House Briefing Room, March 25, 2021, whitehouse.gov/briefing-room/speeches-remarks/2021/03/25/remarks-by-president-biden-in-press-conference/.
66. Ibid.
67. Ibid.
68. Zachery Tyson Brown, "The United States Needs a New Strategic Mindset," *Foreign Policy,* September 22, 2020.
69. Bloomberg, "China Emerges as Only Major Economy to Grow in 2020," *Fortune,* January 17, 2021.
70. Naomi Xu Elegant, "China's 2020 GDP Means It Will Overtake U.S. as World's No. 1 Economy Sooner Than Expected," *Fortune,* January 18, 2021.
71. Brendan Cole, "China Won't Overtake U.S. as World's Largest Economy: Forecast," *Newsweek,* February 19, 2021.
72. "U.S.-China 21: The Future of U.S.-China Relations Under Xi Jinping," Asia Society Policy Institute, asiasociety.org/policy-institute/us-china-21-future-us-china-relations-under-xi-jinping.
73. Zhang Jun, "Economies Need to Rein in Population Risks," *China Daily,* May 10, 2021.
74. "China Birth Rate 1950–2022," Macrotrends, macrotrends.net/countries/CHN/china/birth-rate.
75. Tsuchiya Hideo, "East Asia's Looming Demographic Crisis," Nippon, November 24, 2020, nippon.com/en/in-depth/d00639/.
76. Amy Hampton, "Population Control in China: Sacrificing Human Rights for the Greater Good," *Tulsa Journal of Comparative and International Law* 11, no. 1 (2003): 320–61, digitalcommons.law.utulsa.edu/cgi/viewcontent.cgi?referer=&httpsredir=1&article=1202&context=tjcil.
77. "China Cuts Uighur Births with IUDs, Abortion, Sterilization," AP News, June 29, 2020.

78. Andrew Mullen, "Explainer: Three-Child Policy: How Many Children Can You Have in China?," *South China Morning Post,* June 5, 2021.

79. Bloomberg News, "Why China Is Cracking Down Now on After-School Tutors," *The Washington Post,* July 25, 2021.

80. Lili Pike, "Grim New Climate Report Triggers Calls on China to Slash Carbon Emissions Sooner," *Science,* August 12, 2021.

81. Jianyu Zhang, Xiaolu Zhao, and Hu Qin, "Why China Is at the Center of Our Climate Strategy," Environmental Defense Fund, edf.org/climate/why-china-center-our-climate-strategy.

82. Pike, "Grim New Climate Report."

83. "Death Toll Triples to More Than 300 in Recent China Flooding," AP News, August 2, 2021.

84. Kishore Mahbubani, *Has China Won?: The Chinese Challenge to American Primacy* (New York: Public Affairs, 2020).

85. "China Plans First Crewed Mission to Mars in 2033," Reuters, June 24, 2021.

PART TWO

1. "Anxiety Statistics 2021," SingleCare, March 8, 2021, singlecare.com/blog/news/anxiety-statistics/.

2. "Doomsday Clock Ticks Closer to Disaster," *Physics World,* September 2, 2020, physicsworld.com/a/doomsday-clock-ticks-closer-to-disaster/.

3. Ibid.

4. Ibid.

Chapter 7

1. Joshua Coleman, "A Shift in American Family Values Is Fueling Estrangement," *The Atlantic,* January 10, 2021.

2. Joseph Winchester Brown et al., "Transitions in Living Arrangements Among Elders in Japan: Does Health Make a Difference?," *The Journals of Gerontology: Series B,* 57, no. 4 (2002): S209–20.

3. "Rising Numbers of Elderly People Are Living Alone," editorial, *The Japan Times,* May 3, 2019.

4. Joint Center for Housing Studies of Harvard University, "Demographics of an Aging America," *Housing America's Older Adults—Meeting the Needs of an Aging Population,* September 2,

2014, jchs.harvard.edu/sites/default/files/jchs-housing_americas_older_adults_2014-ch2_0.pdf.

5. "Why *It's a Wonderful Life* Is the Nation's Favourite," BBC News, December 20, 2018.
6. "The Most Popular Christmas Movies, According to Americans," YouGovAmerica, https://today.yougov.com/topics/entertainment/articles-reports/2020/12/14/favorite-christmas-holiday-movie-poll.
7. Matthew Young and Will Hayward, "'The First Brit' Is Known as Cheddar Man and Had Dark Skin and Blue Eyes," WalesOnline, February 7, 2018, walesonline.co.uk/news/uk-news/first-brit-cheddar-man-dark-14257042.
8. Sarah Pruitt, "The Ongoing Mystery of Jesus's Face," History.com, updated March 22, 2021, history.com/news/what-did-jesus-look-like.
9. Antonio Regalado, "More Than 26 Million People Have Taken an At-Home Ancestry Test," *MIT Technology Review,* February 11, 2019, technologyreview.com/2019/02/11/103446/more-than-26-million-people-have-taken-an-at-home-ancestry-test/.
10. Heather Saul, "Craig Cobb: White Supremacist Told He Is 14% African in Televised DNA Test," *The Independent* (U.K.), November 12, 2013.
11. Ruth Padawer, "Sigrid Johnson Was Black. A DNA Test Said She Wasn't," *The New York Times,* November 19, 2018.
12. Saul, "Craig Cobb: White Supremacist."
13. "Multikulti Berlin," *The New York Times,* archive.nytimes.com/www.nytimes.com/fodors/top/features/travel/destinations/europe/germany/berlin/fdrs_feat_28_6.html?n=Top%25252FFeatures%25252FTravel%25252FDestinations%25252FEurope%25252FGermany%25252FBerlin.
14. Ibid.
15. David Goodhart, "Discomfort of Strangers," *The Guardian,* February 24, 2004.
16. Yasemin El-Menouar, "How Do Germans Deal with Cultural Diversity?," Bertelsmann Stiftung Foundation, bertelsmann-stiftung.de/en/our-projects/religion-monitor/projektnachrichten/how-do-germans-deal-with-cultural-diversity.
17. "Figures at a Glance: How Many Refugees Are There Around the World?," UN Refugee Agency, June 10, 2021, unhcr.org/en-us/figures-at-a-glance.html#:~:text=How%20many%20refugees%20are%20there,under%20the%20age%20of%2018.
18. Jada Yuan, "New York's Patron Saint of PPE Went $600,000 in

Debt to Outfit Workers—and Hospitals Keep Turning Her Down," *The Washington Post,* May 5, 2020.

19. "COVID-19: Hospitalization and Death by Race/Ethnicity," Centers for Disease Control and Prevention, September 9, 2021, cdc.gov/coronavirus/2019-ncov/covid-data/investigations-discovery/hospitalization-death-by-race-ethnicity.html.

20. Savannah Smith, Jiachuan Wu, and Joe Murphy, "Map: George Floyd Protests Around the World," NBC News, June 9, 2020, nbcnews.com/news/world/map-george-floyd-protests-countries-worldwide-n1228391.

CHAPTER 8

1. Rob Evans, "Half of England's Property Is Owned by Less Than 1% of the Population," *The Guardian,* April 17, 2019.

2. "1824: Charles Dickens Begins Working at Warren's Blacking Factory," World History Project, worldhistoryproject.org/1824/charles-dickens-begins-working-at-warrens-blacking-factory.

3. Russell McCutcheon, "Stars Upon Thars," *Culture on the Edge,* March 31, 2014, edge.ua.edu/russell-mccutcheon/stars-upon-thars/.

4. Amber Phillips, "'They're Rapists.' President Trump's Campaign Launch Speech Two Years Later, Annotated," *The Washington Post,* June 16, 2017.

5. Lara Jakes, "Pompeo's Parting Message as Secretary of State: Multiculturalism Is 'Not Who America Is,'" *The New York Times,* January 19, 2021.

6. Ellie Harrison, "'I Was Much Older and She Was an Adopted Kid': Woody Allen Admits His Relationship with Wife Soon-Yi Previn 'Looked Exploitative,'" *The Independent* (U.K.), May 26, 2020.

7. Andrea Leadsom, "'I Want to Guide Britain to the Sunlit Uplands'—Full Text of Andrea Leadsom's Leadership Speech," *The Spectator* (U.K.), July 3, 2016.

8. Jon Stone, "Brexit Lies: The Demonstrably False Claims of the Referendum Campaign," *The Independent* (U.K.), December 17, 2017.

9. Chris Giles, "Covid Pandemic Masks Brexit Impact on UK Economy," *Financial Times,* July 1, 2021.

10. Chris Giles, "Coronavirus Sparks Exodus of Foreign-Born People from UK," *Financial Times,* January 14, 2021.

11. Pan Pylas, "UK Job Vacancies Hit Record High amid Worker Shortages," AP News, October 12, 2021.
12. Holly Ellyatt, "After Causing Chaos in the UK, Truck Driver Shortages Could Soon Hit the Rest of Europe," CNBC, October 4, 2021.
13. Kate Holton, "'It's a Catastrophe': Scottish Fishermen Halt Exports Due to Brexit Red Tape," Reuters, January 8, 2021.
14. Lisa O'Carroll, "'A Multiple Pile-Up in the Fog': Wine Agent's Fury at Brexit Red Tape," *The Guardian,* January 18, 2021.
15. Nick Craven et al., "Now They're Taking Our Muesli! Gloating Dutch Customs Staff Reveal MORE Food Seized from Britons Entering the Country After Brexit—but It Includes Spanish Oranges and American Orange Juice," *Daily Mail,* January 12, 2021.
16. Austa Somvichian-Clausen, "The History of Racist Halloween Costumes, and the Progress We've Made in Saying Goodbye to Them," *The Hill,* October 30, 2020.
17. Ibid.
18. Marian Chia-Ming Liu, "A Culture, Not a Costume," *The Washington Post,* October 30, 2019.
19. Somvichian-Clausen, "The History of Racist Halloween Costumes."
20. Ellie Krupnick, "Zendaya Just Said the One Sentence About Cultural Appropriation Everyone Needs," Mic, August 2, 2015.
21. "Amandla Stenberg: Don't Cash Crop on My Cornrows," *Hype Hair Magazine,* YouTube, April 15, 2015, youtube.com/watch?v=O1KJRRSB_XA.
22. Ibid.
23. Shing Yin Khor, "Just Eat It: A Comic About Food and Cultural Appropriation," Bitch Media, February 18, 2014, bitchmedia.org/post/a-comic-about-food-and-cultural-appropriation.
24. "1926, May 01: Ford Factory Workers Get 40-Hour Week," This Day in History, November 13, 2009, history.com/this-day-in-history/ford-factory-workers-get-40-hour-week.
25. Amanda Dixon, "68% of Americans Have Skipped Recreational Activities in the Past Year Because of Cost," Bankrate, August 14, 2019, bankrate.com/surveys/recreational-spending-survey-august-2019/.
26. "The Swedish Cottage Remains Loved, Generation After Generation," Swedish Institute, June 1, 2021, sweden.se/culture-traditions/the-swedish-summer-house-a-love-affair/.
27. Ibid.

Chapter 9

1. Barry Schwartz, *The Paradox of Choice* (New York: Harper Perennial, 2004).
2. Pete Edwards, "How Big Is the Universe . . . Compared with a Grain of Sand?," *The Guardian,* YouTube, February 12, 2013, youtube.com/watch?v=AC7yFDb1zOA.
3. Stephanie Crets, "Online US Home Goods Sales Grow 51.8% in 2020," Digital Commerce 360, September 20, 2021, digitalcommerce360.com/article/online-home-goods-sales/.
4. Technavio,"$82.32 Billion Growth in Global Online Home Decor Market 2020–2024 | Growth in Construction Industry to Drive Market," PR Newswire, March 23, 2021, prnewswire.com/news-releases/-82-32-billion-growth-in-global-online-home-decor-market-2020-2024--growth-in-construction-industry-to-drive-market--technavio-301251230.html.
5. Matt Noltemeyer, "Pandemic-Era Home Bakers Used Yeast in Four Categories on Average," *Food Business News,* October 29, 2021, foodbusinessnews.net/articles/19934-pandemic-era-home-bakers-used-yeast-in-four-categories-on-average.
6. "The McMansion Hell Yearbook: 1981," *McMansion Hell,* November 9, 2021, mcmansionhell.com/post/667428216873664512/the-mcmansion-hell-yearbook-1981.
7. Kerry A. Dolan,"Forbes' 35th Annual World's Billionaires List: Facts and Figures 2021," *Forbes,* April 6, 2021.
8. Miriam Kramer, "Billionaires Are the New Face of the Final Frontier," Axios, July 13, 2021.
9. Ric G., "Do Not Allow Jeff Bezos to Return to Earth," Change.org, change.org/p/the-proletariat-do-not-allow-jeff-bezos-to-return-to-earth.
10. Dylan Byers and Leticia Miranda, "Jeff Bezos Steps Down as Amazon CEO," NBC News, February 2, 2021.
11. Jenna Romaine, "'SNL' Cast Members Who Object to Elon Musk Won't Be Forced to Appear on Show with Him," *The Hill,* April 30, 2021.
12. Sophie Dweck, "Elon Musk Now Lives in a $50,000 Prefab Tiny House in Texas," *Architectural Digest,* July 8, 2021.
13. Cameron Sperance, "Despite Pandemic and Close Quarters, Tiny Homes Are More Popular Than Ever," RealEstate, Boston.com, March 24, 2021, realestate.boston.com/buying/2021/03/24/despite-pandemic-tiny-homes-more-popular.
14. Thomas Gryta, Theo Francis, and Drew FitzGerald, "General

Electric, AT&T Investors Reject CEO Pay Plans," *The Wall Street Journal,* May 4, 2021.

15. "Facts: Wealth Inequality in the United States," Inequality.org, inequality.org/facts/wealth-inequality/.
16. Adam Hadhazy, "The 31 Tallest Buildings in the World," *Popular Mechanics,* June 15, 2021.
17. Jake Powell, "Top 5 World's Biggest Mining Dump Trucks," iseekplant, April 29, 2020, blog.iseekplant.com.au/blog/worlds-biggest-dump-trucks.
18. Dana G. Smith, "Why Do We Think Tiny Things Are Cute?," *Popular Science,* August 28, 2018.
19. "Etsy Shopper Stats: March 2021," Etsy, March 3, 2021, etsy.com/seller-handbook/article/etsy-shopper-stats-march-2021/1030540287389.
20. Ciara McQuillan, "This Irish Baker Sold $1M Worth of Her Scones in 24 Hours. Now She Just Has to Make Them," *The Irish Times,* August 16, 2021.
21. "Our History," Scott Bader, scottbader.com/about-us/history/.
22. Ibid.
23. John Simkin, "Ernest Bader," Spartacus Educational, September 1997, spartacus-educational.com/JbaderE.htm.
24. "Annual Report 2018," Scott Bader, scottbader.com/wp-content/uploads/Annual-Report-2018.pdf.
25. Simkin, "Ernest Bader."
26. "Ernst Friedrich Schumacher," Schumacher Center for New Economics, centerforneweconomics.org/envision/legacy/ernst-friedrich-schumacher/.
27. E. F. Schumacher, "Buddhist Economics," Schumacher Center for New Economics, centerforneweconomics.org/publications/buddhist-economics/.
28. Ibid.
29. Ibid.
30. Peter Yeung, "How '15-Minute Cities' Will Change the Way We Socialise," BBC, January 4, 2021.
31. Antonia Cundy, "What Would a City Designed by Women Look Like?," *Financial Times,* October 6, 2020.
32. Oscar Holland, "Plans Unveiled for High-Tech '10-Minute City' in Seoul," CNN, November 10, 2021.
33. "US States Overlaid on Areas of Europe with Equal Population," MoverDB.com, February 16, 2017, moverdb.com/us-states-europe-population/.

34. "Netherlands—Location, Size, and Extent," Nations Encyclopedia, nationsencyclopedia.com/Europe/Netherlands-LOCATION-SIZE-AND-EXTENT.html.

35. "The Dutch Way of Life," *Lonely Planet,* lonelyplanet.com/the-netherlands/background/other-features/f0bf185d-fd7a-449f-9d20-5c3154326386/a/nar/f0bf185d-fd7a-449f-9d20-5c3154326386/360838.

36. "Homomonument," Wikipedia, en.wikipedia.org/wiki/Homomonument.

37. "LGBT Rights in the Netherlands," Wikipedia, en.wikipedia.org/wiki/LGBT_rights_in_the_Netherlands.

38. "Euthanasia, Assisted Suicide and Non-resuscitation on Request," Government of the Netherlands, government.nl/topics/euthanasia/euthanasia-assisted-suicide-and-non-resuscitation-on-request.

39. Duncan Robinson, "Dutch Parliament Votes to Permit Cannabis Cultivation," *Financial Times,* February 21, 2017.

40. Alyse Messmer, "Calling Code Red, Dutch Official Says Country Faces Climate Change Extremes," *Newsweek,* October 15, 2021.

41. "The Most Common Bathroom Sizes and Dimensions," Badeloft, April 27, 2020, badeloftusa.com/buying-guides/the-most-common-bathroom-sizes-and-dimensions/.

42. "People Living Alone," Statistics Japan, November 13, 2010, stats-japan.com/t/kiji/11902.

43. Bryan Lufkin, "The Rise of Japan's 'Super Solo' Culture," BBC Worklife, January 14, 2020.

44. Lilit Marcus, "Hitori: The Tokyo Bar for Solo Drinkers Only," CNN Travel, November 19, 2019.

45. Lufkin, "Rise of Japan's 'Super Solo' Culture."

46. Varpu, "50 Cultural Facts on Finland That Help You Understand Finns," Her Finland, herfinland.com/facts-on-finland/.

47. Theresa Christine, "What It's Like to Live in Finland, the Happiest Country in the World," *Insider,* March 31, 2021.

48. Karoliina Korhonen, *Finnish Nightmares: An Irreverent Guide to Life's Awkward Moments* (New York: Ten Speed Press, 2019).

49. "30 Top Facts," Backpackerboard, backpackerboard.co.nz/guide/facts-new-zealand/.

50. Chris Weller and Melissa Wiley, "Americans Are Googling How to Move to New Zealand. Here's a Step-By-Step Guide to Becoming a Kiwi After the Pandemic," *Insider,* November 5, 2020.

51. Melia Robinson, "Buying a House in New Zealand Is Silicon Valley Code for Getting 'Apocalypse Insurance,'" *Insider,* February 1, 2017.
52. Mark Broatch, Eleanor Ainge Roy, and Harriet Sherwood, "Thinking Big: New Zealand's Growing Pains as Population Nears 5 Million," *The Guardian,* November 3, 2019.
53. Ross Chapin, *Pocket Neighborhoods: Creating Small-Scale Community in a Large-Scale World* (Newtown, Connecticut: Taunton Press, 2011).
54. Michael Kolomatsky, "The Incredible Shrinking Apartment," *The New York Times,* December 6, 2018.
55. Leanna Garfield, "America's Oldest Shopping Mall Has Been Turned into Beautiful Micro-Apartments—Take a Look Inside," *Insider,* October 10, 2016.
56. Keith Eldridge, "Conestoga Huts for the Homeless a Solution for the Northwest?," Komo News, February 27, 2019, komonews.com/news/local/huts-for-the-homeless-catching-on-in-the-northwest.
57. Tim Levin, "These Custom Sleeper Cabs Are Like Luxurious Tiny Homes for Long-Haul Truckers—See Inside," *Insider,* December 30, 2020.
58. Ken Wells, "Travelers Turn to Tiny Homes During Covid-19," *The Wall Street Journal,* November 11, 2020.
59. Ibid.
60. Janet Eastman, "Portland Builder Brings a Tiny Extra House to You for Temporary, Safe Distancing," *The Oregonian,* November 25, 2020.
61. James Morris, "Tesla's $25,000 Electric Car Means Game Over for Gas and Oil," *Forbes,* September 26, 2020.
62. Britany Robinson, "It's Not That Hard to Buy Nothing," *The New York Times,* December 28, 2020.
63. Scott Galloway, "The Great Dispersion," *No Mercy / No Malice,* December 4, 2020, profgalloway.com/the-great-dispersion/.
64. "Why I'm Betting on Airbnb, Walmart, Robinhood, and Bitcoin to Win Big in 2020," *Insider,* January 9, 2021.

Chapter 10

1. Hillary Hoffower, "Hollywood Billionaire David Geffen Has Been Self-Isolating on His Superyacht in the Caribbean During the

Coronavirus Pandemic. Take a Look at the $590 Million Yacht," *Insider,* April 1, 2020.

2. "Coronavirus Updates from March 31, 2020," CBS News, last updated April 2, 2020.
3. Sydney Jennings, "COVID-19 Updated: Global Confirmed Cases as of March 31, 2020," Patient Care, March 31, 2020, patientcareonline.com/view/covid-19-update-global-confirmed-cases-march-31-2020.
4. Robby Starbuck (@robbystarbuck), Twitter, March 28, 2020, twitter.com/robbystarbuck/status/1243912330645209088.
5. "Real-Time Billionaires: #197 David Geffen," *Forbes,* as on January 10, 2022, forbes.com/profile/david-geffen/?list=rtb/&sh=7a44d8fd17e0.
6. Thomas Lester, "High Design: Luxury Market Forced to Rethink Discretionary Spending," Home Accents Today, October 16, 2020, homeaccentstoday.com/retailers/high-design-luxury-market-forced-to-rethink-discretionary-spending/.
7. J. Clara Chan, "David Geffen Takes Instagram Private After Tone-Deaf Post About Self-Isolating on His Yacht," Yahoo! Entertainment, March 28, 2020.
8. "An Insight into the State of Luxury Branding Today," EHL Insights, hospitalityinsights.ehl.edu/an-insight-into-the-state-of-luxury-branding-today.
9. Jesse Kornbluth, "Serious Money," *Vanity Fair,* November 1988.
10. Public (press conference), "Ian Schrager Relaunches His Transformative New Brand Public for a New Beginning for Both the Hotel and New York City," PR Newswire, June 7, 2021, prnewswire.com/news-releases/ian-schrager-relaunches-his-transformative-new-brand-public-for-a-new-beginning-for-both-the-hotel-and-new-york-city-301306164.html.
11. Ibid.
12. "Choose Your Bike Package," Peloton, onepeloton.com/shop/bike.
13. Elizabeth Gravier, "The Average Millennial Has over $4,000 in Credit Card Debt—Other Generations Have More," CNBC, September 20, 2021.
14. Bridie Pearson-Jones, "Sales of Luxury Goods Such as Chanel Handbags, Designer Trainers and Fine Wine Are at an 'All-Time High' Despite the Pandemic Because They're a 'Safer' Investment Than Gold or Stocks," *Daily Mail,* April 24, 2020.
15. Paul Sullivan, "Can't Afford a Birkin Bag or a Racehorse? You Can Invest in One," *The New York Times,* July 31, 2020.

16. Vanessa Friedman, "The Once and Future Handbag," *The New York Times,* December 10, 2020.
17. Pamela Druckerman, "Why Rich People Make the French Squirm," *The New York Times,* July 8, 2016.
18. Ibid.
19. "Hunterdon Medical Center Gave COVID-19 Vaccine to Donors, Relatives of Top Hospital Executives, Report Says," CBS3 Philly, January 28, 2021.
20. Josh Dawsey, Amy Brittain, and Sarah Ellison, "Andrew Cuomo's Family Members Were Given Special Access to Covid Testing, According to People Familiar with the Arrangement," *The Washington Post,* March 24, 2021.
21. "Steve Jobs' 2005 Stanford Commencement Address," Stanford News, June 14, 2005, news.stanford.edu/2005/06/14/jobs-061505/.
22. "Post-1980s Generation the Major Consumers of Luxury Goods in China," *China Daily,* May 6, 2019.
23. Aimee Kim, Lan Luan, and Daniel Zipser, "The Chinese Luxury Consumer," *McKinsey Quarterly,* August 12, 2019, mckinsey.com/featured-insights/china/the-chinese-luxury-consumer.
24. Ashley Rodriguez, "'Crazy Rich Asians' Is the Top-Grossing Romantic Comedy in 10 Years," *Quartz,* October 1, 2018.
25. Vanessa Friedman, "The Glorious Absurdity of Paris Fashion," *The New York Times,* October 7, 2020.
26. "Chanel Pre-owned 1997 Logo Printed T-shirt," Farfetch, farfetch.com/shopping/women/chanel-pre-owned-1997-logo-printed-t-shirt-item-16229862.aspx.
27. "Balenciaga Men's Leaf Logo Crewneck T-shirt," Neiman Marcus, neimanmarcus.com/p/balenciaga-mens-leaf-logo-crewneck-t-shirt-prod224220499?childItemId=NMN6H39.
28. Mark Ellwood, "Me-Documentaries Are the New Status Symbol," Air Mail, January 30, 2021, airmail.news/issues/2021-1-30/me-documentaries-are-the-new-status-symbol.
29. "High Time to End Legacy Admissions," *The Harvard Crimson,* October 28, 2021, thecrimson.com/article/2021/10/28/high-time-to-end-legacy-admissions/.
30. "Knowledge Is Power (Quotation)," Monticello, monticello.org/site/research-and-collections/knowledge-power-quotation.
31. Monica Hesse, "No, More Sex Is Not the Answer to the Country's Problems," *The Washington Post,* January 29, 2021.
32. Steve Almasy and Amanda Watts, "Ethan Couch, Who Killed

Four People in 'Affluenza' Case, Arrested Again in Texas," CNN, January 2, 2020.

33. Jordan Baker and Kirsty Needham, "A Serious Bout of Affluenza," *The Sydney Morning Herald,* May 28, 2005.
34. Daniel Langer, "Many Luxury Brands Shouldn't Panic About 2022. They Should Be in Shock," *Jing Daily,* November 29, 2021.

Chapter 11

1. "World Poverty Facts," FINCA, finca.org/campaign/world-poverty/?gclid=Cj0KCQjwrJOMBhCZARIsAGEd4VFcLhE-9DatTyPJ7Ccb7ujuCSsEGXDF897T4V8mRJbBPGiCx7vapXsaAg8EEALw_wcB.
2. Department of Economic and Social Affairs, "First-Ever United Nations Resolution on Homelessness," United Nations, March 9, 2020, un.org/development/desa/dspd/2020/03/resolution-homelessness/.
3. Niall McCarthy, "1.7 Billion Adults Worldwide Do Not Have Access to a Bank Account [Infographic]," *Forbes,* June 8, 2018, forbes.com/sites/niallmccarthy/2018/06/08/1-7-billion-adults-worldwide-do-not-have-access-to-a-bank-account-infographic/?sh=21e70e724b01.
4. Bryan Taylor, "A Billion Dollars Just Ain't What It Used to Be," Global Financial Data, November 7, 2018, globalfinancialdata.com/a-billion-dollars-just-aint-what-it-used-to-be.
5. "Measuring Poverty," The World Bank, April 16, 2021, worldbank.org/en/topic/measuringpoverty#1.
6. Office of the Assistant Secretary for Planning and Evaluation, "U.S. Federal Poverty Guidelines Used to Determine Financial Eligibility for Certain Federal Programs," U.S. Department of Health and Human Services, February 1, 2021, aspe.hhs.gov/topics/poverty-economic-mobility/poverty-guidelines/prior-hhs-poverty-guidelines-federal-register-references/2021-poverty-guidelines.
7. Dolan,"Forbes' 35th Annual World's Billionaires List."
8. Ibid.
9. Michela Tindera, "These Billionaire Donors Spent the Most Money on the 2020 Election," *Forbes,* February 25, 2021.
10. Christopher Ingraham, "The Richest 1 Percent Now Owns More of the Country's Wealth Than at Any Time in the Past 50 Years," *The Washington Post,* December 6, 2017.
11. Greg Sargent, "Opinion: The Massive Triumph of the Rich, Illus-

trated by Stunning New Data," *The Washington Post,* December 9, 2019.

12. Ibid.
13. Madeline Darmawangsa, "The Duality of the Dutch Economy," UWEB, April 11, 2021, uweb.berkeley.edu/2021/04/11/the-duality-of-the-dutch-economy/.
14. Shaun Walker, "Unequal Russia: Is Anger Stirring in the Global Capital of Inequality?," *The Guardian,* April 25, 2017.
15. "Brazil: Extreme Inequality in Numbers," Oxfam, oxfam.org/en/brazil-extreme-inequality-numbers.
16. "Asia's 20 Richest Families Control $463 Billion," Bloomberg News, November 28, 2020.
17. Bargaining for the Common Good, Institute for Policy Studies, and United for Respect, "Billionaire Wealth vs. Community Health: Protecting Essential Workers from Pandemic Profiteers," Inequality.org, November 2020, inequality.org/wp-content/uploads/2020/11/Report-Billionaires-EssentialWorkers-FINAL.pdf.
18. Rob Picheta, "Rich People Are Staying Healthy for Almost a Decade Longer Than Poor People," CNN, January 15, 2020.
19. Allison Aubrey, "The Pandemic Led to the Biggest Drop in U.S. Life Expectancy Since WWII, Study Finds," *Morning Edition,* NPR, June 23, 2021.
20. Ruth Batchelor and Bob Roberts, "King of the Whole Wide World," azlyrics.com/lyrics/elvispresley/kingofthewholewideworld.html.
21. Bruce Springsteen, "Badlands," genius.com/Bruce-springsteen-badlands-lyrics.
22. Mark Twain, *Mark Twain on the Damned Human Race,* ed. Janet Smith (New York: Hill and Wang, 1962).
23. Daniel Kahneman and Angus Deaton, "High Income Improves Evaluation of Life but Not Emotional Well-Being," *PNAS* 107, no. 38 (September 21, 2010): 16489–93, doi.org/10.1073/pnas.1011492107.
24. Richard Brody, "The Women," *The New Yorker,* November 11, 2009.
25. Abigail Disney, "It's Time to Call Out Disney—and Anyone Else Rich off Their Workers' Backs," *The Washington Post,* April 23, 2019.
26. Leena Rao, "The 2009 List of Tech Billionaires and How Much They Lost," Tech Crunch, March 13, 2009.

27. Tom Huddleston, Jr., "These 5 Billionaires Added the Most to Their Net Worths in 2020," CNBC, December 21, 2020.
28. Willis Wee, "Mark Zuckerberg in Forbes 400 Richest Americans 2009," Tech in Asia, October 2, 2009, techinasia.com/mark-zuckerberg-in-forbes-400-richest-americans-2009.
29. Huddleston, Jr., "These 5 Billionaires Added the Most to Their Net Worths in 2020."
30. "Grasping Large Numbers," The Endowment for Human Development, ehd.org/science_technology_largenumbers.php.
31. Robert Reich, "Trickle-Down Economics Doesn't Work but Build-Up Does—Is Biden Listening?," *The Guardian,* December 20, 2020.
32. "Extreme Carbon Inequality," Oxfam, December 2, 2015, oi-files-d8-prod.s3.eu-west-2.amazonaws.com/s3fs-public/file_attachments/mb-extreme-carbon-inequality-021215-en.pdf.
33. Associated Press, "Memorable Quotes from Global Climate Change Conference," ABC News, November 1, 2021.
34. Ibid.
35. "Śāntideva: Quotes," Good Reads, goodreads.com/author/quotes/29132._ntideva.
36. Chance the Rapper (@chancetherapper), Twitter, January 3, 2015, twitter.com/chancetherapper/status/551568052530450433?lang=en.
37. "A Commitment to Philanthropy," Giving Pledge, givingpledge.org.
38. "The Rockefellers, Part 1," *The Rockefellers,* PBS, 2000, cosmolearning.org/documentaries/the-rockefellers-397/3/.
39. Samuel Bowles, Herbert Gintis, and Melissa Osborne Groves, "Unequal Chances: Family Background and Economic Success," Research Gate, January 2005, researchgate.net/publication/24117936_Unequal_Chances_Family_Background_and_Economic_Success.
40. Zoë Beery, "The Rich Kids Who Want to Tear Down Capitalism," *The New York Times,* November 27, 2020.
41. Jonah E. Bromwich and Alexandra Alter, "Who Is MacKenzie Scott?," *The New York Times,* January 12, 2019.
42. Nicholas Kulish, "MacKenzie Scott Announces $4.2 Billion More in Charitable Giving," *The New York Times,* December 15, 2020.
43. Ellie French, "Billionaire MacKenzie Scott Gifts Vermont Foodbank $9 Million, Largest Donation in Its History," VTDigger,

December 18, 2020, vtdigger.org/2020/12/18/billionaire-mackenzie-scott-gifts-vermont-foodbank-9-million-largest-donation-in-its-history.

44. "Morgan State University Receives Historic Gift of $40M from Philanthropist MacKenzie Scott," Morgan State University, December 15, 2020, news.morgan.edu/40m-gift-from-mackenzie-scott/.
45. "Howard University Receives Transformative Gift from Philanthropist MacKenzie Scott," Howard University, July 28, 2020, newsroom.howard.edu/newsroom/article/12951/howard-university-receives-transformative-gift-philanthropist-mackenzie-scott.
46. Belinda Luscombe, "MacKenzie Scott Gave Away $6 Billion Last Year. It's Not as Easy as It Sounds," *Time,* May 25, 2021.
47. Ibid.
48. Jasmine Ng, "More Than a Third of the Earth's Population Faces Malnutrition Due to Covid," Bloomberg, July 19, 2021.
49. Laura J. Colker, "The Word Gap: The Early Years Make the Difference," *Teaching Young Children* 7, no. 3 (February–March 2014), naeyc.org/resources/pubs/tyc/feb2014/the-word-gap.
50. Jessica Dickler, "Virtual School Resulted in 'Significant' Academic Learning Loss, Study Finds," CNBC, March 30, 2021.
51. Emma Dorn, Bryan Hancock, Jimmy Sarakatsannis, and Ellen Viruleg, "COVID-19 and Learning Loss—Disparities Grow and Students Need Help," McKinsey & Company, December 8, 2020, mckinsey.com/industries/public-and-social-sector/our-insights/covid-19-and-learning-loss-disparities-grow-and-students-need-help.
52. Ibid.
53. Emma Dorn, Bryan Hancock, Jimmy Sarakatsannis, and Ellen Viruleg, "COVID-19 and Student Learning in the United States: The Hurt Could Last a Lifetime," McKinsey & Company, June 1, 2020, mckinsey.com/industries/public-and-social-sector/our-insights/covid-19-and-student-learning-in-the-united-states-the-hurt-could-last-a-lifetime.
54. United States Census Bureau, "QuickFacts," https://www.census.gov/quickfacts/fact/table/tucsoncityarizona,newcanaancdpconnecticut,newcanaantownfairfieldcountyconnecticut/INC110219.
55. Ursula K. Le Guin, *The Wind's Twelve Quarters* (New York: Harper & Row, 1975), 275–84.
56. "Tesco Halts Production at Chinese Factory over Alleged 'Forced' Labour," BBC News, December 22, 2019.

57. Jesse Kornbluth, "If I Were President . . . ," *The New York Times,* August 20, 2021.
58. Brandon Presser, "The Gated Family in the Age of Coronavirus," *Avenue,* November 18, 2020, avenuemagazine.com/private-clubs-luxury-covid-safety-gated-families/.
59. Christopher Cameron, "Rich People Are Buying Homes Just for a Place to Park Their Yachts," *New York Post,* October 26, 2020.
60. Presser, "Gated Family in the Age of Coronavirus."
61. Saahil Desai, "The Pandemic Really Did Change How We Tip," *The Atlantic,* June 29, 2021.
62. GoFundMe, "The Data Behind Donations During the COVID-19 Pandemic," September 24, 2020, medium.com/gofundme-stories/the-data-behind-donations-during-the-covid-19-pandemic-c40e0f690bfa.
63. "Risk of Severe Illness or Death from COVID-19: Racial and Ethnic Health Disparities," Centers for Disease Control and Prevention, December 10, 2020, cdc.gov/coronavirus/2019-ncov/community/health-equity/racial-ethnic-disparities/disparities-illness.html.
64. "Covid Vaccines: Widening Inequality and Millions Vulnerable," UN News, September 19, 2021, news.un.org/en/story/2021/09/1100192.
65. "Coronavirus (COVID-19) Vaccinations," Our World in Data, ourworldindata.org/covid-vaccinations?country=IRQ.
66. Hillary Hoffower and Juliana Kaplan, "*Sex and the City*'s Newest Accessory Says a Lot About How Status Symbols Have Changed over the Past 20 Years," *Insider,* July 20, 2021.

PART THREE

1. "10 Trends for 2001," Young & Rubicam Department of the Future, November 2000.

Chapter 12

1. Margaret Talbot, "Joni Mitchell's Youthful Artistry," *The New Yorker,* November 29, 2020.
2. Robert Longley, "Profile of Women in the United States in 2000," Thought Co., March 3, 2021, thoughtco.com/women-in-the-us-in-2000-3988512.
3. Anneli Miettinen et al., "Increasing Childlessness in Europe: Time Trends and Country Differences," Families and Societies Working

Paper Series, 2015, http://www.familiesandsocieties.eu/wp-content/uploads/2015/03/WP33MiettinenEtAl2015.pdf.

4. Maya Oppenheim, "Unmarried, Childless Women Are Happiest People of All, Says Expert," *The Independent* (U.K.), May 28, 2019.

5. Nancy Weiss Malkiel, *Keep the Damned Women Out: The Struggle for Coeducation* (Princeton, NJ: Princeton University Press, 2018), 87.

6. Ibid., 185.

7. Richard V. Reeves and Ember Smith, "The Male College Crisis Is Not Just in Enrollment, but Completion," Brookings Institution, October 8, 2021, brookings.edu/blog/up-front/2021/10/08/the-male-college-crisis-is-not-just-in-enrollment-but-completion/.

8. Zhang Zhouxiang, "More Women in Higher Education," *China Daily,* December 24, 2020, global.chinadaily.com.cn/a/202012/24/WS5fe3dcb7a31024ad0ba9de9a.html.

9. "Regional Percentage of People Aged Between 30 and 34 Years with University Education in Italy in 2018, by Gender," Statista, February 8, 2021, statista.com/statistics/777040/people-aged-30-34-with-university-education-by-gender-italy/.

10. "Girls' Education," The World Bank, worldbank.org/en/topic/girlseducation#1.

11. "The Data on Women Leaders," Pew Research Center, September 13, 2018, pewsocialtrends.org/fact-sheet/the-data-on-women-leaders/.

12. Emily Jane Fox, "Ex-Lehman Exec Says Dick Fuld Finally Apologized in New Memoir," *Vanity Fair,* March 23, 2016.

13. Andrew Clark, "Lehman Brothers' Golden Girl, Erin Callan: Through the Glass Ceiling—and off the Glass Cliff," *The Guardian,* March 19, 2010.

14. Raakhee Mirchandani, "The 50 Most Powerful Women in NYC," *New York Post,* June 1, 2008.

15. Dominic Elliott, "Ex-CFO's Book Reveals Why Lehman Failed," CNBC, March 31, 2016.

16. Ibid.

17. "Factbox: Examiner's Findings of Claims Against Lehman Board," Reuters, March 11, 2020, reuters.com/article/us-lehman-examiner-factbox/factbox-examiners-findings-of-claims-against-lehman-board-idUSTRE62A5NU20100311.

18. Clark, "Lehman Brothers' Golden Girl, Erin Callan."

19. Elisabeth Grant, "New Catalyst Report: Senior Women 3 Times

More Likely to Lose Job than Senior Men," The Glass Hammer, February 25, 2010, theglasshammer.com/2010/02/new-catalyst-report-senior-women-3-times-more-likely-to-lose-job-than-senior-men/.

20. Sheryl Sandberg, "On Mother's Day, we celebrate all moms," Facebook, May 6, 2016, facebook.com/sheryl/posts/10156819553860177.
21. Scott Carlson, "CBS to Pay $8 Million to Settle Sex Discrimination Lawsuit," Knight Ridder/Tribune News Service, October 25, 2000, web.archive.org/web/20160911033207/https://www.highbeam.com/doc/1G1-72470958.html.
22. Elizabeth Chuck, "Fox News Host Gretchen Carlson Sues CEO Roger Ailes for Sexual Harassment," NBC News, July 6, 2016.
23. Emma Brown, "The Uncovering of Sexual Assault Scandals: #MeToo and the Netherlands," *Dutch Review,* November 11, 2017, dutchreview.com/featured/sexual-assault-scandals-metoo-and-the-netherlands/.
24. "#MeToo Revelations Rock the Dutch Art World," E-Flux Conversations, December 2020, conversations.e-flux.com/t/metoo-revelations-rock-the-dutch-art-world/10180.
25. Ibid.
26. Jason Horowitz, "In Italy, #MeToo Is More Like 'Meh,'" *The New York Times,* December 16, 2017.
27. Molly Ball, "Donald Trump Didn't Really Win 52% of White Women in 2016," *Time,* October 18, 2018.
28. Todd Franko, "Meet Ohio's Director of Health; Not the Story You Would Expect," *Cincinnati Herald,* April 5, 2020.
29. Paige Williams, "How America Can Avoid Dual Cataclysms," *The New Yorker,* November 1, 2020.
30. "Dr. Amy Acton Inspires the Next Generation of Heroes," Governor Mike DeWine, March 30, 2020, YouTube, youtube.com/watch?v=M9YFuM0ZAhU.
31. Associated Press and Mike Foley, "Duwve Withdrew Name from Consideration to Protect Family from Harassment Acton Faced," WCBE, September 11, 2020, wcbe.org/post/duwve-withdrew-name-consideration-protect-family-harassment-acton-faced.
32. "Amy Acton Named Director of Kind Columbus," The Columbus Foundation, August 4, 2020, columbusfoundation.org/news-reports/news/amy-acton-named-director-of-kind-columbus.
33. Ailsa Chang, Noah Caldwell, and Courtney Dorning, "Investigation Lays Out Plot to Kidnap Michigan's Governor," *All Things Considered,* NPR, July 28, 2021.

34. "Quotation of the Day: Whitmer Said to Be Targeted in Kidnap Plot," *The New York Times,* October 8, 2020.

35. Kathleen Walsh, "The Gretchen Whitmer Abduction Plot Is a Window into American Misogyny," *The Week,* October 9, 2020.

36. Anna North, "'The Woman in Michigan': How Gretchen Whitmer Became a Target of Right-wing Hate," *Vox,* October 9, 2020.

37. Ibid.

38. United Nations, "From the Field: The Women Fighting for Generation Equality," UN News, March 7, 2021, news.un.org/en/story/2021/03/1086552.

39. Allyson Bear and Roselle Agner, "Why More Countries Need Female Leaders," *U.S. News & World Report,* March 8, 2021.

40. Luca Coscieme et al., "Women in Power: Female Leadership and Public Health Outcomes During the COVID-19 Pandemic," medRxiv, July 16, 2020, doi.org/10.1101/2020.07.13.20152397.

41. Dina Kesbeh, "New Zealand Prime Minister's Baby Makes History at U.N. General Assembly," NPR, September 25, 2018.

42. Shibani Mahtani, "New Zealand Passes Law Banning Most Semiautomatic Weapons, Less Than a Month After Mosque Massacres," *The Washington Post,* April 10, 2019.

43. Guardian staff, "Jacinda Ardern on the Christchurch Shooting: 'One of New Zealand's Darkest Days,'" *The Guardian,* March 15, 2019.

44. Uri Friedman, "New Zealand's Prime Minister May Be the Most Effective Leader on the Planet," *The Atlantic,* April 19, 2020.

45. "Jacinda Ardern Holds Coronavirus Q&A from Home as New Zealand Lockdown Begins," Bloomberg Quicktake: Now, March 26, 2020, YouTube, youtube.com/watch?v=CNGqEAjasOo.

46. Alexander Smith, "New Zealand's Jacinda Ardern Wins Big After World-Leading Covid-19 Response," NBC News, October 20, 2020.

47. Marisa Peñaloza, "New Zealand Declares Victory over Coronavirus Again, Lifts Auckland Restrictions," NPR, October 7, 2020.

48. Martin Abel, "Women Bosses Face More Discrimination (from Both Men and Women)," *Fast Company,* October 18, 2019.

49. Sophia Rahman, "Why Men Treat Female Bosses Differently Than Their Male Counterparts," *Vice,* April 11, 2017.

50. Ibid.

51. Ibid.

52. Jack Zenger and Joseph Folkman, "Research: Women Score

Higher Than Men in Most Leadership Skills," *Harvard Business Review,* June 25, 2019.

53. "Global Gender Gap Report 2020," World Economic Forum, December 16, 2019, weforum.org/reports/gender-gap-2020-report-100-years-pay-equality.
54. "Pandemic Leads 1 in 4 U.S. Women to Consider Career Change; 2 in 5 Considering STEM," MetLife, October 28, 2020, metlife.com/about-us/newsroom/2020/october/pandemic-leads-1-in-4-us-women-to-consider-career-change-2-in-5-considering-stem/.
55. "Women in the Workplace 2021," McKinsey & Company, September 27, 2021, mckinsey.com/featured-insights/diversity-and-inclusion/women-in-the-workplace.
56. Claire Cain Miller, "The Pandemic Created a Child-Care Crisis. Mothers Bore the Burden," *The New York Times,* May 17, 2021.
57. "Women in the Workplace 2021."
58. "Seven Charts That Show COVID-19's Impact on Women's Employment," McKinsey & Company, March 8, 2021, mckinsey.com/featured-insights/diversity-and-inclusion/seven-charts-that-show-covid-19s-impact-on-womens-employment.
59. Maddy Savage, "How Covid-19 Is Changing Women's Lives," BBC, June 30, 2020.
60. Miller, "Pandemic Created a Child-Care Crisis."
61. Ibid.
62. Kelli Rogers, "The Future of Women at Work Is Alarming—and Promising, New Report Shows," Devex, June 4, 2019, devex.com/news/the-future-of-women-at-work-is-alarming-and-promising-new-report-shows-95041.
63. "Rise of the Modern FeMEnist—Latest Netmums Survey Results," Netmums, https://www.netmums.com/coffeehouse/other-chat-514/news-12/836486-rise-modern-femenist-latest-netmums-survey-results.html.
64. Caroline Simon, "Not Your Mother's (or Grandmother's) Feminism: How Young Women View the Fight for Equality," *USA Today,* March 16, 2017.
65. Kimberlé Crenshaw, "The Urgency of Intersectionality," TED Women 2016, accessed December 2, 2020, ted.com/talks/kimberle_crenshaw_the_urgency_of_intersectionality/transcript.
66. "Gender Equality, the Status of Women and the 2020 Elections," Supermajority/PerryUndem National Survey, August 19, 2019, int.nyt.com/data/documenthelper/1647-supermajority-survey-on-women/429aa78e37ebdf2fe686/optimized/full.pdf#page=1.
67. Ibid.

68. "Woman Get Back in the Kitchen T-Shirt," Zazzle, zazzle.com/woman_get_back_in_the_kitchen_t_shirt-235612024899574859.
69. Alistair Potter, "Topman Pulls T-shirts with 'Sexist and Offensive' Slogans from UK Stores," *Metro* (U.K.), September 14, 2011.
70. Laura Bates, *Everyday Sexism* (London: Simon & Schuster, 2014).
71. Associated Press, "Female Boxers Furious After Sporting Body Says It May Force Women Fighters to Wear Skirts in the Ring," *Daily Mail,* November 8, 2011.
72. Jenny Gross, "Women's Handball Players Are Fined for Rejecting Bikini Uniforms," *The New York Times,* July 20, 2021.
73. Andrew McMurtry and AFP, "Women Fined $2409 for Wearing Shorts Instead of Bikini Bottoms During Beach Handball Game at European Championships," News.com.au, July 21, 2021, news.com.au/sport/more-sports/bikini-drama-overshadows-beach-handball-european-championships/news-story/0f3710004fc48453799032733b79fb0b.
74. Katelyn Ohashi, "Young Gymnasts Are Taught That Their Bodies Are Not Their Own. Simone Biles Refused to Accept That," *Time,* July 28, 2021.
75. Ashlie D. Stevens, "'Framing Britney Spears' Makes Viewers Reflect on How Everyone Accepted the Abusive Sexism She Faced," *Salon,* February 9, 2021.
76. Anastasia Tsioulcas, "Britney Spears' Conservatorship Has Finally Ended," NPR, November 12, 2021.

Chapter 13

1. FCA, "All-New 2021 Ram 1500 TRX: Quickest, Fastest and Most Powerful Mass-Produced Truck in the World with 702-Horsepower 6.2-Liter Supercharged HEMI V-8 Engine," press release, PR Newswire, August 17, 2020, prnewswire.com/news-releases/all-new-2021-ram-1500-trx-quickest-fastest-and-most-powerful-mass-produced-truck-in-the-world-with-702-horsepower-6-2-liter-supercharged-hemi-v-8-engine-301112769.html.
2. Rita DeMichiel, "The 2021 Ram 1500 TRX Is Simply the Best-Looking Truck Out," Motor Biscuit, January 31, 2021, motorbiscuit.com/the-2021-ram-1500-trx-is-simply-the-best-looking-truck-out/.
3. Ibid.

4. Timothy Cain, "Dodge Ram/Ram Pickup Sales Figures," Good Car Bad Car, goodcarbadcar.net/dodge-ram-sales-figures/.
5. "Pickup Truck Owner Demographics: Who Buys Pickup Trucks?," Hedges & Company, hedgescompany.com/blog/2018/10/pickup-truck-owner-demographics/.
6. Ian Bremmer, "The 'Strongmen Era' Is Here. Here's What It Means for You," *Time,* May 3, 2018.
7. "Number of Mass Shootings in the United States Between 1982 and May 2021, by Shooter's Gender," Statista, November 25, 2021, statista.com/statistics/476445/mass-shootings-in-the-us-by-shooter-s-gender/.
8. Nicole M. Fortin, Philip Oreopoulos, and Shelley Phipps, "Leaving Boys Behind: Gender Disparities in High Academic Achievement," National Bureau of Economic Research, Working Paper 19331, August 2013, nber.org/system/files/working_papers/w19331/w19331.pdf.
9. Chloe Taylor, "Firms with a Female CEO Have a Better Stock Price Performance, New Research Says," CNBC, October 18, 2019.
10. Michael Baggs, "Body Image Affects Half of Men's Mental Health, New Study Shows," BBC News, April 28, 2021.
11. Tarik Carroll, "Every Man," EveryMAN, theeverymanproject.com/about.
12. "Changing the Face of What It Means to Be a Man," Humen, wearehumen.org/about.
13. "Discover What's Missing," Evryman, evryman.com/.
14. "Our Story," The Man Cave, themancave.life/our-story/.
15. Jennifer Medina, "The Macho Appeal of Donald Trump," *The New York Times,* October 14, 2020.
16. Jeva Lange, "61 Things Donald Trump Has Said About Women," *The Week,* October 16, 2018.
17. Andrew Kaczynski and Megan Apper, "Donald Trump Thinks Men Who Change Diapers Are Acting 'Like the Wife,'" BuzzFeed, April 24, 2016.
18. "'Harmful' Gender Stereotypes in Adverts Banned," BBC, June 14, 2019.
19. "We Heal, Inspire, Educate and Celebrate Black Fathers," Dope Black Dads, dopeblack.org/dopeblackdads.
20. "The World According to Slater," *Harvard Magazine,* March–April 2013, harvardmagazine.com/2013/03/the-world-according-to-slater.

21. Ibid.
22. Associated Press, "Canadian Incel Found Guilty in Van Attack That Killed 10 People, Mostly Women, in Toronto," *USA Today*, March 3, 2021.
23. Jennifer Wright, "Why Incels Hate Women," *Harper's Bazaar*, April 27, 2018.

Chapter 14

1. Alyssa Rosenberg, "Madison Cawthorn Accidentally Trolls His Way into a Great Point About Men and Work-Life Balance," *The Washington Post*, May 24, 2021.
2. Stephen Whittle, "A Brief History of Transgender Issues," *The Guardian*, June 2, 2010.
3. *Lawrence v. Texas*, 529 US 558 (2003), oyez.org/cases/2002/02-102.
4. Corinne Segal, "David Bowie Made Androgyny Cool, and It Was About Time," *PBS NewsHour*, January 11, 2016.
5. Kristin Anderson, "The New York Dolls's Sylvain Sylvain on the Band's Groundbreaking Style and His Clothing Line," *Vogue*, November 19, 2015.
6. Koh Mochizuki, "Ohio School Officials Shut Down Outraged Parents After Lesbian Couple Crowned Prom King and Queen," Comic Sands, May 4, 2021, comicsands.com/ohio-school-lesbian-couple-prom-2652863402.html.
7. Russell Goldman, "Here's a List of 58 Gender Options for Facebook Users," ABC News, February 13, 2014.
8. Dennis Baron, "Pronoun Backlash," *The Web of Language*, October 4, 2020, blogs.illinois.edu/view/25/49786652#image-11.
9. "How a Review Changed Both Sarah Silverman and Our Critic," *The New York Times*, May 19, 2021.
10. Lily Wakefield, "Railway Firm Apologises to Non-binary Passenger for 'Ladies and Gentlemen' Announcement," Pink News, May 14, 2021, pinknews.co.uk/2021/05/14/non-binary-train-london-north-eastern-railway-ladies-gentlemen/.
11. Sara Kettler, "How Ellen DeGeneres' Historic Coming-Out Episode Changed Television," Biography, April 14, 2020, biography.com/news/ellen-degeneres-sitcom-coming-out-episode.
12. David Bauder, "Ellen DeGeneres Mad at ABC's Warning for 'Ellen,'" Associated Press, October 8, 1997.
13. Samantha Grossman, "Ellen DeGeneres Addresses Anti-gay 'One Million Moms' Group," *Time*, February 8, 2012.

14. Trish Bendix, "Backlash: What Happened to Ellen DeGeneres *After* She Came Out?," New Now Next, April 27, 2017, newnownext.com/backlash-what-happened-to-ellen-degeneres-after-she-came-out/04/2017/.
15. J. K. Rowling (@jk_rowling), Twitter, June 6, 2020, twitter.com/jk_rowling/status/1269382518362509313?lang=en.
16. Jennifer O'Connell, "There Are No Winners in Trans-Rights Culture War," *The Irish Times,* June 13, 2020.
17. Schmidt, "1 in 6 Gen Z Adults Are LGBT."
18. Ibid.
19. Gwen Aviles, "'I'm Not Male or Female': Sam Smith Comes Out as Gender Nonbinary," NBC News, March 18, 2019.
20. Josie Fischels and Sarah McCammon, "2021 Miss Nevada Will Be the First Openly Transgender Miss USA Contestant," *All Things Considered,* NPR, July 3, 2021.
21. Camp Aranu'tiq, camparanutiq.org.
22. Associated Press, "'Bathroom Bill' to Cost North Carolina $3.76 Billion," CNBC, March 27, 2017.
23. Yuki Noguchi, "He, She, They: Workplaces Adjust as Gender Identity Norms Change," *Morning Edition,* NPR, October 16, 2019.
24. "Swimwear for You," Humankind, humankindswim.com/pages/our-story.
25. "Levi's, Now Without the Labels," Levi's, levi.com/GB/en_GB/features/unlabeled.
26. "Beauty of Becoming," Levi's, January 2021, levi.com/US/en_US/blog/article/beauty-of-becoming/.
27. Mattel (@Mattel), Twitter, September 25, 2019, twitter.com/Mattel/status/1176726868294135808.
28. Eric R. Varner, "Transcending Gender: Assimilation, Identity, and Roman Imperial Portraits," *Memoirs of the American Academy in Rome. Supplementary Volumes* 7 (2008): 185–205, jstor.org/stable/40379354.
29. Cecily Hilleary, "Native American Two-Spirits Look to Reclaim Lost Heritage," Voice of America, June 15, 2018, voanews.com/usa/native-american-two-spirits-look-reclaim-lost-heritage.

Chapter 15

1. Alex Williams, "How the Selfie Conquered the World," *The New York Times,* March 2, 2018.
2. "Mason Cooley," brainyquote.com/quotes/mason_cooley_395737.

3. Mollie A. Ruben et al., "Is Technology Enhancing or Hindering Interpersonal Communication? A Framework and Preliminary Results to Examine the Relationship Between Technology Use and Nonverbal Decoding Skill," *Frontiers in Psychology,* January 15, 2021, doi.org/10.3389/fpsyg.2020.611670.
4. Vanessa Romo, "Whistleblower's Testimony Has Resurfaced Facebook's Instagram Problem," NPR, October 5, 2021.
5. Alicia Phaneuf, "The Number of Health and Fitness App Users Increased 27% from Last Year," eMarketer, July 20, 2020, emarketer.com/content/number-of-health-fitness-app-users-increased-27-last-year.
6. Dave Chaffey, "Global Social Media Statistics Research Summary 2022," Smart Insights, October 26, 2021, smartinsights.com/social-media-marketing/social-media-strategy/new-global-social-media-research/.
7. Greg Iacurci, "The Gig Economy Has Ballooned by 6 Million People Since 2010. Financial Worries May Follow," CNBC, February 4, 2020.
8. Tina Brown, "The Gig Economy," The Daily Beast, January 12, 2009.
9. Tyler Horvath, "What Is a Solopreneur?," Solopreneur Institute, solopreneurinstitute.com/what-is-solopreneur/.
10. David G. Blanchflower, Andrew Oswald, and Alois Stutzer, "Latent Entrepreneurship Across Nations," August 27, 2000, downloaded from Cite Seer X, hosted by Pennsylvania State University, citeseerx.ist.psu.edu/viewdoc/download?doi=10.1.1.503.7501&rep=rep1&type=pdf.
11. Robert Putnam, *Bowling Alone: The Collapse and Revival of American Community* (New York: Simon & Schuster, 2000).
12. Dawne Gee, "Know Thy Neighbor? Survey Shows Many Don't Know Their Neighbors by Name," WAVE 3 News, March 3, 2021, wave3.com/2021/03/04/know-thy-neighbor-survey-shows-many-dont-know-their-neighbors-by-name/.
13. Grand View Research, Inc., "Smart Home Security Camera Market Size Worth $11.89 Billion by 2027," press release, PR Newswire, November 25, 2020, prnewswire.com/news-releases/smart-home-security-camera-market-size-worth-11-89-billion-by-2027-grand-view-research-inc-301180410.html.
14. Elizabeth Segran, "Social Clubs Died Out in America. Now, Venture Capital Is Bringing Them Back," *Fast Company,* May 28, 2019.
15. Ben Bromley, "In Depth: Shrinking Service Clubs Try to Reach

Millennials," *Baraboo News Republic,* May 10, 2019, wiscnews .com/baraboonewsrepublic/news/local/in-depth-shrinking-service -clubs-try-to-reach-millennials/article_99763e68-f425-5253-875c -d6603a0c9dd9.html.

16. Jeffrey M. Jones, "U.S. Church Membership Falls Below Majority for First Time," Gallup, March 29, 2021, news.gallup.com/poll/ 341963/church-membership-falls-below-majority-first-time.aspx.
17. Shabnam Berry-Khan, "The Cultural Experience of Loneliness: Why South Asians Need to Take Heed During the Coronavirus Pandemic," Global Indian Series, January 11, 2021, globalindianseries .com/the-cultural-experience-and-neuroscience-of-loneliness-why -south-asians-need-to-take-heed-during-the-coronavirus-pandemic/.
18. Department for Digital, Culture, Media and Sport; Office for Civil Society; and Baroness Barran, "Loneliness Minister: 'It's More Important Than Ever to Take Action," Gov.UK, press release, June 17, 2021, gov.uk/government/news/loneliness-minister -its-more-important-than-ever-to-take-action.
19. "How Lonely Are Europeans?," EU Science Hub, European Commission, June 12, 2019, ec.europa.eu/jrc/en/news/how-lonely-are -europeans.
20. Eric Klinenberg, *Going Solo: The Extraordinary Rise and Surprising Appeal of Living Alone* (New York: Penguin, 2013), 3.
21. "People Living Alone," Statistics Japan, November 13, 2010, stats -japan.com/t/kiji/11902.
22. "People Living Alone to Account for 40% of Japanese Households in 2040," *The Jakarta Post*, January 15, 2018, thejakarta post.com/life/2018/01/15/people-living-alone-to-account-for-40 -of-japanese-households-in-2040.html.
23. "Over Half of Sweden's Households Made Up of One Person," Eurostat, September 5, 2017, ec.europa.eu/eurostat/web/products -eurostat-news/-/DDN-20170905-1?inheritRedirect=true.
24. Jeff Smith, "Cities with the Most Adults Living Alone," *Self,* self .inc/blog/adults-living-alone.
25. Ibid.
26. Albert Esteve et al., "Living Alone over the Life Course: Cross-National Variations on an Emerging Issue," *Population and Development Review* 46, no. 1 (March 2020): 169–89, https:// doi.org/10.1111/padr.12311.
27. Esteban Ortiz-Ospina, "The Rise of Living Alone: How One-Person Households Are Becoming Increasingly Common Around the World," Our World in Data, December 10, 2019, ourworldindata.org/living-alone.

28. Evan L. Ardiel and Catharine H. Rankin, "The Importance of Touch in Development," *Paediatrics Child Health* 15, no. 3 (March 2010): 153–56, doi.org/10.1093%2Fpch%2F15.3.153.

29. Sheldon Cohen, Denise Janicki-Deverts, Ronald B. Turner, and William J. Doyle, "Does Hugging Provide Stress-Buffering Social Support? A Study of Susceptibility to Upper Respiratory Infection and Illness," *Psychological Science* 26, no. 2 (February 2015): 135–47, doi.org/10.1177%2F0956797614559284.

30. Cuddle Party, cuddleparty.com.

31. Scott Simon, "Opinion: The Comfort of Cow Cuddles," *Weekend Edition Saturday,* NPR, March 13, 2021.

32. "New Report of Global Weighted Blanket (Gravity Blanket) Market Overview, Manufacturing Cost Structure Analysis, Growth Opportunities 2021 to 2026," *Market Watch,* November 15, 2021.

33. Serena Gove, "How Calming Compression Clothing Can Be Beneficial (for Adults and Children)," Caring Clothing, April 12, 2019, caringclothing.com.au/blogs/adaptive-clothing-disabled/how-calming-compression-clothing-can-be-beneficial-for-adults-children.

34. "SAC Releases Report Comparing 3 Years of COVID-19's Effect on US Animal Shelters," Shelter Animals Count, shelteranimalscount.org/blog.

35. Jeffery Ho, Sabir Hussain, and Olivier Sparagano, "Did the COVID-19 Pandemic Spark a Public Interest in Pet Adoption?," *Frontiers in Veterinary Science,* May 7, 2021, doi.org/10.3389/fvets.2021.647308.

36. L. F. Carver, "How the Coronavirus Pet Adoption Boom Is Reducing Stress," The Conversation, May 24, 2020, theconversation.com/how-the-coronavirus-pet-adoption-boom-is-reducing-stress-138074.

37. National Service Animal Registry, nsarco.com.

38. Anna Burke, "What Is a Crisis Response Dog? Comfort Dogs vs. Therapy Dogs," American Kennel Club, May 12, 2021, akc.org/expert-advice/training/what-is-a-crisis-response-dog/.

39. "Smart Speaker Market Revenue Worldwide from 2014 to 2025," Statista, April 7, 2021, statista.com/statistics/1022823/worldwide-smart-speaker-market-revenue/.

40. "iLife: Perceptions and Expectations Regarding Technology," Havas, havas.cz/en/meaningful-difference-en/ilife-perceptions-and-expectations-regarding-technology/.

41. Scott Dewing, "Rise of the Sexbots," Medium, June 20, 2021, medium.com/predict/rise-of-the-sexbots-550c93f4d310.

42. Ibid.

43. Maureen Dowd, "A.I. Is Not A-OK," *The New York Times,* October 30, 2021.

44. Ibid.

45. Tamara Bhandari, "Stroke-Recovery Device Using Brain-Computer Interface Receives FDA Market Authorization," Washington University School of Medicine in St. Louis, April 27, 2021, medicine.wustl.edu/news/stroke-recovery-device-using-brain-computer-interface-receives-fda-market-authorization/.

46. Eillie Anzilotti, "Watch This Device Translate Silent Thoughts into Speech," MIT Media Lab, May 16, 2019, media.mit.edu/articles/watch-this-device-translate-silent-thoughts-into-speech/.

47. "Saturday Night Passover Featuring Dan Levy, Finn Wolfhard, Billy Porter, Idina Menzel and More," Tasty, April 11, 2020, YouTube, youtube.com/watch?v=QGRsH2Qti_Q.

48. Carol Glatz, "Vatican Registers High Growth, Engagement Online for Holy Week, Easter," *Crux,* April 14, 2020.

49. Rosie Murphy, "Local Consumer Review Survey 2020," Bright Ideas, December 9, 2020, brightlocal.com/research/local-consumer-review-survey/.

PART FOUR

1. Tom Gillespie, "COVID-19: In Charts—One Year Since the Coronavirus Outbreak Was Declared a Global Pandemic," Sky News, March 11, 2021, news.sky.com/story/covid-19-in-charts-one-year-since-the-coronavirus-outbreak-was-declared-a-global-pandemic-12242044.

2. Jack Goodman and Flora Carmichael, "Coronavirus: Bill Gates 'Microchip' Conspiracy Theory and Other Vaccine Claims Fact-Checked," BBC, May 20, 2020.

3. RedNewspaper, "Vaccinated People Are Walking Time Bombs and a Threat to Society," Foreign Affairs Intelligence Council, April 8, 2021, web.archive.org/web/20210421183422/https://foreignaffairsintelligencecouncil.wordpress.com/2021/04/08/vaccinated-people-are-walking-biological-time-bombs-and-a-threat-to-society/.

4. Ibid.

5. Mark Zuckerberg, "Bringing the World Closer Together," Face-

book, m.facebook.com/nt/screen/?params=%7B%22note_id%22%3A393134628500376%7D&path=%2Fnotes%2Fnote%2F&_rdr.

6. Stephen Loiaconi, "'Avalanche' of Allegations Against Facebook Raises New Questions," ABC 4 News, October 25, 2021, abcnews4.com/news/nation-world/avalanche-of-allegations-against-facebook-raises-new-questions.
7. Eliza Mackintosh, "Facebook Knew It Was Being Used to Incite Violence in Ethiopia. It Did Little to Stop the Spread, Documents Show," CNN, October 25, 2021.
8. Clare Duffy, "Facebook Has Known It Has a Human Trafficking Problem for Years. It Still Hasn't Fully Fixed It," CNN, October 25, 2021.
9. Craig Timberg, Elizabeth Dwoskin, and Reed Albergotti, "Inside Facebook, Jan. 6 Violence Fueled Anger, Regret over Missed Warning Signs," *The Washington Post,* October 22, 2021.
10. Jonathan Rothwell and Sonal Desai, "How Misinformation Is Distorting COVID Policies and Behaviors," Brookings Institution, December 22, 2020, brookings.edu/research/how-misinformation-is-distorting-covid-policies-and-behaviors/.
11. Julia Manchester, "Analyst Says US Is Most Divided Since Civil War," *The Hill,* October 3, 2018.
12. Jon Henley, "Europeans' Confidence in EU Hit by Coronavirus Response," *The Guardian,* June 8, 2021.
13. Kat Devlin, Moira Fagan, and Aidan Connaughton, "People in Advanced Economies Say Their Society Is More Divided than Before Pandemic," Pew Research Center, June 23, 2021, pewresearch.org/global/2021/06/23/people-in-advanced-economies-say-their-society-is-more-divided-than-before-pandemic/.
14. Wai Lin, "XFS Patches for Linux 5.10 Delays the Year 2038 Problem to 2486," Linux Reviews, October 17, 2020, linuxreviews.org/XFS_Patches_For_Linux_5.10_Delays_The_Year_2038_Problem_To_2486.
15. Vishal Thakur, "What Is the 2038 Problem?," Science ABC, November 13, 2021, scienceabc.com/innovation/what-is-the-2038-problem.html.
16. Conspiracy Theory Trivia Board Game, Neddy Games, shopneddy.com/products/conspiracy-theory-trivia-board-game.
17. Ian Graber-Stiehl, "To Study Swarming Cicadas, It Takes a Crowd," *Science,* June 1, 2021.

18. Ian Frazier, "When Bob Dylan Heard the Cicadas," *The New Yorker,* June 2, 2021.
19. "Well . . . This Is the Million Dollar Question. And One That's Very Hard to Answer," World Wildlife Federation, wwf.panda.org/discover/our_focus/biodiversity/biodiversity/.
20. Ibid.

Chapter 16

1. John Harris, "What Does Tech Take from Us? Meet the Writer Who Has Counted 100 Big Losses," *The Guardian,* November 3, 2021.
2. Ibid.
3. Jackie Salo, "China Using 'Emotion Recognition Technology' for Surveillance," *New York Post,* March 4, 2021.
4. Thomas Humphry Ward, ed., *The English Poets,* vol. 4, *Wordsworth to Rossetti* (London: Macmillan, 1919).
5. Ron Baker, "The (Modern) Father of the Billable Hour and Timesheet," VeraSage Institute, verasage.com/verasage-institute/blog/the_modern_father_of_the_billable_hour_and_timesheet.
6. Charlie Svensson, "6-Hour Workdays in Sweden Boost Productivity, Energy, and Happiness," Daily Scandinavian, January 25, 2021, dailyscandinavian.com/6-hour-workdays-in-sweden-boost-productivity-energy-and-happiness/.
7. Simon Kemp, "Digital 2021: 60 Percent of the World's Population Is Now Online," We Are Social, April 22, 2021, wearesocial.com/blog/2021/04/60-percent-of-the-worlds-population-is-now-online/.
8. Tyler Cowen, "Cryptocurrency Is Not Necessarily the Future," Bloomberg, December 29, 2020.
9. Stephen Johnson, "'The Time Is Now' for Cryptocurrencies, PayPal CEO Says," Big Think, December 4, 2020, bigthink.com/technology-innovation/future-of-cryptocurrency?rebelltitem=3#rebelltitem3.
10. Luke Conway, "10 Important Cryptocurrencies Other Than Bitcoin," Investopedia, November 19, 2021, investopedia.com/tech/most-important-cryptocurrencies-other-than-bitcoin/.
11. James McWhinney, "Why Governments Are Wary of Bitcoin," Investopedia, September 21, 2021, investopedia.com/articles/forex/042015/why-governments-are-afraid-bitcoin.asp.
12. Rupert Neate, "SpaceX Could Make Elon Musk the World's First

Trillionaire, Says Morgan Stanley," *The Guardian,* October 20, 2021.

13. Chris Taylor, "The Future of Free Money," Mashable, 2020, mashable.com/feature/universal-basic-income-future/.
14. "What Is Digital Fabrication," IGI Global, igi-global.com/dictionary/digital-fabrication/53850.
15. Emma Newberger and Adam Jeffery, "Photos Show Impact of Temporary Air Pollution Drops Across the World from Coronavirus Lockdown," CNBC, April 23, 2020.
16. Erik Stokstad, "The Pandemic Stilled Human Activity. What Did This 'Anthropause' Mean for Wildlife?," *Science*, August 13, 2020.
17. Damian Carrington, "New Super-Enzyme Eats Plastic Bottles Six Times Faster," *The Guardian,* September 28, 2020.
18. Jordan Davidson, "Scientists Find Bacteria That Eats Plastic," EcoWatch, March 27, 2020, ecowatch.com/scientists-find-bacteria-that-eats-plastic-2645582039.html.
19. Frank Jordans, "Germany Is First Major Economy to Phase Out Coal and Nuclear," AP News, July 3, 2020.
20. "Finland Approves Ban on Coal for Energy Use from 2029," Reuters, February 28, 2019.
21. "Fact Sheet: President Biden Sets 2030 Greenhouse Gas Pollution Reduction Target Aimed at Creating Good-Paying Union Jobs and Securing U.S. Leadership on Clean Energy Technologies," White House Briefing Room, April 22, 2021, whitehouse.gov/briefing-room/statements-releases/2021/04/22/fact-sheet-president-biden-sets-2030-greenhouse-gas-pollution-reduction-target-aimed-at-creating-good-paying-union-jobs-and-securing-u-s-leadership-on-clean-energy-technologies/.
22. Dan Gearino, "What Germany Can Teach the US About Quitting Coal," Inside Climate News, October 15, 2020, insideclimatenews.org/news/15102020/germany-coal-transition/.
23. "Renewable Heat Incentive," Energy Saving Trust, energysavingtrust.org.uk/grants-and-loans/renewable-heat-incentive/.
24. "Smart Export Guarantee," Energy Saving Trust, energysavingtrust.org.uk/advice/smart-export-guarantee/.
25. Sara Schonhardt, "U.K. Will Stop Using Coal in Just Three Years," E&E News, *Scientific American,* July 1, 2021.
26. "18 Surprising Projections About the Future of Water," Seametrics, seametrics.com/blog/future-water/.
27. Sandy Milne, "How Water Shortages Are Brewing Wars," BBC Future, August 16, 2021.

28. Meaghan O'Neill, "The World's Tallest Timber-Framed Building Finally Opens Its Doors," *Architectural Digest,* March 22, 2019, architecturaldigest.com/story/worlds-tallest-timber-framed-building-finally-opens-doors.

29. "Wooden Satellite Due for Launch by End of 2021," Engineering and Technology, April 23, 2021, eandt.theiet.org/content/articles/2021/04/selfie-stick-wielding-wooden-satellite-to-launch-by-end-of-2021/.

30. Kim Severson, "How Will Americans Eat in 2022? The Food Forecaster Speaks," *The New York Times,* December 28, 2021.

31. "Exploring the Green Canopy in Cities Around the World," Treepedia, senseable.mit.edu/treepedia.

32. City of Melbourne, "Urban Forest Strategy," https://www.melbourne.vic.gov.au/community/greening-the-city/urban-forest/Pages/urban-forest-strategy.aspx.

33. University of Wisconsin–Madison, "Trees Are Crucial to the Future of Cities," *Science News,* March 25, 2019.

34. Qing Li, "'Forest Bathing' Is Great for Your Health. Here's How to Do It," *Time,* May 1, 2018.

35. Chris Taylor, "The Future's Getting Smarter," Mashable, 2019, mashable.com/feature/smart-drugs-future-brain/.

36. "Brain Implants to Restore Lost Memories," Future Timeline.net, futuretimeline.net/21stcentury/2023.htm#memory-chip-brain-implant.

37. Hiroyuki Katoh, Kazuya Yokota, and Michael G. Fehlings, "Regeneration of Spinal Cord Connectivity Through Stem Cell Transplantation and Biomaterial Scaffolds," *Frontiers in Cellular Neuroscience,* June 6, 2019, doi.org/10.3389/fncel.2019.00248.

38. Anthony L. Komaroff, "Why Are mRNA Vaccines So Exciting?," Harvard Health Publishing, November 1, 2021, health.harvard.edu/blog/why-are-mrna-vaccines-so-exciting-2020121021599.

39. Aparna Vidyasagar and Nicoletta Lanese, "What Is CRISPR?," Live Science, October 20, 2021, livescience.com/58790-crispr-explained.html.

40. "Noncommunicable Diseases," World Health Organization, April 13, 2021, who.int/news-room/fact-sheets/detail/noncommunicable-diseases.

41. Alison Abbott, "COVID's Mental-Health Toll: How Scientists Are Tracking a Surge in Depression," *Nature,* February 3, 2021.

42. Ibid.

43. Yasemin Saplakoglu, "'Diseases of Despair' on the Rise Across

the US," Live Science, November 10, 2020, livescience.com/diseases-despair-rising-us.html.

44. "Policy Brief: COVID-19 and the Need for Action on Mental Health," United Nations, May 13, 2020, un.org/sites/un2.un.org/files/un_policy_brief-covid_and_mental_health_final.pdf.

45. Yascha Mounk and Roberto Stefan Foa, "This Is How Democracy Dies," *The Atlantic,* January 29, 2020.

46. Rob Toews, "Deepfakes Are Going to Wreak Havoc on Society. We Are Not Prepared," *Forbes,* May 25, 2020.

47. Mark Fischetti, "Africa Is Way Bigger Than You Think," *Scientific American,* June 16, 2015, blogs.scientificamerican.com/observations/africa-is-way-bigger-than-you-think/.

48. Klaus Schwab, "The Fourth Industrial Revolution: What It Means, How to Respond," World Economic Forum, January 14, 2016, weforum.org/agenda/2016/01/the-fourth-industrial-revolution-what-it-means-and-how-to-respond/.

49. "Foresight Africa: Top Priorities for the Continent 2020–2030," Brookings Institution, January 8, 2020, brookings.edu/multi-chapter-report/foresight-africa-top-priorities-for-the-continent-in-2020/.

50. "Africa Growth," Future Agenda, futureagenda.org/foresights/africa-growth/.

51. "Forecast of the Total Population of Africa from 2020 to 2050," Statista, August 10, 2021, statista.com/statistics/1224205/forecast-of-the-total-population-of-africa/.

52. "The Future Is African," Council on Foreign Relations, December 11, 2020, cfr.org/podcasts/future-african.

53. "Africa Growth."

54. Ibid.

55. Alyssa Maio, "What Is Nollywood and How Did It Become the 2nd Largest Film Industry?," Studio Binder, December 5, 2019, studiobinder.com/blog/what-is-nollywood/.

56. Simon Varrella, "Life Expectancy in Africa 2021," Statista, August 12, 2021, statista.com/statistics/274511/life-expectancy-in-africa/#:~:text=For%20those%20born%20in%202021,for%20females%20in%20mid%2D2021.

57. "Iceland Has Most Developed Information Society Worldwide, According to UN Report," *Iceland Magazine,* November 21, 2017, icelandmag.is/article/iceland-has-most-developed-information-society-worldwide-according-un-report.

58. Patrick J. Kiger, "How Venezuela Fell from the Richest Country in

South America into Crisis," History, May 9, 2019, history.com/news/venezuela-chavez-maduro-crisis.

59. Dany Bahar and Meagan Dooley, "Venezuela Refugee Crisis to Become the Largest and Most Underfunded in Modern History," Brookings Institution, December 9, 2019, brookings.edu/blog/up-front/2019/12/09/venezuela-refugee-crisis-to-become-the-largest-and-most-underfunded-in-modern-history/.
60. "A Century of Decline: The Tragedy of Argentina," *The Economist,* February 15, 2014.
61. "The World Bank in Argentina: Overview," The World Bank, October 4, 2021, worldbank.org/en/country/argentina/overview.
62. "Democracy in Post-Pandemic Latin America: Enhanced Vulnerabilities," National Endowment for Democracy, Democracy Digest, December 9, 2020, demdigest.org/democracy-in-post-pandemic-latin-america-enhanced-vulnerabilities/.
63. "Back to Basics: Getting Serious About Advancing Democracy," National Endowment for Democracy, Democracy Digest, December 4, 2020, demdigest.org/get-serious-about-advancing-democracy/.
64. Craig Dempsey, "The Rise of Entrepreneurship in Latin America," Data Driven Investor, February 9, 2019, medium.datadriveninvestor.com/the-rise-of-entrepreneurship-in-latin-america-18370c0f30ed.
65. "Latin America Most Optimistic Region—According to C-Suite Barometer," Mazars, mazars.com/Home/Insights/Latest-insights/C-suite-Latam-most-optimistic-region.
66. "Welcome to Accumulus Synergy," accumulus.org.
67. "Commit. Act. Impact.," climatecollaborative.com/about.

Conclusion

1. Marshall McLuhan and Bruce R. Powers, *The Global Village: Transformations in World Life and Media in the 21st Century* (New York: Oxford University Press, 1989).
2. Città Slow, citta-slow.com.
3. "International Network of Cities Where Living Is Good," Città Slow International, cittaslow.org.
4. Neil Ruiz, Luis Noe-Bustamante, and Nadya Saber, "Coming of Age," *Finance & Development* 57, no. 1 (March 2020), imf.org/external/pubs/ft/fandd/2020/03/infographic-global-population-trends-picture.htm.
5. Sophie Jeong, "Exhausted and Without Hope, East Asian Youth Are 'Lying Flat,'" CNN Business, August 29, 2021.

6. "'Selfie' Named by Oxford Dictionaries as Word of 2013," BBC, November 19, 2013.
7. Ray Kurzweil, "The Dawn of the Singularity, a Visual Timeline of Ray Kurzweil's Predictions," Futurism, October 13, 2015, kurzweilai.net/futurism-the-dawn-of-the-singularity-a-visual-timeline-of-ray-kurzweils-predictions#!prettyPhoto.
8. Ibid.
9. Ibid.

INDEX

Abel, Martin, 171
Abzug, Bella, 188
Accumulus Synergy, 238
acid rain, 34
Action 2000, 10, 11
Acton, Amy, 166–167
Adams, Eric, 224
Adams, Martin, 68
ADP Research Institute, 198
affluenza, 137
Africa, 234–235
After the Warning to 2038 (Cyr), 214
"age of rage," 25
"ages without stages," xxi
AI devices, 203–205, 221
Ailes, Roger, 165
Ajibade, Jola, 36–37
Alger, Horatio, 103
Allen, Woody, 104, 105
Allied Market Research, 75
allyship, rise of, 5
Alston, Philip, 37
"alternative facts," 6, 234
always-on media environment, xxi, 15
Amazon, 42–43
American Beauty (film), 104
American Dialect Society, xx
American exceptionalism, 65
American Family Association, 192
American Museum of Natural History, 215
American Red Cross, 11
Amnesty International, 50, 75
Ancestry, 93
Anderson, Thomas F., 47–48
Andeweg, Julian, 165
antiabortion activists, 175–176
anti-expert mindsets, 15
anti-immigration sentiment, 22, 94–95, 104, 105–106
anti-science mindset, 23–24
antisocial tendencies, 24–25
anti-vaxxer movement, xxvii, 23–24, 212
antiwar movement, 103, 188
anxiety, 87, 232–233
Ardern, Jacinda, 169–171
Argentina, 236
Armed Forces Network, 12
Army Public School shooting, 20
Arrhenius, Svante, 33
Arthur, Bea, 159
art/music, impact of, 189
Asia Society, 81
AT&T, 10
authentic, embrace of, 6–7
autocrats/autocracy, 105, 180, 237
automation, 221, 222
autonomy, 175, 177–178
AXA, 52

Back to the Future Part II, 29
Bader, Ernest, 117–118
"Badlands" (Springsteen), 142
Baez, Joan, 188

Baidu, 79
Ban the Scan campaign, 75
Barbie dolls, gender-neutral, 195
Barlow, John Perry, xxii–xxiii
Bates, Laura, 176
"bathroom bills," 194
Belarus, 3–4
Ben & Jerry's, 123
Bennett, Robert, 10
Berejiklian, Gladys, 39
Berry-Khan, Shabnam, 199–200
Bessette, Lauren, xix
Best Countries ranking, *U.S. News & World Report*'s, 64
Beyond Meat, xvi
Bezos, Jeff, 42, 114, 144
Biden, Joe, 40, 80
Biles, Simone, 177
billionaires, 114, 128, 141–142, 224
Birkin bags, 129, 131–132
birth control, 188
birth rates, decline in, 136–137
Black, Hugo, 57
Black Lives Matter protests, 24, 152
Black Rifle Coffee Company, 4
Blue Origin, 114
body image, 182
Body Shop, 123
Boko Haram, 22
Bolsonaro, Jair, 16, 17, 22, 237
Bonaparte, Napoleon, 79–80
boredom, 217
Borland, Janet, 49
boundaries, resetting, 101–110, 219
Bowie, David, 189
Bowling Alone (Putnam), 199
Boy George, 189
Branson, Richard, 114, 146
Brazil, 16
Brexit, 16, 22, 105–106
BrightLocal, 206–207
Brookings Institution, 136, 235
Brown, Ethan, xvi
Brown, Michael, 98
Brown, Tina, 199
Brown, Zachery Tyson, 80
Buffett, Warren, 146
Bulletin of the Atomic Scientists, 87
bullies, 165–166
bunker mentality, 231
Burke, Tarana, 165
Bush, George W., 15
Bushnell, Candace, 159
business
  in China, 76, 77–79
  climate change and, 40–41
  reevaluation of practices in, 6
  scale and, 123–124
  small, 116–117
  women in, 162–164, 171–173, 181

Calacal, Celisa, 174
Callan, Erin, 163–164, 180
CALM (Campaign Against Living Miserably), 182
Camp Aranu'tiq, 194
Candid, 147
carbon emissions, 34, 40–42, 145. *See also* climate change
Carlson, Gretchen, 165
Carroll, Diahann, 159
Carroll, Tarik, 182
Carson, Rachel, 33
Carter, Jimmy, 33
Carver, L. F., 202
caste system, 102
Castile, Philando, 97
Catalyst, 164
CBS, lawsuit against, 165
CDC Foundation's Coronavirus Emergency Response Fund, 206
center, difficulties of, xxv–xxvi
Chai, Elizabeth, 127
Chance the Rapper, 145

change
  lack of in some areas, 30–31
  pace of, 26–27
Change.org, 114
chaos
  of 1968, 45–46
  as megatrend, 218
  of now, 45–55
  responses to, 98–99
Chapin, Ross, 124–125
Chavez, Hugo, 236, 237
Cheddar Man, 92
Chiang Kai-shek, 67
Chicago Board Options Exchange's Volatility Index, 51
childlessness, 161
China
  Africa and, 235
  businesses in, 76, 77–79
  changing demographics of, 81–82
  climate change and, 82
  COVID-19 pandemic and, 71–73
  cryptocurrency and, xxviii, 70
  deep control and, 220
  development of, 236
  economy of, 21, 80–81
  efforts to counter, 83
  eradication of poverty in, 76–77
  Hollywood and, 78, 79
  Hong Kong and, 75
  infrastructure in, 73
  localism and, 79
  Long March and, 67–68
  Mao Zedong and, 67–68
  Napoleon on, 79–80
  rise of, xxv
  social credit system in, 74
  as superpower, 218
  surveillance in, 74–75
  Uighur Muslims in, 76, 81
  women in, 69–70
  Xi Jinping and, 68–69, 70
  youth of, 70–71
China Online, 69
Chindia, xxi
Chinese Basketball Association, 77
choice, paradox of, 111
Chrysalis Effect, The (Slater), 186
Cicada Safari, 214
cicadas, 214–215
Città Slow, 242
Civil Rights Act (1964), 24
Civil Rights movement, 103
climate apartheid, 37
climate change
  China and, 82
  cicadas and, 214–215
  denial of, 35
  early warnings about, 33–34
  efforts to counter, 40–42
  extreme weather events and, 22–23
  growing awareness of, 37–38
  impact of, 35–37, 38–40, 100
  infrastructure problems and, 53
  predictions regarding, xxviii, 43–44
  wealth gap/inequality and, 145
Climate Collaborative, 238
climate migration, 36–37
Climate Modelling Laboratory, 36
Clinton, Bill, 10, 11
Clinton, Hillary, 58, 166, 183, 184
Cobb, Craig, 93
coeducation, 161–162
collectivism versus individualism, 96
Collins, Chuck, 147
Columbine High School shooting, 20
commercial divides, 4
Communist Party in China, 67
community, COVID-19 pandemic and, 95–97
commuters, 30–31
Comparitech, 52
compartmentalization, 111
Complete Y2K Home Preparation Guide, The, 11

compression wear, 202
Computerworld, 10
concierge doctors, 133
Conestoga huts, 125
Conference of the Parties of the United Nations Framework Convention on Climate Change, 82
conservatorships, 177–178
Conspiracy Theory Trivia Board Game, 214
contraception, 188
control culture, 186
Cooley, Mason, 197
cooperatives, 97, 238
COP26 climate conference, 145
costumes, cultural appropriation and, 107–108
Couch, Ethan, 137
Council on Foreign Relations, xxv
Council on Year 2000, 11
Country Driving (Hessler), 73
country living, 230–231
COVID-19 pandemic
  billionaires and, 141–142
  changes in time of, 4–7
  in China, 71–73
  concept of community and, 95–97
  conspiracy theories about, 212
  Delta variant and, 54
  disinformation/misinformation on, 54–55
  doomsday preppers and, 231
  economic costs of, 17
  education and, 148
  false news reports about, 6
  female leadership during, 169–171
  food insecurity and, 40
  impact of, 27–28, 31, 49–51, 172–173, 241–242
  introspection during, 4–5, 7, 30
  lack of grounding during, 46–47
  lack of prediction of, xxi
  in Latin America, 237
  life during, 28–29
  malnutrition and, 148
  obesity and, 23
  pets and, 202–203
  race and, 50, 152
  remote living during, 205–206
  responses to, 17–18
  small things and, 113–114
  start of, 14–15
  vaccinations and, xxvi–xxvii, 133–134
  work disruptions and, 108–109
cow cuddling, 201
Cracco, Carlo, 135
Crazy Rich Asians (film), 134–135
Credit Suisse, 21
Crenshaw, Kimberlé Williams, 174
crisis concierge service, 51
CRISPR techniques, 232
crowdfunding, 152
cryptocurrency, xxviii, 70, 224, 234
CryptoPunk 7523, xxviii
cuddle parties, 201
cultural appropriation, 107–108
cultural boundaries, 102–103, 107–108
Cuomo, Andrew, 105, 133
cybersecurity, 52
Cybersecurity Ventures, 52
cybersurveillance, 220–221
Cyr, Bruce, 214

Damaske, Sarah, 173
de Jager, Peter, 10
deaths
  from COVID-19 pandemic, 27
  from flooding, 82
  heat-associated, 38
  power outages and, 53
  racial disparities in, 50
  by suicide, 233
  from wildfires, 39
Deaton, Angus, 143

decision paralysis, 111
"Declaration of the Independence of Cyberspace, A" (Barlow), xxii–xxiii
deepfake technology, 234
DeGeneres, Ellen, 191–192
DeGraffenreid, Emma, 174
democracy, 233–234, 238
Deng Xiaoping, 68
deplorables, Clinton's use of, 58
depression, 232–233
Dern, Laura, 191
despair, diseases of, 232–233
desperation, 218–219
details, tendency to obsess over, 28, 29
DeWine, Mike, 166–167
Dewing, Scott, 204
Dickens, Charles, 102
dictatorships, 237. *See also* autocrats/autocracy
digifabs (digital fabricators), 225–226
digital detox, xxvi
digital divide, 25–26
digital environment, 207
digitalization, pervasiveness of, 217
disinformation/misinformation, 6, 16, 18, 22, 212–213, 233–234
Disney, Abigail, 144
displacement, 22
divisiveness, 14, 15, 100, 213
divorce rates, increase in, 47
DNA test kits, 93
Dobson, James, 11
documentaries, private, 135
Dodd, Chris, 10
Dodge Ram pickup truck, 179
Dolan, Paul, 161
Doomsday Clock, 87–88
"doomsday prepper" movement, xxi, 231
Dope Black Dads, 185
dot-com bubble, 21
downsizing, 5
droughts, 38, 227–228
drug use, 188
Drummond, Ree, 115–116
Duterte, Rodrigo, 22
Duwve, Joan, 166–167

early-warning systems, 220–221
Earth Summit, 34
Earthquake Children (Borland), 49
echo chambers, 16, 35
economic inequality, xxiv, 21, 61–62. *See also* wealth gap/inequality
Economic Statistics Centre of Excellence, 106
Economist Intelligence Unit, 42
economy, booms and busts in, 21
economy/economic issues. *See also* business; wealth gap/inequality
  of China, 21, 80–81
  COVID-19 pandemic and, 17
  finance, 223
  gig workers/gig economy, 198–199
  poverty, 76–77, 140
  tax code, 141
  universal basic income (UBI), xxviii, 153, 225
Edmunds, 206
education, 136, 148, 161–162, 181, 223
Edwards, Pete, 113
EHL Insights, 130
Ehrlich, Paul R., 215
Elagabalus (Roman emperor), 195
elder care, 64
Election (film), 104
electric vehicles, 41, 42
Eler, Alicia, 198
Ellen, 191
Elliott, Dominic, 163
emotional intelligence quotient (EQ), 181

emotion-recognition technology, 74, 75, 220
energy crisis, 8
energy sources, 227
Enos, Tony, 195
"enoughness," 123
entertainment, xxvii
environmental issues, 22–23, 218, 226–227
Epochalypse, xxiii
Epstein, Jeffrey, 105
Équité, 138
equity, as megatrend, 219
escapes, 109–110
essential, reevaluation of, 5–6
essential workers, 50, 96, 126, 152
ETH Zürich, 73
Etheridge, Melissa, 191
Etsy, 116
Euronews, 36
European Social Survey, 200
European Union, Brexit and, 105–106
Eurostat, 47
EU's Joint Research Committee, 200
Evergrande Group, 70
Everyday Sexism (Bates), 176
EveryMAN Project, 182
Everyway People, 157
Evryman, 183
expectations, 29, 47–48
extinction rate, increase in, 215
extreme weather events, 36–37. *See also* climate change
extreme weather exiles, 36
extremism, 22

Facebook, 198, 212–213. *See also* social media
facial recognition software, 74, 75
fact-checking, 6
Fair Labor Standards Act (1938), 222
"fake news," 6, 25
Falwell, Jerry, 11
family, lack of contact with, 90–91
FamilyTreeDNA, 93
fashion
  ethical, 42
  gender-neutral, 195
Fast Company (Abel), 171
Faust, Drew Gilpin, 65
FEMA, 11
Feminine Mystique, The (Friedan), 188
feminism, 174
Fenton, Chris, 79
Fidelity National Financial, 115
fifteen-minute city, 117–118
Figueres, Christiana, 37
finance, 223
Finland, 121–122
Finnish Nightmares: An Irreverent Guide to Life's Awkward Moments, 122
"fire moats," 37
fishing industry, 106
fitness apps, 198
Fitzgerald, F. Scott, 143
flooding, 39, 52–53, 82
Flower, Gwynneth, 11
Floyd, George, 5, 24, 97–98, 152
Focus on the Family, 11
food
  cultural fusion and, 108
  insecurity regarding, 40
  shortages of, 7–8
Forbes, 114, 128
Ford Motor Company, 109
Foreign Affairs Intelligence Council, 212
fossil fuel, phasing out, 226–227
Fourth Industrial Revolution, 234–235
Fox News, 165
France, yellow vest protests in, 3
Francis, Pope, 206
Franken, Al, 105
Frazier, Ian, 214
Frederiksen, Mette, 169

#FreeBritney campaign, 177–178
"freedom dividend," 153
freelance work, 198–199
Friedan, Betty, 188
From Blackface to Black Twitter (Moody-Ramirez), 107
Full Circle: Leaning In Too Far and the Journey Back (Callan), 164
Future We Choose, The (Figueres and Rivett-Carnac), 37

Gaines, Chip and Joanna, 116
Galloway, Scott, 127
Gandhi, Indira, 180
Garissa University shooting, 20
Garner, Eric, 97
Gates, Bill, 14–15, 146
Gates, Frederick T., 146
gay rights, 191–192. *See also* LGBTQ+ community
Geffen, David, 128, 129
Gemmell, Andrew, 135
gender discrimination, 165. *See also* LGBTQ+ community
gender fluidity, xxviii, 104, 188–196, 219. *See also* nonbinary people; transgender rights
gender roles, 181–182
geriatric research, 231–232
Getaway, 126
Getty Images survey, 42
gezelligheid (coziness/conviviality), 120
ghost kitchens, 97
gig workers/gig economy, 198–199
gigantism, 123
Giving Pledge, 146
glass ceiling/glass cliff, 162–164
Glee, 192
Global Consumer Insights pulse survey, 42
Global Gender Gap Report 2020, 172
global recession, 21
Global Risks Report (World Economic Forum), 52
Global Village, The (McLuhan), 241
globalization, 117
"globesity" (global obesity), xxi, 23
Glossier, xvi
GoFundMe, 152
Going Solo (Klinenberg), 200
Gordon, Erik, 78
Gore, Al, 34
Gosschalk, Job, 165
government, predictions regarding, xxv
GoZen! 49
Great Dispersion, 127
Great Divide, 3–4
Great Kanto Earthquake, 49
Great Reboot, 4–8
Great Society programs, xviii
greenhouse effect, 34, 100
Gucci, 135
guns, increase in sales of, 11
guochao, 79

Haiti, 16
Halloween, 106–107
Handy, Charles, 58
Hansen, James, 34
haptic technologies, 223
Harris, Janna, 126
Harris, Kamala, 166
Harvard Business Review, 171–172
Has China Won? (Mahbubani), 82–83
hate and hate speech, xxv
Haugen, Frances, 198
Hawking, Stephen, xxvii
health and fitness apps, 198
healthcare. *See also* COVID-19 pandemic
  climate change and, 38
  concierge doctors and, 133

healthcare (*cont'd*):
COVID-19 pandemic and, 49–50
DNA and, 93
future of, 231–232
global crisis in, 23–24, 31
ransomware attacks involving, 52
wealth gap/inequality and, 142
Her (film), 204
Hermès, 131–132
Hessler, Peter, 73
Hidalgo, Anne, 118
Hitchcock, Alfred, 89–90
Hollywood, 78, 79
homelessness, 125
Hong Kong, 3, 75
House Hunters, 111
housing
decrease in size of, 125–126
off-the-grid, 126
single-person households and, 47, 200, 202
Houston Rockets, 77–78
Howard University, 147
Humankind, 195
Humans of New York, 116–117
Humen, 183
Hunt, Nelson Bunker, 140
hurricanes, 22–23, 53
hybridization, 101–102
hygge, 242
hypermasculinity, 186–187

Iceland, 236
ICT Development Index, 236
identity, flexibility of, 219. *See also* gender fluidity
identity markers, 93–94
incels (involuntarily celibate men), xxi, 187
inclusiveness, 170
income inequality, 161, 172. *See also* wealth gap/inequality
Inconvenient Truth, An (film), 34
Index of Economic Freedom, 64
individualism versus collectivism, 96
inequity, addressing, 225. *See also* wealth gap/inequality
infrastructure, 52–53, 73
in-group/out-group thinking, 95
Intergovernmental Panel on Climate Change, 82
International Boxing Association, 177
International Handball Federation, 177
International Monetary Fund, 17, 80
international poverty line, 140
International Y2K Cooperation Center, 11
internet. *See also* technology
access to, 25–26
development of, 211–212
disinformation/misinformation on, 22
effects of, xxii
ISIS, 22
isolation, increase in, 99, 198–201
It's a Wonderful Life (film), 91

Japan, 121
Jefferson, Thomas, 136
Jenner, Caitlyn, 193
Jesus, 92
Jetsons, The, 29
job displacement, 221, 222, 226–227
Jobs, Steve, 134, 144
Johnson, Boris, 52
Johnson, Sigrid, 93
Joint Center for Housing Studies (Harvard University), 90–91
Jones, Grace, 189
Jonze, Spike, 204
Just Eat It (Khor), 108

Kahneman, Daniel, 143
"Karen," 60
Keep the Damned Women Out (Malkiel), 162
Keilar, Brianna, 54
Kennedy, Carolyn, xix
Kennedy, John F., 103
Kennedy, John F., Jr., xix
Kennedy, Robert F., 45
Khor, Shing Yin, 108
Kidnapped (Stevenson), 218
Kind Columbus, 167
King, Martin Luther, Jr., xxvi, 45
Kinks, The, 189
Klinenberg, Eric, 200
Koskinen, John, 11, 12
Krishnan, Mekala, 173
Kurzweil, Ray, 244
Kyoto Protocol, 34

"Lady, or the Tiger? The" (Stockton), 244–245
lagom (just the right amount), 109
Lai, Jimmy, 75
Lamb, Charles, 221
Lancet Countdown report, 38
Langer, Daniel, 138
Last Best Hope (Packer), 61
Latin America, 236–238
Lawrence v. Texas decision, 24
Lazarus, Emma, 56
Le Guin, Ursula K., 149–150
Lean In (nonprofit), 172
Lean In (Sandberg), 164
Lederberg, Joshua, 14
legacy applicants, 136
Lehman Brothers, 163–164, 180
Levi's, 195
LGBTQ+ community. *See also* gender fluidity
  acceptance of, 24
  among Gen Zers, 193
  celebrities and, 193–194
  fashion and, 195
life expectancy, 142
Lifeboat (film), 89–90
Livekindly, 41
localism, 79
Lohan, Lindsay, 184–185
Lolita (Nabokov), 104
London North Eastern Railway, 191
loneliness, crisis of, 95, 199–200. *See also* isolation, increase in
Long March, 67–68
Lore, Marc, xxvii
Louis Vuitton, 135
"Lowest Animal, The" (Twain), 143
Lukashenko, Alexander, 17
luxury/luxury goods, xxix, 128–138, 219

Macron, Emmanuel, 145
Maduro, Nicolás, 237
Mahbubani, Kishore, 82–83
Malkiel, Nancy Weiss, 162
Man Cave, The, 183
Manhattan (film), 104
Manjoo, Farhad, 13–14
manufacturing and production, reshoring of, 78–79
Mao Zedong, 67–68, 70, 71
Marjory Stoneman Douglas High School shooting, 20
marriage rate, decline in, 47, 161
Mary Tyler Moore Show, The, 159
mass murder/shootings, 20–21, 180–181
Mattel, 195
Mayors for a Guaranteed Income coalition, 153
Mazars C-suite barometer, 238
McKinsey, 134, 148, 172
McLuhan, Marshall, 241
McMansion Hell (Wagner blog), 114
"me time," 109
Meals on Wheels, 147

meat consumption, 41–42. *See also* plant-based foods
Medina, Jennifer, 184
medRxiv, 169
megacities, xxvii
Megatrends: Ten New Directions Transforming Our Lives (Naisbitt), xix
Meir, Golda, 180
Meituan, 77
men/male behavior, 179–187
mental health issues, 232–233
Merkel, Angela, 169
metanarratives, 16–17
metaverse, 204–205
MetLife, 172
#MeToo movement, 24–25, 69, 105, 165–166, 176, 181, 185
metrosexualism, xx–xxi
Michaels, Lorne, 115
micro-apartments, 125
middle class, shrinking of, 61–62
Midea, 77
Midnight Trains service, xxviii
millennium bug. *See* Y2K
Millman, Noah, 59
Mind Set! (Naisbitt), xxv
mindful consumption, 5
minimalism, 5
minimum-basic-living guarantee plan (*dibao*), 76
Ministry of Utmost Happiness, The (Roy), 7
misinformation/disinformation, 6, 16, 18, 22, 212–213, 233–234
missing middle, xxv–xxvi
Mizutori, Mami, 38
Modi, Narendra, 17
money, predictions regarding, xxviii
Moody-Ramirez, Mia, 107
Moore, Demi, 191
Moreno, Carlos, 118
Morey, Daryl, 77
Morgan State University, 147
movie industry, 235
Moynihan, Daniel Patrick, 10–11
M-Pesa, 235
mRNA technology, 232
"multi" mandate, 238
multiculturalism, 94–95
Munro, Alice, 160
mushrooms, 228–229
Musk, Elon, 114–115, 146, 225
My Pillow, 4
MyHeritage, 93

Nabokov, Vladimir, 104
Naisbitt, Doris, xxv
Naisbitt, John, xviii–xix, xxv
Napier, Erin and Ben, 116
narrowcasting, xxi
NASA Goddard Institute for Space Studies, 34
National Agency for New Technologies, Energy, and Sustainable Economic Development (ENEA; Italy), 36
National Day Golden Week, 72–73
National Endowment for Democracy, 238
National Institute of Population and Social Security Research (Japan), 200
National Service Animal Registry, 203
nationalism, 22, 94, 106
nativism, 95
Nature Food, 148
Netherlands, 120–121
Netmums survey, 173–174
New Canaan, Connecticut, 149
New Shepard, 114
New York Dolls, 189
New Zealand, 122–123, 169–171
NewsGuard, 6
Next (Matathia and Salzman), 243

NFTs (non-fungible tokens), xxviii
Nichols, Mike, 12
9/11 attacks/Commission, 13, 21
99 Giving Day campaign, 77
Nomura Holdings, 80
nonbinary people, 190–191, 193, 195–196. *See also* gender fluidity
North, Anna, 168–169
North Korea, 25
nostalgia, xv–xvi
Nunberg, Geoffrey, 190
nutrigenomics, 93

Obama, Barack, 15, 25, 65, 192
Occupy Wall Street, 21
O'Halloran, Mary, 116–117
Ohashi, Katelyn, 177
ohitorisama (party of one), 121
Olympics, 57, 177
One Million Moms, 192
one-child policy, 81
"Ones Who Walk Away from Omelas, The" (Le Guin), 149–150
online reviews, 206–207
Open Society European Policy Institute, 35
Osaka, Naomi, 177
Osnos, Evan, 69–70
Our World in Data, 200
outsourcing, 13
Oxfam, 145

Packer, George, 61
Page, Elliot, 193–194
Palmer Drought Severity Index, 38
paradox of choice, 111
parenthood, as choice, 136, 161
Patagonia, 4
Paul, Pamela, 217
pay equity, 161, 172. *See also* wealth gap/inequality
PEN America, 78
Pence, Mike, 166
P'eng Te-huai, 67
Penny, Brenda, 178
Perón, Juan, 237
personal pronouns, changes in, 190–191. *See also* gender fluidity; transgender rights
pessimism, increase in, 48
Petrus wine, 112–113
pets, 202–203
Pew Research Center, 6, 26, 47, 57–58, 62, 64–65, 213
philanthropy, 146–147, 225
Pioneer Woman, The, 115–116
plant-based foods, xvi, 41, 228–229
plastics problem, 226
Playbook for Early Response to High-Consequence Emerging Infectious Disease Threats and Biological Incidents, 15
pocket neighborhoods, 124–125
polarization, 3–4
political boundaries, 105–106
politics, women in, 166–171, 175
Pompeo, Mike, 104
population
  changing demographics of, 63, 81–82
  consolidation of, 58–59
  density of, 119–122, 235
  redistribution of, xxvii
Population Reference Bureau, 58–59
Potential Energy Coalition, 35
poverty. *See also* wealth gap/inequality
  China's efforts to eradicate, 76–77
  measuring, 140
Prada, Miuccia, 135
Prague Spring, 46
Presley, Elvis, 142
Princeton University, 162
prison labor, 150
privacy, xxvi, 133

private-public partnerships, 239
Proud Boys, xxi
Public, 130
Putnam, Robert D., 199
PwC, 42

qualitative analysis, xvii
quantitative analysis, xvii
Queer Eye, 192

race issues, 24, 50, 146, 152
Radcliffe, Daniel, 192
Ragged Dick (Alger), 103
Raiser, Martin, 76
Rally, 132
Ram pickup truck, 179
Ramkalawan, Wavel, 145
ransomware attacks, 52
Rapoport, Adam, 107
Raviola, Giuseppe, 46
Reagan, Ronald, xix
RealDoll, 204
Rebellyous Foods, 41
Red Star over China (Snow), 67–68
Redmayne, Eddie, 192
reducetarianism, 42
Reed, Lou, 189
Reed, Sean, 97
refugee crisis, 22
Reich, Robert, 145
Renewable Heat Initiative (United Kingdom), 227
reproductive rights, 175–176
resiliency, 49
retail, hyperspecialized, xxi
Rice, Condoleezza, 78
Rice, Tamir, 98
Rising Sun, 128
Rittenhouse, Kyle, 152
Rivett-Carnac, Tom, 37
Road to Resilience, 49
Robertson, Pat, 191
robots, 203–204, 221
Rochefoucauld, François de La, xx
Rockefeller, John D., 146
Rodriguez, Mj, 194
Room + Wheel, 126
Roosevelt, Franklin, 222
Roosevelt, Theodore, 143
Rosenbaum, S. I., 46
Rowling, J. K., 192
Roy, Arundhati, 7
Russell, Joellen, 35–36
Ryan, Michelle, 164

Sadik-Khan, Janette, 118
Samhain, 107
Sandberg, Sheryl, 164, 172
Sandel, Michael, 150–151
Sandy Hook Elementary School massacre, 20
Sannino, Gianmaria, 36
Saturday Night Live, 114–115
Saturday Night Seder, 206
Schieffelin, Eugene, xxii
Schmidt, Eric, 204–205
school shootings, 20
Schrager, Ian, 130–131, 134
Schumacher, E. F., 117, 123
Schwartz, Barry, 111
science, polarization of, xxvi–xxvii
Science Moms, 35
Scott, MacKenzie, 146–147, 225
Scott Bader Commonwealth, 117–118
Selected Works of Mao Zedong, The, 71
self-absorption, 243
self-centeredness, xxiv, 197–208, 219, 243–244
selfie culture, 197–198
Selfie Generation, The (Eler), 198
selflessness, 244
service/support animals, 203
Sex and the City, 153, 159–160
sexbots, 204

sexual harassment, 24–25, 165, 176
sexual orientation, 189–190
Shantideva, 145
shared experiences, value placed on, xxiv
Sharp Eyes program, 74–75
Shearer, Rhonda Roland, 96
Shelter Animals Count, 202
shopping, xxviii–xxix, 116–117
"Significance of the Frontier in American History, The" (Turner), 103
Silent Spring (Carson), 33
Silverman, Sarah, 191
Simpson, Mark, xx
single-parent households, 47, 164
single-person households, 47, 200, 202
skin hunger, 201–202
"skyboxification," 151
Slater, Philip, 186
slow (food) movement, 242
Small Is Beautiful (Schumacher), 117, 123
small things
  appeal of, 115–116
  COVID-19 pandemic and, 113–114
  defining, 112–113
  focus on, 109–110
  as megatrend, 219
  urban development and, 117–118
Smart Export Guarantee program (United Kingdom), 227
smart speakers, 203–204
smartphones, 18. *See also* technology
Smith, Jaden, 195
Smith, Robert Angus, 34
Smith, Sam, 193
Snow, Edgar, 67–68
social boundaries, 102–103
social credit system, 74
social hierarchy, 102
social media. *See also* technology
  disinformation/misinformation on, 25, 212–213
  hate and hate speech on, xxv
  impact of on young people, 198
  Trump and, 15
  untruths and, 6
social progress, 24–25
solidarity, 96, 98
solopreneurs, 199
South America, 236
South Korea, 25, 236
space race, 114
Spears, Britney, 177–178
sports, 177
Springsteen, Bruce, 142
Stanton, Brandon, 117
Starbucks, 4
starlings, xxi–xxii
Statue of Liberty, 56
Steinem, Gloria, 160
Stenberg, Amandla, 108
Stevens, Ashlie D., 178
Stevenson, Robert Louis, 218
Stockton, Frank R., 244–245
Strategic Arms Reduction Treaty, 87
strongmen, 180, 237
student protests, 45–46
Studio 54, 130
Styron, William and Rose, 12
subprime housing crisis, 21
success, redefining, 123
suicide, 233
Summer of Love, 188
Sun Shuyun, 68
Sun Tzu, 51–52
Supermajority/PerryUndem Research, 175–176
surrogacy, commercial, 137
surveillance, 74–75, 220–221
syndemic, 46

Taliban, xxi
tang ping (lying flat), 242–243
tax code, 141

technology. *See also* internet; social media
AI devices, 203–205, 221
centrality of, 19
climate change and, xxviii
divisiveness and, 16
emotion-recognition technology, 74, 75, 220
facial recognition software, 74, 75
impact of, 14–15, 26
increase in use of, 25–26
questions regarding, 18
smartphones, 18
3D printing, 225
Y2K and, 7–8, 9–14, 16–17
TED Talks, 14, 174
television shows, 159–160
Telosa, xxvii
Tencent, 77
terrorism, 20–21
That Girl, 159
Thatcher, Margaret, xix, xxv, 180
Thich Nhat Hanh, 197
Thiel, Peter, 122–123
third-gender people, 195. *See also* gender fluidity
Thomas (sourcing specialist), 78
Thomas, Marlo, 159
Thoreau, Henry David, 140
thought technologies, 205
3D printing, 225
Thunberg, Greta, xxviii, 226
time
freedom of, 130–131, 138
perceptions of, 30
as privilege, 134, 219
reclaiming of, 109–110
work changes and, 222
tiny houses, 126
Titchmarsh, Alan, 116
Tlatelolco Massacre, 46
Tocqueville, Alexis de, 58
"together apart," xxiv
touch deprivation, 201–202
toxic masculinity, 180
traffic jams, 30–31
Transformer (Reed), 189
transgender rights, 192–193. *See also* gender fluidity
transgender workers, protections for, 24
travel, xvii–xviii
Treasure Island (Stevenson), 218
Treepedia, 229
trees/wood, 228, 229–230
trends, fads versus, 211
trendspotting, overview of, xv–xvii
tribalism, xxvi, 4, 16, 65–66
trillionaires, 223–224
TripAdvisor, 206
Trump, Donald, 15, 51, 58, 64–65, 103–104, 122, 165–166, 184–185
Tsai Ing-wen, 169
tsunamis, 22–23
Tucson, Arizona, 35, 149
Turner, Frederick Jackson, 103
Twain, Mark, 142–143
23andMe, 93

Uighur Muslims, 76, 81
Umbrella, 63
UN Peoples' Climate Vote, 35
uncertainty, navigating, xx
UNICEF, 24
unisex bathrooms, 194
unisex clothing, 195
United Kingdom
Brexit and, 16, 22, 105–106
sustainable power sources in, 227
United Nations High Commissioner for Refugees, 22
United States
division in, 56–66, 213
luxury goods in, 135
race issues in, 146
shifting boundaries in, 102–104
as superpower, 218
tax code in, 141

universal basic income (UBI), xxviii, 153, 225
universe, immensity of, 113
Unix time, 213
unpaid care work, division of, 173
untruths, 6
upskilling, 223
urban development, 117–118
urban exodus, xxvii, 230–231
urbanization, 235
U.S. citizenship, renunciation of, 57
U.S. Federal Reserve, 146
U.S. News & World Report, 64, 169
USA Today, 48

vacation days, 109–110
vaccines, distrust of, 23–24
Van Gogh, Vincent, 111
Venezuela, 236
Vermont Foodbank, 147
verzuiling (pillarization), 120
Villages, The (Florida), 63
violence
  COVID-19 pandemic and, 50–51
  mass murder/shootings, 20–21, 180–181
Virgil, 117
Virgin Galactic, 114
Virginia Tech shooting, 20
vocabulary development, 148

Wagner, Kate, 114
Wakefield, Andrew, 23
Walsh, Kathleen, 168
war, 185–186
Ward, Vicky, 163
water scarcity, 38–39
Waters, Maxine, 110
Watson, Emma, 192
WCCO-TV, 165
"we," defining, 90–92, 99
wealth
  defining, 140
  poverty and, 141
wealth gap/inequality, 62, 114–115, 139–154, 224–225. *See also* income inequality
weighted blankets, 201–202
Weinstein, Harvey, 105
Weiss, Emily, xvi
Wellcome Trust, 23
We're a Culture, Not a Costume, 107
Westminster Arcade, 125
white supremacy, 94
Whitmer, Gretchen, 167–168
"why," focus on, 5–6
Wiklund, Anna, 110
wildfires, 39
Will & Grace, 192
Williams, William Carlos, 30
Wilson, Woodrow, 238
Winfrey, Oprah, 191
Wolverine Watchmen, 168
women. *See also* sexual harassment
  in business, 162–164, 171–173, 181
  in China, 69–70
  education and, 161–162, 181
  equality for, 24–25
  independence and, 136, 175, 177–178
  leadership of, 169–172
  in politics, 166–171, 175
  shifting boundaries and, 103, 104–105
  in sports, 177
  stalled progress of, 160–161
  television shows and, 159–160
Women in the Workplace study, 172
women's lib, 188–189
Wong, Darrick J., 213
wood/trees, 228, 229–230
work, changes in, 221–222
work/working from home (WFH), 108–109

World Bank, 11, 31, 38, 76
World Business Council for Sustainable Development, 40–41
World Economic Forum, 14, 52, 161, 235
World Health Organization (WHO), 23, 31, 87
World Meteorological Organization, 33
World Trade Center attack, 13
World Wildlife Fund, 215
Wright, Jennifer, 187

Xi Jinping, 68–69, 70, 74, 76, 80, 82

Y2K, xxiii, 7, 9–14, 16–17, 211
Y2K: A Christian's Survival Guide to the Millennium Bug (film), 11
Y2038, xxiii, 213–214
Yale Program on Climate Communication, 35
Yang, Andrew, 153
yellow vest protests, 3

Zendaya, 108
Zuckerberg, Mark, 144, 146, 212–213
Zwarte Piet (Black Pete), 24

About the Author

Marian Salzman has worked at the leading edge of advertising, public relations, and technology for more than three decades. Since cofounding the first online market research company, she has served as a communications executive at companies in the United States and Europe. Her annual forecasting report on the coming year's trends, released each November, garners global media attention. A graduate of Brown University and the recipient of numerous awards, Marian Salzman lives in Connecticut and Switzerland.